# Cognitive Behavioral Therapy for Social Anxiety Disorder

## PRACTICAL CLINICAL GUIDEBOOKS SERIES

# Cognitive Behavioral Therapy for Social Anxiety Disorder

### Evidence-Based and Disorder-Specific Treatment Techniques

## Stefan G. Hofmann
## Michael W. Otto

Routledge
Taylor & Francis Group
New York   London

Routledge
Taylor & Francis Group
711 Third Avenue
New York, NY 10017, USA

Routledge
Taylor & Francis Group
2 Park Square
Milton Park, Abingdon
Oxon OX14 4RN

**Visit the Taylor & Francis Web site at**
**http://www.taylorandfrancis.com**

**and the Routledge Web site at**
**http://www.routledge.com**

*To Benjamin and Lukas, for giving me daily exposure to happiness*

—SGH

*To my parents, with love*

—MWO

# Contents

# Preface

Social anxiety disorder (SAD), also known as social phobia, is one of the most common mental disorders in the population. During the past two decades, an enormous amount of research has been conducted that has led to effective treatment strategies for this debilitating disorder. This book describes many of these techniques.

We wrote this book with a number of readers and applications in mind. First and foremost, this book is designed for clinicians with basic knowledge in cognitive behavioral therapy who want to increase or establish their skills for treating SAD. For this purpose, we have provided a wealth of detail on the nature of SAD, with attention to core maintaining factors and common clinical presentations (chapter 1). In chapter 2, we provide an overview of the principles of treatment that inform the specific interventions discussed in chapter 3. We discuss the research basis of these principles in chapter 4. Attention to these principles of treatment will help clinicians adapt interventions to the needs of individual patients (chapter 5). Some of these variations on the theme of treatment are captured in chapter 6 where complicating factors in treatment are discussed. General issues in the close of treatment and in enhancing relapse prevention are discussed in chapter 7. Nonetheless, we also provide enough information on a structured format for therapy and examples of that therapy in action in chapter 5, so that clinicians will never be without guidance on a state-of-the-art approach to treating SAD.

In addition to the primary application of this book as a treatment guide, we have provided readers with a wealth of information on the nature of SAD and treatment efficacy as informed by controlled trials. Our purpose is to ensure that this book serves as a resource for clinical researchers as well as clinicians. In particular, chapters 1 and 4 provide comprehensive reviews of the psychopathology and outcome studies that inform our model of SAD and its treatment. These chapters ensure continuity between the empirical literature and the intervention strategies discussed in the book, and together this combination of empirical guidance and principle-based treatment provides the scientist–practitioner perspective that we particularly value.

In writing this book, we were also mindful of the various practice characteristics in which clinicians work. Our manual is designed for interventions that can be administered in individual treatments or in group settings, and accordingly, throughout the book we have provided examples of interventions in both of these formats. Group treatment brings with it the ease of having a ready-made audience available for social exposures. Yet, the formation of groups for treatment in a timely fashion requires a steady flow of patients with SAD. For practices without this flow, individual treatment will be the most efficient. Many exposure practices are conducted in vivo outside the therapist's office as part of what we call *social mishap exposures*. Some of the initial exposures happen ideally in the therapist's office. The use of clinic staff as an impromptu audience can aid clinicians in the application of individual treatment. These and other techniques outlined in this book are specifically geared toward the adult patient with SAD. Clinicians who would like to advance their understanding on SAD in children and adolescents may consult the excellent books by Beidel and Turner (2007) and Albano and DiBartolo (2007).

Overall, we hope our book will give a range of readers what they need to provide their patients with the best possible treatment that is currently available. We emphasize principle-guided treatment, complement this broad perspective with specific protocol with examples of interventions, and link all of these interventions to the wealth of guidance provided by the empirical literature. For clinicians, researchers, and students alike, we believe this approach will provide an accessible accounting of the treatment strategies important for individuals with SAD.

Stefan G. Hofmann, PhD

Michael W. Otto, PhD

# Acknowledgments

Our conceptualization of the nature of social anxiety disorder (SAD) and its treatment has been shaped by a wide range of individuals. As witnessed by a wealth of studies we have cited in chapters 1 and 4, we have been informed and influenced by numerous talented and achieving clinical researchers who have shaped the field with their cutting-edge studies. We were tempted to try to name some of these luminaries here, but the list is so long that perhaps our reference list itself will have to serve as a testament to our gratitude for the way in which their thinking has shaped our thinking about this prevalent and disabling disorder. We also want to express our gratitude to the colleagues with whom we have worked over the last two decades. Most prominently they include David Barlow at the Center for Anxiety and Related Disorders (CARD) at Boston University and Mark Pollack at the Center for Anxiety and Stress Related Disorders at Massachusetts General Hospital. We have each benefited from their collaboration and friendship for years and want to acknowledge their shaping influence on the research and clinical interventions we have come to value. We also would like to thank the Boston University students and staff of CARD who play such an important and ongoing role in keeping our research perspectives fresh and making clinical research, and the academic enterprise more broadly, an exciting and rewarding activity. Finally, we would like to thank our patients who have also played a powerful role in shaping our thinking about SAD. It is in relation to the successes and treatment difficulties that these patients have faced that we have been able to refine our perspective about what individuals need when they struggle with this disorder.

# CHAPTER 1

# Characterizing Social Anxiety Disorder

Some 50,000 years ago, probably somewhere in Africa, the modern human was born. Mutations to the human genome led to changes in the human brain, which enabled this new species to have the capacity to make sophisticated tools, to develop language and culture, and to develop a sense of self. These changes further led to the development of complex social systems that gave the species enormous independence from environmental conditions. To support these social systems, humans evolved high-level motivations to compete for the approval and support of others (Barkow, 1989; Gilbert, 2001). Our species needs to be liked, valued, and approved of in order to elicit parental investment, develop supportive peer relationships, attract desirable mates, and engage successfully in many types of social relationships (Tooby & Cosmides, 1996). Ostracism from the social group impacts negatively on a variety of health-related variables, including one's self-esteem and sense of belonging (Baumeister & Leary, 1995; Baumeister & Tice, 1990). As a result, humans naturally fear negative evaluation by their peers.

The maladaptive expression of this evolutionarily adaptive concern is social anxiety disorder (SAD). With the core feature of fears of negative evaluations from others, one can imagine the range of social interactions that can cue social anxiety: performance situations such as eating or writing in public, initiating or maintaining conversations, going to parties, dating, meeting strangers, or interacting with authority figures. Among social fears, a particularly challenging event is public speaking, and indeed this is the most commonly feared social situation among individuals with SAD (e.g., Pollard & Henderson, 1988). Aside from this commonality, there is considerable variability among patients with SAD in the number and type of situations they fear. This chapter will review the diagnostic criteria of SAD, treatment-relevant facts about the psychopathology and etiology of the disorder, and the treatment-outcome literature.

## WHAT IS SOCIAL ANXIETY DISORDER?

Anthony's Story

Anthony is a 50-year-old, single postal worker. He recently decided to see a doctor because of his depression. During the diagnostic interview, Anthony told the therapist that he has been feeling constantly depressed since first grade, without a period of "normal" mood for more than a few days at a time. He often feels lethargic with little or no interest or pleasure in anything, frequently has trouble concentrating, and generally feels inadequate and very pessimistic about the future. Anthony also told the therapist that he cannot ever remember feeling comfortable in social situations. Even in grade school, his mind would go blank when somebody asked him to speak in front of a group of his parents' friends. He would avoid going to birthday parties and other social gatherings when he could, or he would just sit there quietly if he had to go. He used to be a very quiet kid in school and would only answer questions in class when he wrote down the answers in advance. But even then, he would frequently mumble or not be able to get the answer out well. He usually met new children with his eyes lowered, fearing that they would make fun of him.

As he grew older, Anthony had a few playmates in his neighborhood, but he never really had a best friend. His school grades were fairly good, except for subjects that required classroom participation. As a teenager, he was especially anxious in interactions with members of the opposite sex. Although he would like to have a relationship with a woman, he has never gone on a date or asked a woman out on a date because of the fear of rejection. Anthony attended college and did well for a while. But when he was expected to give oral presentations in some of his classes, he stopped coming to class and eventually dropped out. For a few years after that, he had trouble finding a job because he didn't think that he was able to go to the job interviews. Eventually, he found some jobs for which only a written test was required. A number of years ago, he passed the civil service exam and was offered a job in the post office on the evening shift. He was offered several promotions but refused them because he feared the social pressures. Anthony told the therapist that he has a number of acquaintances at work but no friends, and avoids all invitations to socialize with co-workers after his shifts.

## Barbara's Story

Barbara is a 33-year-old businesswoman who has been living with her husband and two children outside a major metropolitan area. Her husband takes care of the children at home while she works at a large insurance company. She has been extraordinarily successful in her career and recently became the vice president of her company. Shortly after she got promoted, she decided to see a therapist because of her panic attacks that she sometimes gets when she has to give presentations in front of people at work. During the diagnostic interview, Barbara described herself as having been outgoing and popular throughout adolescence and young adulthood, with no serious problems until her third year in college. This is when she began to become extremely tense and nervous when she had to give oral presentations in front of people, especially large crowds in a formal setting. When asked what it was about these situations that make her so nervous, she said that she was concerned about what the audience would think of her. "The audience might sense how nervous I am, and I may not be comprehensible and look foolish." As a result, she spends many hours preparing her speech, writing out explicit scripts for all of her presentations. Curiously, she experiences little or no anxiety in informal social settings, such as parties or large dinner meetings.

Barbara said that she has been functioning at only 20% of her work capacity since she got promoted, which she attributes to the increased demands of oral presentations now required of her. Barbara and her husband entertain guests at their home regularly and enjoy socializing with friends at picnics, parties, and formal affairs. Barbara lamented, "It's just when I'm expected to give a formal presentation. That's when I feel like I'm on stage, all alone, with everyone watching me."

## Donny's Story

Donny Osmond was the lead singer of the Osmond Brothers in the 1960s. He became a teenage star after a string of early '70s solo hits, and then again landed a late '80s comeback hit. In an interview with *People* magazine ("Broken heartthrob" May 17, 1999), Osmond revealed:

> I'd been a little nervous about every one of my performances all my life, but for as long as I can remember—whether I was onstage or in a business meeting—I knew that if I just got that applause at the end of the first song, a laugh when I made a joke, my nervousness would diminish, though never go away. Sometime around 1994, I began feeling a kind of anxiousness

unlike anything I'd ever felt before .... Once the fear of embarrassing myself grabbed me, I couldn't get loose. It was as if a bizarre and terrifying unreality had replaced everything that was familiar and safe. In the grip of my wildest fears, I was paralyzed, certain that if I made one wrong move, I would literally die. Even more terrifying, I'd have felt relieved to die. The harder I tried to remember the words, the more elusive they became. The best I could do was not blackout, and I got through the show, barely, telling myself repeatedly, "Stay conscious, stay conscious." And these attacks of nerves weren't only about performing onstage. I remember being so wound up at the prospect of cohosting *Live With Regis and Kathie Lee* that I didn't sleep at all the night before and got nauseous before I went on. Another time, my anxiety was so overwhelming during my audition to play the voice to Hercules in the Disney animated feature, my performance was embarrassing. I started to wonder if I could continue a singing career at all.

Donny, Barbara, and Anthony tell very different stories. Barbara is a highly successful businesswoman who is only slowed by her public speaking anxiety, which has become a significant problem with a recent job promotion. In contrast, Anthony's lifelong social anxiety makes it difficult for him to maintain even the most minimal social contact. Donny Osmond is an example of a celebrity who suffers from stage fright that had become so severe that it interfered with his professional and personal life. Other examples of successful public figures with stage fright include Barbara Streisand, Carly Simon, and professional athletes including baseball players Steve Sax, Mike Ivie, and Steve Blass.

## DIAGNOSTIC CRITERIA FOR SAD

Social anxiety has been noted and recorded throughout history. However, the definition of social phobia (or SAD) as we know it today dates back to Marks and Gelder (1966) who described a condition in which a person becomes very anxious when subject to scrutiny by others while performing a specific social task. SAD as a diagnostic entity was first characterized in 1980 with the publication of the third edition of the *Diagnostic and Statistical Manual for Mental Disorders* (DSM–III), published by the American Psychiatric Association (APA).

The most recent revision of these criteria was published in 1994 in the fourth edition, the *DSM–IV*. (The World Health Organization's International Classification of Mental Disorders, or ICD–10, criteria for social phobia are very similar to that provided by the *DSM–IV*.) According to the *DSM–IV*, the core feature of the disorder (Criterion A) is defined by a persistent and marked fear of social or performance situations (where the person is exposed to unfamiliar people or potential scrutiny by others) linked to fears that she or he will be humiliated or embarrassed. Exposure to the feared social situation should reliably provoke anxiety (Criterion B) and may take the form of panic attacks in or around the feared situation. Criterion C requires that the fear is excessive or unreasonable, and Criterion D underscores the importance of social avoidance, defining the disorder by either avoidance of the feared social or performance situations or the experience of intense anxiety or distress if these situations are endured. For example, if Anthony had told us that he avoids people, not because he feels anxious around them but because he simply gets irritated by them, or if he does not think that he is more nervous is social situations than most people are, he would probably not have received the diagnosis of SAD. Criterion E characterizes the disorder in terms of significant interference of normal routine, occupational or academic functioning, or social interactions, or marked distress about having the phobia. For example, if Barbara had told us she realizes that she gets pretty nervous when she has to give presentations, but that this doesn't really bother her too much and does not cause her to avoid the situation, she would also not have met the criteria for social phobia. The bottom line is that social anxiety is only a diagnosable disorder if (1) the person realizes that the fear is excessive and (2) if this fear significantly interferes with the person's life by causing either distress or avoidance. It is obviously very subjective whether social anxiety is in fact "excessive" and "interfering," and this is ultimately a clinical judgment. Additional criteria are directed toward differentiating the disorder of SAD from other conditions (e.g., not due to the direct effects of a medical indication or drug) and present for at least 6 months in individuals under age 18.

The variability in the breadth and severity of social anxiety within this definition is striking and can be characterized by the differences in the developmental characteristics, chronicity, and disability as exemplified by the cases of Anthony and Barbara. Some individuals are only afraid of certain performance situations (such as public speaking, eating in a restaurant, using a public lavatory, writing while people are watching), whereas others show a broad array of fears that may include numerous performance situations and interactional fears (such as meeting new people, going out on a date, saying no to unreasonable requests). Anthony is an example of somebody with the "generalized subtype" social phobia, defined by fears of most or all social situations. In contrast, Barbara's social anxiety is limited to the fear of public speaking and is an example of what was defined in *DSM–III* as a performance subtype. However, one commonality across subtypes is the degree to which public speaking tends to be feared by all individuals with SAD (whether or not they meet criteria for the generalized subtype).

## DISORDER PREVALENCE AND CHARACTERISTICS

Based on a review of the epidemiological literature, the lifetime prevalence of SAD in Western countries ranges between 7% and 12% of the population (Furmark, 2002; Kessler et al., 2005). The disorder affects females and males fairly equally, with the average gender ratio (female:male) ranging between 1:1 (Moutier & Stein, 1999) and 3:2 (Kessler et al., 2005) in community studies. SAD often begins in the midteens but can also occur in early childhood. During childhood, SAD is often associated with overanxious disorder, mutism, school refusal, separation anxiety, behavioral inhibition, and shyness. If untreated, the disorder typically follows a chronic, unremitting course and leads to substantial impairments in vocational and social functioning (Davidson, Hughes, George, & Blazer, 1993; Liebowitz, Gorman, Fyer, & Klein, 1985; Schneier et al., 1994; Schneier, Johnson, Hornig, Liebowitz, & Weissman, 1992; Stein & Kean, 2001; Stein, Torgrud, & Walker, 2000; Stein, Walker, & Forde, 1996).

When first introduced as a diagnostic category in the *DSM-III* (APA, 1980), SAD was conceptualized similar to specific phobia. Specifically, the *DSM–III* stated, "Both Social and Simple Phobias generally involve a circumscribed stimulus .... When more than one type is present, multiple diagnoses should be made" (p. 225). *DSM–III* did not recognize the fact that most individuals with SAD fear multiple social situations when it stated that "generally an individual has only one Social Phobia" (p. 227). Furthermore, the diagnosis of SAD was ruled out if the individual met diagnostic criteria for avoidant personality disorder (APD). These diagnostic criteria underwent significant changes with the publication of the *DSM–III–R* (APA, 1987) and then later the *DSM–IV* (APA, 1994). Specifically, the diagnostic specifier "generalized subtype" was included if the person feared "most or all" social situations (p. 417), and the diagnosis of SAD was no longer ruled out if the criteria for APD were met. Studies consistently report a high degree of overlap between the generalized subtype of SAD and the Axis II disorder APD (e.g., Heimberg, 1996; Schneier, Spitzer, Gibbon, Fyer, & Liebowitz, 1991). This finding is not overly surprising because six of the seven diagnostic criteria for APD include social interactional components. Moreover, one of the nonsocial-specific criteria for APD was removed in the transition from *DSM–III–R* to *DSM–IV* (APA, 1994), making the overlap between the two diagnoses even greater. As a result, many researchers have questioned the utility of maintaining two diagnostic categories on two separate *DSM–IV* axes.

## The Generalized Subtype

According to the *DSM–IV*, the generalized specifier for SAD should be used "when the [individual's] fears are related to most social situations" (p. 451). Unfortunately, the DSM does not specify the number and type of social situations that define the generalized subtype. Therefore, different research groups have developed slightly different operational definitions for the generalized subtype of SAD and the residual subgroup. This has made it difficult to directly compare empirical studies on the subtype issue. Turner, Beidel, and Townsley (1992) and Stemberger, Turner, Beidel, and Calhoun (1995) assigned a generalized subtype if the individual feared attending parties (social gatherings), initiating conversations, or maintaining conversations. A "specific" subtype (not specified in *DSM–IV*) was assigned if the person feared only performance-oriented situations, such as giving speeches, speaking up in meetings, eating or writing in public, and using public restrooms. People who were assigned to this group could fear multiple "specific" social situations, but could not fear more "general" social situations, such as parties or conversations.

Heimberg, Holt, Schneier, Spitzer, and Liebowitz (1993) discussed three possible subtypes of SAD: generalized, nongeneralized, and circumscribed. Individuals with nongeneralized SAD function in at least one broad social domain without experiencing clinically significant anxiety, whereas people with circumscribed SAD experience anxiety in only one or two discrete situations. Because the number of individuals with circumscribed SAD is very small, most studies either did not include the circumscribed subtype (Herbert, Hope, & Bellack, 1992) or pooled them with the nongeneralized group (Brown, Heimberg, & Juster, 1995; Hofmann, Newman, Ehlers, & Roth, 1995; Hofmann & Roth, 1996; Holt, Heimberg, & Hope, 1992). Only very few studies have included a subgroup corresponding to Heimberg et al.'s (1993) circumscribed subtype (Heimberg, Hope, Dodge, & Becker, 1990; Levin et al., 1993; McNeil et al., 1995; Stein et al., 1996). In these studies, the subtype was restricted to individuals with public speaking anxiety, the most commonly feared social situation.

Feared Social Situations

Some researchers quantified the number and type of feared social situations based on items reported in social anxiety questionnaires and other self-report instruments. For example, Holt, Heimberg, Hope, and Liebowitz (1992) proposed four situational domains based on their inspection of the 24 items of the Liebowitz Social Anxiety Scale (LSAS; Liebowitz, 1987): formal speaking/interaction, informal speaking/interaction, assertive interaction, and observation by others. Factor analytic techniques, however, provided mixed support for this classification system (Baker, Heinrichs, Kim, & Hofmann, 2002; Safren et al., 1999; Slavkin, Holt, Heimberg, Jaccard, & Liebowitz, 1990). Other investigators have employed latent class analysis (Kessler, Stein, & Berglund, 1998), cluster analysis (Eng, Heimberg, Coles, Schneier, & Liebowitz, 2000; Kashdan & Hofmann, in press), and taxometric analyses (Kollman, Brown, Liverant, & Hofmann, 2006) to examine the subtypes of SAD. The studies with the two largest samples were the studies by Kessler and colleagues (1998) and Kollman and colleagues (2006).

Kessler et al. (1998) analyzed fear ratings of six social situations that were assessed as part of the National Comorbidity Survey. The results of the latent class analysis showed that one third of the individuals with SAD reported speaking fears only, whereas the other two thirds had speaking fears with at least one other social fear. The two subtypes had similar ages of onset, family histories, and demographic characteristics.

Kollman et al. (2006) examined the latent structure of SAD in a sample of 2,035 outpatients with anxiety and mood disorders to determine whether the disorder operates in a categorical or dimensional fashion. Using three mathematically distinct taxometric procedures with indicators constructed from clinical interview ratings and questionnaire measures of social anxiety symptoms, they supported the notion that the latent structure of SAD is dimensional. However, the choice of other indicator variables might identify qualitatively different subgroups in the future (e.g., Kashdan & Hofmann, in press).

Differences Between Diagnostic Subtypes

The diagnostic category of SAD shows a great degree of heterogeneity. It is important to more closely examine the nature of this heterogeneity because we believe that this has direct implications for therapy for the disorder (for a review, see Hofmann, Heinrichs, & Moscovitch, 2004).

Studies have found that the generalized subtype of SAD and the highly overlapping Axis II diagnosis APD are associated with severe levels of social anxiety, poor overall psychosocial functioning, greater overall psychopathology, high trait anxiety, and depression (e.g., Boone et al., 1999; Brown et al., 1995; Herbert, Hope, et al., 1992; Holt, Heimberg, & Hope, 1992; Tran & Chambless, 1995; Turner et al., 1992). Therefore, it has been suggested that these diagnoses may simply represent increasingly more severe manifestations of social anxiety, which range on a continuum from specific (nongeneralized) SAD to generalized SAD without APD to generalized SAD with APD (Hofmann, 2000b; McNeil, 2001). Other studies, however, suggest that not all differences between these diagnostic groups can be explained by differences in social anxiety severity. These studies have reported subtype differences in a number of important variables, including prevalence, demographics, developmental characteristics, psychophysiological response during exposure, and treatment response.

### Prevalence

Irrespective of the differences between studies in the operational definition, the literature consistently reports that at least 50% of individuals with SAD meet criteria for the generalized subtype (Brown et al., 1995; Mannuzza et al., 1995).

### Demographics

Two thirds of patients with generalized SAD and one third of patients with nongeneralized SAD have never been married (Mannuzza et al., 1995). Moreover, some studies have reported that individuals with generalized SAD tend to have a lower socioeconomic status than the residual subgroup of individuals (Brown et al., 1995; Heimberg, Hope, et al., 1990; Levin et al., 1993). However, other studies have found no differences between subtypes with respect to age, gender, and socioeconomic status (Herbert, Hope, et al., 1992; Hofmann & Roth, 1996; Holt, Heimberg, Hope, & Liebowitz, 1992; Mannuzza et al., 1995; McNeil et al., 1995; Stemberger et al., 1995).

### Developmental Characteristics

Generalized SAD is associated with a significantly earlier age of onset (mean = 10.9) than nongeneralized SAD (mean = 16.9), with half of the former group developing the disorder before age 10 (Mannuzza et al., 1995). With early onset of social fears and avoidance behavior, one can imagine the developmental challenges faced by these children. With impairments in opportunities for social success, early onset may be one driving force in the generalization of social fears and avoidance patterns.

## Clinical Severity

Studies consistently report that individuals with generalized SAD show higher scores on self-report measures of social anxiety than the residual subtype (Stein & Chavira, 1998), including the Fear of Negative Evaluation Scale (FNE; Watson & Friend, 1969), the Social Avoidance and Distress Scale (SADS; Watson & Friend, 1969) (Brown et al., 1995; Gelernter, Stein, Tancer, & Uhde, 1992; Heimberg, Hope, et al., 1990; Hofmann & Roth, 1996; Holt, Heimberg, & Hope, 1992; Turner et al., 1992), and the Social Phobia and Anxiety Inventory (SPAI; Turner, Beidel, Dancu, & Stanley, 1989) (Bögels & Reith, 1999; Hofmann & Roth, 1996; Turner et al., 1992). Individuals with generalized SAD who also meet criteria for avoidant personality disorder tend to score the highest on these measures (e.g., Brown et al., 1995) and are also more likely to have other comorbid Axis I diagnoses and more overall psychopathology, such as general anxiety, depression (Herbert, Hope, et al., 1992; Hofmann, Newman, Ehlers, et al., 1995; Hofmann & Roth, 1996; Holt, Heimberg, & Hope., 1992), and neuroticism (Stemberger et al., 1995) than individuals in the residual categories. However, individuals with generalized SAD do not typically rate themselves as more impaired by their disorder than those of the residual group, suggesting that the results cannot be explained by differences in the subjective severity of the illness (Gelernter et al., 1992).

## Psychophysiological Response During Exposure

At least five studies have compared SAD subtypes in their psychophysiological response during an exposure task. In the first study, individuals with SAD whose fears were restricted to public speaking situations were compared with individuals who met criteria for generalized SAD (Heimberg, Hope, et al., 1990). Individuals who only feared public speaking showed higher heart rates but reported less subjective anxiety to a behavioral challenge than individuals with generalized SAD. One major limitation of the study was that the behavioral challenge test was individually tailored for the generalized SAD group and therefore not uniform for all individuals.

The second study by Turner and colleagues (1992) compared individuals with "discrete" SAD, generalized SAD without APD, and generalized SAD with APD on heart rate levels recorded during an impromptu speech. The results showed no differences in heart rate between the three groups. However, the study did not specify what participants' main fears were. The third study by Levin et al. (1993) compared patients with generalized SAD and discrete SAD with controls on heart rate, subjective measures, and biochemical measures, including plasma epinephrine and norepinephrine. In contrast to Heimberg, Hope, and colleagues' (1990) design, Levin et al. (1993) included a standard public speaking task.

Consistent with findings reported by Heimberg, Hope, et al. (1990), individuals with discrete SAD showed higher heart rates but reported less subjective anxiety during their speeches than individuals with generalized SAD. The groups did not differ in their plasma catecholamine levels, and heart rates did not significantly correlate with plasma catecholamine levels. The fourth study reported similar subtype differences in the autonomic measures (Hofmann, Newman, Ehlers, et al., 1995). In this study, public-speaking anxious individuals with generalized SAD (and APD), those with nongeneralized SAD (and no APD), and nonanxious controls were instructed to give a speech while cardiovascular parameters, behavioral measures, and subjective anxiety were recorded. The results showed that the generalized SAD group scored highest on SAD severity measures. However, the nongeneralized SAD group showed the highest heart rate level in response to the public speaking exposure. The fifth study by Boone et al. (1999) replicated these findings. These five studies question the notion that the diagnostic subgroups differ solely in the severity of their social anxiety on the basis of autonomic measures. The nature of these differences, however, remains unknown. It is possible that the psychophysiological differences are not directly due to the diagnostic subtypes per se, but are related to associated features that affect psychophysiological responses to social threat, such as behavioral inhibition (Hofmann & Kim, 2006) and self-monitoring (Hofmann, 2006).

*Treatment Response*

Some studies suggest that the presence of avoidant personality disorder or depression predicts poor treatment outcome (Alden & Capreol, 1993; Chambless, Tran, & Glass, 1997; Erwin, Heimberg, Juster, & Mindlin, 2002; Feske, Perry, Chambless, Renneberg, & Goldstein, 1996), whereas others have not replicated these results (Brown et al., 1995; Dreessen & Arntz, 1998; Hofmann, Newman, Becker, Taylor, & Roth, 1995; Hope, Herbert, & White, 1995; Mersch, Jansen, & Arntz, 1995; Van Velzen, Emmelkamp, & Scholing, 1997). Inconsistent results have also been reported in studies investigating the generalized subtype of SAD as a predictor of poor treatment outcome (Brown et al.; Gorman, Liebowitz, Fyer, Campeas, & Klein, 1985; Liebowitz et al., 1992; Turner et al., 1992; Uhde, Tancer, Black, & Brown, 1991). Our clinical experience is that even the individual with most severe SAD and avoidant personality disorder responds very well to a tailored, long-term cognitive behavioral therapy (CBT) intervention (see Hofmann, in press-b, for a case report).

The inconsistent findings in the literature may be partly due to the small sample size in some of the studies, differences in the operational definition of generalized subtype, and differences in the assessment procedure of APD. Systematic dismantling studies would provide valuable data. Furthermore, future studies investigating the moderating role of diagnostic subgroups of SAD will need to consider the effects of treatment expectancy (Chambless et al., 1997; Safren, Heimberg, & Juster, 1997), homework compliance (Edelman & Chambless, 1995; Leung & Heimberg, 1996), and depression (Chambless et al., 1997), as well as therapeutic alliance, adherence to and competence of the treatment protocol, sociodemographic variables, and diagnostic data.

For example, the study by Chambless, Tran, and Glass (1997) considered depression, treatment expectancy, personality disorder traits, clinical severity, and frequency of negative thoughts during social interactions as possible predictors for treatment outcome in 62 patients with SAD. Treatment consisted of 12 weekly cognitive behavioral group sessions following Heimberg's cognitive behavioral group therapy (CBGT; Heimberg & Becker, 1991, 2002). Participants were assessed at pretreatment, posttreatment, and 6-month follow-up. Outcome measures included self-report questionnaires and behavioral tests. The results showed that none of the predictors was related to outcome across all domains of measurement. However, higher levels of depression, as measured with the Beck Depression Inventory (Beck & Steer, 1987), more avoidant personality disorder traits, and lower treatment expectancy were each related to poorer treatment response on one or more outcome criteria. The most salient predictor for poor treatment outcome was depression.

It is important to note that depression is not a consistent predictor of poor outcome for patients with SAD, despite the frequent exclusion of individuals with comorbid depression from clinical trials. A meta-analysis of 30 cognitive and behavioral treatments of SAD, published between 1996 and 2002, found only 11 studies that included patients with SAD and comorbid depression (Lincoln & Rief, 2004). Nonetheless, this meta-analysis indicated that inclusion of at least some patients with comorbid depression appeared to make little difference to the overall study outcome, with near identical estimates of mean pre- to posttreatment effect sizes for studies that did and did not exclude patients with depression. Other individual studies support this result. Van Velzen et al. (1997) found, in a sample of 18 patients with SAD, that comorbid anxiety or depression did not affect treatment outcome of exposure treatment. Similarly, in a larger scale study ($N = 141$) by Erwin et al. (2002), responses to 12 sessions of CBGT were compared among three groups of patients with SAD: those with no comorbid diagnoses, those with a comorbid anxiety disorder, and those with a comorbid mood disorder. They found that SAD patients with comorbid mood disorders, but not comorbid anxiety disorders, were more severely impaired than those with no comorbid diagnosis both before and after treatment; however, the *rate* of improvement in therapy was the same in both groups.

An additional perspective on the influence of comorbidity on the treatment of SAD is provided by studies offering more detailed analyses of changes in symptoms across treatment. Moscovitch, Hofmann, Suvak, and In-Albon (2005) assessed anxiety and depression symptoms on a weekly basis in 66 adults with SAD who were treated with CBGT. They found that improvements in SAD symptoms mediated 91% of the improvements in depression symptoms over time. On the other hand, decreases in depression accounted for only 6% of the change in social anxiety over time.

In summary, studies that examined the diagnostic subtypes of SAD provided limited support for the usefulness of subtyping individuals based on the number of feared social situations. More recent studies, however, suggest that certain temperamental factors and personality traits (Hofmann & Bitran, 2007; Hofmann & Loh, 2006; Kashdan & Hofmann, in press) might identify meaningful subgroups (for a review, see Hofmann, Moscovitch, & Kim, 2006). This is an area of future research. These subgroups, if they exist, are all very likely to benefit from specifically tailored intervention strategies, all of which are outlined in this book.

Available evidence further suggests that patients with SAD and comorbid depression are likely to be more severe prior to treatment and to retain some of this severity after treatment. Nonetheless, SAD patients with comorbid depression appear to be likely to improve at the same rate as their nondepressed counterparts and that response to treatment may drive improvement in comorbid depression. Accordingly, we believe the available literature provides clinicians with confidence that brief CBT targeting social phobia has a good chance of success despite the presence of depression (see chapter 5).

## INFORMATION PROCESSING IN SAD

Contemporary theories of social anxiety and SAD emphasize the role of cognitive processes for the maintenance of the disorder (Clark & Wells, 1995; Leary & Kowalski, 1995; Rapee & Heimberg, 1997; Turner, Beidel, & Jacob, 1994) with the notion that effective psychological treatment changes a person's representation of the self in a more positive direction (Rapee & Heimberg, 1997). Supporting evidence comes from a study by Woody, Chambless, and Glass (1997), who observed that self-focused attention decreased during the course of cognitive-behavioral group treatment in individuals with SAD, whereas external focus of attention remained unchanged. Similarly, Hofmann (2000b) reported that individuals with SAD who underwent exposure therapy showed a significant decline of negative self-focused thoughts, which was correlated with changes in self-reported social anxiety. Another study by Wells and Papageorgiou (1998) suggested that exposure therapy combined with instructions to focus on the external environment is more effective than standard exposure therapy. Wells and colleagues (1995) hypothesized that self-focused attention and evaluating one's own behaviors is part of the person's misguided attempts to prevent an embarrassing and humiliating situation. However, this strategy interferes with the processing of information that could provide disconfirming evidence against their negative beliefs (Wells et al., 1995).

Greater detail on presumed cognitive biases in SAD are provided by Clark and Wells (1995). Clark and Wells discussed at least four psychopathological processes that prevent individuals with SAD from disconfirming their beliefs. First, when individuals with SAD enter a social situation they shift their attention to detailed monitoring and observations of themselves. This attentional shift produces an enhanced awareness of feared anxiety responses, interferes with processing the situation and other people's behavior, and produces interoceptive information, which is used to construct an impression of oneself. Second, individuals with SAD engage in a variety of safety behaviors to reduce the risk of rejection. These behaviors prevent them from critically evaluating their feared outcomes (e.g., "I will shake uncontrollably") and catastrophic beliefs (e.g., "I will be humiliated and will be unable to every show my face there again"). Third, Clark and Wells assumed that individuals with SAD show an anxiety-induced performance deficit. Furthermore, they overestimate how negatively other people evaluate their performance. Fifth, the model suggested that prior to and after a social event, individuals with SAD think about the situation in detail primarily focusing on past failures, negative images of themselves in the situation, and other predictions of poor performance and rejection. The cognitive model assumed that these anxious feelings and negative self-perception are strongly encoded in memory because they are processed in such detail.

Therefore, this cognitive model is consistent with many empirical studies suggesting that cost and probability estimations of social events are biased (Amir, Foa, & Coles, 1998; Foa, Franklin, Perry, & Herbert, 1996; Lucock & Salkovskis, 1988). Moreover, the model explains the crucial role of interpretational processes in the maintenance of SAD and predicts a self–other discrepancy when social situations are judged. Empirical evidence supports this notion (e.g., Mellings & Alden, 2000; Rapee & Lim, 1992). However, the model also suggests that this bias is evident in specific physical and behavioral signs of anxiety, but this has not consistently been found (Rapee & Lim, 1992).

The cognitive model also explicitly assumes the existence of a memory bias (encoding, elaboration, and retrieval) because it assumes that individuals with SAD show a memory bias toward socially threatening information

(e.g., anxious feelings, negative self-perceptions). The model further emphasizes the importance of encoding material in a public-self-referent fashion,
suggesting that encoding processes may be more crucial for maintaining
SAD than retrieval processes, but they also assume that individuals with
SAD are more likely to recall socially threatening information. Although
this has been supported by memory studies with subclinical samples,
we have found no compelling evidence of this effect in clinical samples.
Another assumption of the cognitive model that has not been confirmed is
the notion of enhanced recall of past failures. Rapee, McCallum, Melville,
Ravenscroft, and Rodney (1994) did not find that individuals with SAD
recall threat-related memories from their own lives better than controls.
Finally, the cognitive model suggests that social success experiences can lose
their positive connotation during post-event processing. However, Wallace
and Alden's study (1997) indicates that although social success can be recognized, it does not elicit positive affect. Instead, it is associated with negative affect because individuals with SAD are afraid that their interaction
partners also expect them to perform well in the future.

## ETIOLOGY OF SAD

There is little evidence to suggest that traumatic speaking experiences play
a dominant role in the onset of social fears. Of the few studies addressing
this issue, Stemberger et al. (1995) examined the presence of traumatic
social experiences among 22 individuals who met criteria for generalized SAD, 16 participants who met criteria for a specific subtype, and 25
healthy control participants. The study reported that 56% of individuals
with specific SAD and 40% of those with generalized SAD, but only 20%
of normal controls, reported the presence of these traumatic social-condi-
tioning experiences. Only the difference between the specific subtype and
the control group reached the level of statistical significance. Contrary
to this finding, a previous study found that traumatic external events, as
well as vicarious and informational learning, were notably uncommon
among individuals anxious about public speaking. Instead, individuals tended to attribute their fear most often to panic attacks (Hofmann,
Ehlers, & Roth, 1995). Although 89% of the speech phobics in the study
reported traumatic experiences in the past, which is consistent with those
of Öst and Hugdahl (1981, 1983), none of them developed SAD after
they experienced these traumatic speaking situations. The study further
showed that only 15% reported that the traumatic experience occurred at
the same time as the onset of SAD. The traumatic experience occurred on
average 21.5 years *after* the onset of SAD. Stemberger et al. (1995) did not
examine the temporal relationship between the traumatic event and the

onset of the disorder. Therefore, the existing data question the hypothesis that traumatic experiences play a significant role in the etiology of SAD.

Some scholars assume that social fears are the result of a biologically determined readiness to easily associate fear with angry, critical, or rejecting facial stimuli (Öhman, 1986; Öhman, Dimberg, & Öst, 1985). Consistent with this notion are studies that have shown that angry faces and happy faces elicit different patterns of electromyographic activity in normals (Dimberg, 1982), and fear conditioning to angry faces shows much more resistance to extinction than do responses to happy or neutral expressions (Dimberg, 1982; Öhman & Dimberg, 1978). It is important to note that this conditioning effect is only obtained when the stimulus person directs his or her anger toward the subject; angry faces looking away are as ineffective as happy faces in conditioning paradigms (Dimberg & Öhman, 1983). This finding suggests that direct eye contact is crucial. In primates, direct eye contact seems to be very frightening. Moreover, various species display eyelike spots to frighten potential predators. Although the response to eye contact is greatly altered by contextual and learning factors among humans, it is also a hard-wired evolutionary response that is common to all mammals. Therefore, it has been suggested that the fear of being watched among individuals with SAD is an exaggeration of the normal human sensitivity to eyes (Marks, 1987).

Consistent with this assertion is a study that compared 9 individuals with SAD and 9 normal controls in their eyeblink rate and skin conductance response during exposure to slides of angry faces, happy faces, and neutral objects (Merckelbach, van Hout, van den Hout, & Mersch, 1989). The results showed that in both groups angry faces elicited greater skin conductance response and stronger inhibition of eyeblink rate than the other stimuli. No difference was found between individuals with SAD and the normal controls in their responses to these stimuli. This study was obviously limited by the small sample size and the choice of the dependent variables.

In contrast to psychophysiological data, there is some evidence to suggest that individuals with SAD and healthy controls differ in their memory for faces. In a study by Lundh and Öst (1996), individuals with SAD (most of them met criteria for the generalized subtype) and normal controls were presented with a number of photos of faces and asked to judge whether the people in the photos were critical or accepting. After this encoding task, participants were asked to perform an unrelated task for 5 minutes and were then unexpectedly presented with a facial recognition task. The findings showed that individuals with SAD recognized more critical than accepting faces, whereas the controls tended to recognize more accepting than critical faces. These findings suggest that individuals with SAD show either a recognition bias or a response bias for critical faces. Interestingly, this effect has not been found in studies that used words as stimulus material (e.g., Cloitre, Cancienne, Heimberg, Holt, & Liebowitz, 1995; Rapee et al., 1994). Future studies that employ signal detection analyses of subjects' responses could determine whether the results, if replicable, are due to a response bias or due to a true recognition bias.

Evidence for a genetic contribution to social anxiety comes from family studies, twin studies, and high-risk studies (Fyer, Mannuzza, Chapman, Liebowitz, & Klein, 1993; Horwarth et al., 1995; Kendler, Neale, Kessler, Heath, & Eaves, 1992; Mancini, van Ameringen, Szatmari, Fugere, & Boyle, 1996; Reich & Yates, 1988; Skre, Onstad, Torgersen, Lygren, & Kringlen, 1993). For example, the results of a direct family interview study showed that the risk for developing SAD was approximately 3 times higher for relatives of individuals with SAD than for relatives of never mentally ill controls (Fyer et al., 1993). Similarly, the twin study by Kendler et al. (1992), which was based on over 1,000 female twin pairs, found substantial concordance rates for SAD in identical (24%) and fraternal (15%) twin pairs. Another study by Mancini and colleagues (1996) reported that 23% of the children (with the mean age of 11 years) of adults with SAD met diagnostic criteria for SAD.

The genetic disposition to develop SAD may be nonspecific but seems to be closely connected to certain temperament variables. In particular, shyness, one of the most heritable temperament factors (Plomin & Daniels, 1985), seems to be closely related to SAD (Turner, Beidel, & Townsley, 1990) and also subclinical forms of social anxiety (Hofmann, Moscovitch, & Kim, 2006). Another likely precursor of SAD is behavioral inhibition, which refers to the child's fearfulness, timidity, and weariness when encountering novel people, objects, or events (Kagan, Reznick, & Snidman, 1988). Numerous studies have found that behavioral inhibition in childhood is closely associated with social anxiety and SAD during adolescence (Mick & Telch, 1998; Rosenbaum, Biederman, Hirshfeld, Bolduc, & Chaloff, 1991; Rosenbaum, Biederman, Pollock, & Hirshfeld, 1994; Schwartz, Snidman, & Kagan, 1999). For example, Kagan's group found that parents of children who were identified as inhibited at 21 months of age were significantly more likely to meet *DSM–III* diagnostic criteria for SAD (17.5%) than parents of uninhibited children (0%) and control parents whose children were neither inhibited or uninhibited (2.9%; Rosenbaum et al., 1991). These findings seem to suggest that behaviorally inhibited children are more likely to have parents with SAD than noninhibited children. However, it has yet to be examined whether parents with SAD are also more likely to have behaviorally inhibited children and whether behavioral inhibition in childhood leads to SAD in adulthood. If this relationship between behavioral inhibition and SAD holds true, future studies will need to identify the factors that protect behaviorally inhibited children from developing SAD in adulthood. Examples of such protective factors might be family factors and peer relationships. However, little empirical evidence exits on the specific relationship those variables have on social functioning during childhood and adulthood (Masia & Morris, 1998; Rapee & Heimberg, 1997).

Barlow's anxiety model as it relates to SAD assumes that relatively minor negative life events involving performance or social interactions can lead to anxiety, particularly if anxiety attacks (alarms) are associated with these events (Hofmann & Barlow, 2002). These factors then form the platform from which a false and true alarm can develop. The pathway via true alarms appears to be more common for individuals with a nongeneralized (specific, circumscribed) subtype of SAD than for people with generalized SAD. This assumption is consistent with the notion that individuals with nongeneralized SAD exhibit more of a *fear* reaction (similar to individuals with specific phobias), whereas individuals with a generalized subtype experience more of an *anxiety* response, which is often associated with feelings of embarrassment and shame. This distinction corresponds to Buss's classification of shy individuals into "fearful shys" and "self-conscious shys" (Buss, 1980). One of the characteristic features of the former group is the fear of autonomic reactivity, whereas the second group is characterized by excessive "public self-awareness" (i.e., increased attention that is focused on public aspects of the self). This would explain why individuals with SAD attribute their fear of public speaking more often to "panic attacks" than to fear of evaluation, traumatic events, or indirect conditioning events (Hofmann, Ehlers, & Roth, 1995). In contrast, our model assumes that the etiologic pathway for the generalized subtype of SAD is more likely to occur without alarm or via false alarms associated with social evaluative situations. Supporting evidence for this idea comes from a study showing that in contrast to individuals with generalized SAD, those with a specific SAD subtype are more likely to report the presence of traumatic conditioning experiences than controls (Stemberger et al., 1995). The repeated experience of such false alarms may be the reason why individuals with SAD often perceive a lack of internal control (Leung & Heimberg, 1996) and believe that events are controllable only by people other than themselves (Cloitre, Heimberg, Liebowitz, & Gitow, 1992). Once established, SAD persists unless treated.

## ASSESSMENT OF SOCIAL ANXIETY AND SAD

Given the focus of this book, we will only briefly review some of the most popular assessment instruments. A comprehensive review of assessment measures for social anxiety and SAD can be found in Hofmann and DiBartolo (2001).

A popular clinician-rated scale is the Liebowitz Social Anxiety Scale (LSAS) to measure the severity of anxiety and avoidance in social situations (Liebowitz, 1987). This scale consists of 24 items that include a number of social interactional situations (13 items) and performance situations (11 items). Each item is rated for fear and avoidance. More recently, the scale has been modified as a self-report measure (Baker, Heinrichs, Kim, & Hofmann, 2002). Another clinician-rated scale is the Brief Social Phobia Scale (Davidson et al., 1991). This scale consists of 7 items describing a number of common social situations that are rated on both fear and avoidance. Another 4 items are included to measure physiological symptoms.

The most frequently used self-report scales for social anxiety and SAD include the Fear of Negative Evaluation Scale (FNE) and the Social Avoidance and Distress Scale (SADS) by Watson and Friend (1969); the Social Phobia Scale (SPS) and the Social Interaction Anxiety Scale (SIAS) by Mattick and Clarke (1998); and the Social Phobia and Anxiety Inventory (SPAI) for adults (Turner et al., 1989) and children between the ages of 8 and 17 (Beidel, Turner, & Morris, 1995).

Although the SADS and FNE are among the most widely used assessment measures, the appropriateness for social phobia patients has been questioned because the two instruments seem to lack discriminant validity (Turner & Beidel, 1988; Turner, McCanna, & Beidel, 1987). Moreover, the scales are limited by the true–false format of their items. Therefore, Leary (1983) developed a shorter 12-item version of the FNE (Brief FNE) that is uses a 5-point Likert-type scale. Moreover, the scoring procedure in the original publication of the SADS is erroneous (Hofmann, DiBartolo, Holaway, & Heimberg, 2004).

The SPS and SIAS were designed to be used together in the assessment of SAD. The SPS assesses fears of being scrutinized or observed by others, whereas the SIAS measures anxiety concerning interpersonal interactions. Both scales show good psychometric properties and consist of 20 items each.

The SPAI is a 109-item scale to assess the cognitive, somatic, and behavioral aspect of social anxiety. This instrument consists of two subscales: the social phobia subscale and the agoraphobia subscale. A difference score is derived by subtracting the agoraphobia subscale score from the social phobia subscale score. Turner et al. (1989) recommended using the difference score as an indicator of social anxiety, whereas Herbert, Bellack, Hope, and Mueser (1992) suggested that the best SPAI subscale score depends on the intended use of the instrument.

A study by Ries and colleagues (1998) compared the SPS, SIAS, and SPAI and evaluated these instruments in patients with SAD. The results suggested that each of these instruments offers a unique contribution to the assessment of SAD in terms of behavioral and cognitive self-report criteria, as well as distinction among subtypes. For example, the SIAS was consistently related to negative and positive self-reported thoughts in a speech and conversation test, whereas the SPS showed a significant negative relationship with time spent during the impromptu speech. The SIAS and the SPAI were most sensitive to treatment change and for distinguishing the diagnostic subtypes of SAD. Although reliable and valid, these measures are somewhat limited for research purposes because they provide only an overall score as a general indicator of distress and avoidance in social situations.

Despite the theoretical importance of cognitions in SAD, few studies on SAD have utilized any type of cognitive assessment. The only two instruments that were specifically designed to measure cognitions in social phobic individuals are the Social Interaction and Self-Statement Test (SISST; Glass, Merluzzi, Biever, & Larsen, 1982) and the Self-Statement during Public Speaking Scale (SSPS; Hofmann & DiBartolo, 2000). Unlike the SISST, the SSPS can be administered without a social challenge test.

## CONTEMPORARY PSYCHOLOGICAL TREATMENTS

A number of effective treatments for SAD exist, including cognitive therapy, CBT, exposure treatment, and social skills training (e.g., Heimberg, Salzman, et al., 1990, 1998; Heimberg, Holt, et al., 1993; Heimberg, Salzman, Holt, & Blendell, 1993; Hofmann, 2007; Hofmann & Scepkowski, 2006; Mattick & Peters, 1988; Turner, Beidel, Cooley, Woody, & Messer, 1994; Turner, Beidel, & Cooley-Quille, 1995). Of those treatments, Heimberg's CBGT for SAD (Heimberg & Becker, 1991, 2002) is often considered the gold standard intervention. The efficacy of CBGT has been demonstrated in a number of well-designed studies (Gelernter et al., 1991; Heimberg, Becker, Goldfinger, & Vermilyea, 1985; Heimberg, Dodge, et al., 1990; Heimberg, Salzman, et al., 1993; Heimberg et al., 1998; Hofmann, Schulz, Meuret, Moscovitch, & Suvak, 2006). Treatment drop outs are generally low and not systematically associated with any patient variables (Hofmann & Suvak, 2006). CBGT is administered by 2 therapists in 12 weekly 2.5-hour sessions to groups consisting of 4 to 6 participants. In the most recent study on the efficacy of CBGT, 133 patients with SAD were randomly assigned to phenelzine (a monoamine oxidase inhibitor commonly used to treat SAD), educational support group therapy (ESGT), a pill placebo, or CBGT (Heimberg et al., 1998). After 12 weeks, both the phenelzine (65%) and the CBGT conditions (58%) had higher proportions of responders than the pill placebo (33%) or ESGT (27%), which served as a psychotherapy placebo condition.

Although the study showed that the treatment groups were statistically better than the placebo conditions, the percentages of responders in these conditions were modest. The criterion for treatment response was based on a 7-point rating of change on the Social Phobic Disorders Severity Change Form (Liebowitz et al., 1992). Patients rated as markedly or moderately improved were classified as responders. Using a stricter improvement criterion, Mattick and Peters (1988) found that only 38% of individuals with SAD who completed a treatment very similar to Heimberg's protocol achieved "high end state functioning." More recently developed CBT protocols include Comprehensive Cognitive Behavioral Therapy (CCBT; Foa et al., unpublished data, 1994) and a cognitive therapy protocol developed by Clark et al. (2003). The treatment protocol by Foa et al. (1994) was included as a treatment condition in a recently published clinical trial (Davidson et al., 2004). The treatment protocol is derived in part from CBGT (Heimberg & Becker, 1991, 2002) and combines exposure techniques, Beckian cognitive restructuring therapy, and social skills training. It is conducted in the form of 14 weekly group sessions. The treatment differs from CBGT primarily in that it includes specific social skills training. Furthermore, the role plays are shorter and the treatment is two sessions longer than CBGT. The study by Davidson et al. (2004) suggested that Foa's treatment shows efficacy rates similar to CBGT. Specifically, the study randomized 295 patients with generalized SAD to one of five groups: (1) fluoxetine, (2) CCBT, (3) placebo, (4) CCBT combined with fluoxetine, or (5) CCBT combined with placebo. The results showed that all active treatments were superior to placebo, and the combined treatment was not superior to the other treatments. The response rates in the intention-to-treat sample (using the Clinical Global Impressions scale) were 50.9% (fluoxetine), 51.7% (CCBT), 54.2% (CCBT + fluoxetine), 50.8% (CCBT + placebo), and 31.7% (placebo). These findings are comparable with other clinical trials using conventional CBT and suggest that many participants remain symptomatic after standard cognitive behavioral intervention. The authors, therefore, wondered whether "changes in the delivery of CBT would improve the results" (p. 1012). Preliminary evidence in support of the notion that changes in the intervention strategies could lead to improved outcomes came from a recent study by Clark et al. (2003). The treatment used in this trial also focused on modifying safety behaviors and self-focused attention, among more conventional CBT strategies that have been used in earlier protocols.

The cognitive therapy protocol by Clark and colleagues (2003, 2006) is an individual approach consisting of 16 sessions. Treatment efforts are directed toward the systematic teaching of an alternative cognitive frame for understanding social situations, social performance, and social risk. Interventions are richly cognitive, asking patients to examine their expectations about social situations and the social costs of imperfect social performances, and then to specifically examine the veracity of these expectations as evaluated by logical evaluation and, particularly, specific "behavioral experiments" that are designed to test anxiogenic expectations. As compared with more behavioral treatments emphasizing exposure alone, the Clark and colleagues protocol devotes more attention to the testing of assumptions in select, carefully arranged—but often exposure-based—social experiments. What then, is the distinction between cognitive therapy using behavioral experiments to aid therapeutic learning versus a standard exposure protocol? One answer is that cognitive protocols try to substitute in *specific learning moments* for what may be more nonspecific learning of safety in social situations that come from repeated exposure assignments that may rely on less cognitive preparation or testing of specific anxiogenic predictions.

Regarding the performance of this approach, an abbreviated version of the Clark and associates' protocol was developed by Wells and Papageorgiou (2001). The Clark et al. (2003) trial randomly assigned 60 patients with generalized SAD to one of three conditions: (1) cognitive therapy alone, (2) fluoxetine combined with self-exposure, or (3) self-exposure combined with placebo. Treatment efficacy was measured by calculating a SAD composite score that was based on six frequently used self-report measures of SAD and a rating based on a structured clinical interview. The results at posttreatment and 12-month follow-up assessments showed that cognitive therapy was superior to the other two conditions, which did not differ from one another.

The study did not include a method to assess responder status. Furthermore, most of the results were based on self-report instruments. Nonetheless, the uncontrolled effect size of the severity rating based on the clinical interview was 1.41 (pretest to posttest) and 1.43 (pretest to 12-month follow-up) in the cognitive therapy group. The composite score was associated with an uncontrolled pre/post effect size of 2.14. However, another recently published study by Stangier, Heidenreich, Peitz, Lauterbach, and Clark (2003) reported a considerably smaller uncontrolled prepost effect size after administering Clark's protocol (ES = 1.77) and an even smaller effect size when administering this treatment in a group format (ES = 0.60).

The CBT protocols that we have reviewed here are based on the assumption that treatment progress occurs as a result of changes in cognitive schemata. More specifically, it is assumed that effective psychotherapy provides patients with a range of learning experiences that modify the patient's anxiogenic beliefs and expectations or deactivates them while making other interpretations and beliefs available. Following this model, individuals with SAD believe they are in danger of behaving in an inept and unacceptable fashion, and such behavior would have disastrous consequences in terms of loss of status, loss of worth, and interpersonal rejection (Clark & Wells,

1995; Rapee & Heimberg, 1997). This model predicts that once a situation is perceived as holding the potential for social evaluation, individuals with SAD become preoccupied with negative thoughts about themselves and the way other people perceive them. The model further proposes that this negative impression typically occurs in the form of an image from an "observer" perspective in which people with SAD can see themselves as if from another person's vantage point. Therefore, this model predicts that treatment is most effective if it is aimed at changing dysfunctional cognitions directly and systematically via cognitive therapy.

Several authors have suggested that treatment for SAD should include a focused approach on changing dysfunctional beliefs about social situations using logical evaluation on specific behavioral experiments that use experience in social situations to challenge these thoughts (Heinrichs & Hofmann, 2001; Stopa & Clark, 1993, 2000; Wells, Clark, & Ahmad, 1998; Wells & Papageorgiou, 1998). However, it is not clear whether this approach has advantages over exposure-based treatment with a less explicit focus on cognitive-restructuring and logical evaluation. A number of review articles and meta-analyses have shown that cognitive-behavioral treatment is not more effective than exposure therapy that specifically addresses negative cognitive appraisals and probability overestimation (Feske & Chambless, 1995; Gould, Buckminster, Pollack, Otto, & Yap, 1997; Taylor, 1996). For example, the meta-analysis by Gould and colleagues (1997) showed that exposure interventions yielded the largest effect size, whether alone (ES = .89) or in combination with cognitive restructuring (ES = .80). Similar results were reported by Feske and Chambless (1995) who also found no evidence of differential dropout or relapse rates between the two treatment modalities. Another meta-analysis by Taylor (1996) compared the effect sizes of cognitive treatments, exposure treatments, CBT, social skills training, placebo treatments, and waitlist control groups. The results showed that the effect size of the waitlist control group was significantly smaller than the effect sizes of the different treatment conditions at posttreatment. The strongest effect size was for combined cognitive-restructuring/exposure treatments. Finally, the results of a dismantling study conducted by Hope, Heimberg, and Bruch (1995) suggested that exposure alone is at least as effective as exposure plus cognitive intervention in the treatment of SAD. This study randomly assigned 40 individuals with SAD to Heimberg's CBGT group, an exposure condition without cognitive intervention, or a waitlist control group. As expected, individuals in both active treatments improved more than those in the waitlist control group. However, participants who received CBGT did not improve more than those who received exposure without cognitive intervention. In fact, individuals in the exposure-only condition improved even more on some measures than those who received CBGT.

However, it should be pointed out that in practice it is difficult to directly contrast the efficacy of exposure treatment and cognitive therapy in isolation. Unexpected positive experiences during exposure to fearful social situations inevitably change the patient's beliefs and attitudes about a situation, even without explicit cognitive-restructuring techniques. Indeed, when comparing cognitive interventions utilizing behavioral experiments in feared social situations with more traditional exposure therapy, it is only with difficulty that one can operationalize the differences in these approaches. Both rely on experience to change patients' beliefs and expectations about social performance. The former relies on a more focused program of hypothesis generation ("What do you think will happened in this situation?") and specific testing of those hypotheses ("How do you interpret what happened?"). The latter relies on repeated exposure practices, but also assumes that patients will abstract new conceptualizations about the nature of social performance, a process that is often aided by review and processing what was learned from the exposure relative to a broader model of the nature of the disorder. Both models assume that social "safety" will be learned from real-life practice with social situations, and both guide this practice by providing patients with a framework for understanding the value of exposure. Indeed, given that the process of extinction learning is best understood as new learning (e.g., the acquisition of a sense of safety in a social situation) rather than weakening of a previously learned fear association (for a review, see Powers, Smits, Leyro, & Otto, 2006), any strategy that is used to maximize this new learning (e.g., making the learning especially salient, including the use of procedures to direct attention and the interpretation of what is being learned during exposure) fits both a traditional extinction model and a cognitive model of the value of programmed experience via exposure or behavioral experiments. The functional question for the clinician is how much time to devote to cognitive interventions versus exposure interventions in providing an efficient and effective treatment approach for patients with SAD. That is, by adding cognitive techniques to an exposure-based intervention, less time is available for exposure in any given session or series of sessions. This issue is particularly apt for cognitive interventions relying on logical evaluation versus behavioral experiments. Until the experimental literature indicates otherwise, our current recommendation is to utilize cognitive interventions in conjunction with exposure therapy to provide patients with a model for (1) how the experience can be constructed differently from expectation and (2) guiding an adaptive interpretation of the meaning of a successful exposure. In sum, the treatment outcome literature underscores the importance of programmed learning intervention in the treatment of SAD and suggests that both conventional CBT and exposure alone are effective treatments.

The data are also consistent with our earlier etiology model of SAD, which emphasizes the role of false alarms. This model predicts that repeated and prolonged exposure to social threat in the absence of all manners of avoidance strategies (safety signals and behavior) will lead to changes in harm expectancy (Hofmann, in press-b), relearning of safety (extinction) relative to the learned alarm response, improvement of perceived social skills, and decrease in anxious apprehension, including self-focused attention. These changes are more likely to occur if internal fear cues and other significant contexts are systematically produced (e.g., Bouton, Mineka, & Barlow, 2000), and if the outcome of the social situation is unexpectedly positive because it forces the person to reevaluate the actual threat of the social situation.

Another controversial area of research on SAD concerns the issue of SAD subtypes. Our model states that social threat leads primarily to "anxiety" (an integrated affective and cognitively mediated anticipation of potential danger) in individuals with generalized SAD/APD and primarily to "fear" or panic (a more basic and less cognitively mediated emotional response) in individuals with nongeneralized SAD (and those without APD), although anxiety may come to be focused on the next alarm response in a social context. Patients who primarily show an anxiety reaction to a social threat are likely to respond to strategies that target the underlying cognitive processes, including self-related processes and expectations about the outcome and cost of social mishaps, whereas patients who show a fear response are likely to benefit most from exposure strategies that enhance their perception of emotional control. This model emphasizes the importance of cognitive and exposure-based procedures that are specifically targeted to the individual. We believe that an effective intervention will need to target a number of different aspects because SAD comprises a heterogeneous group (Hofmann, Heinrichs, & Moscovitch, 2004).

## PHARMACOLOGICAL TREATMENTS

Although this text focuses on psychological treatment of SAD, here we will briefly review some pharmacological alternatives. With the recognition of SAD as a prevalent and serious condition, the number of pharmacological studies has increased substantially in recent years. The most common drug treatments for SAD include monoamine oxidase inhibitors (MAOIs; e.g., phenelzine), selective serotonin reuptake inhibitors (SSRIs), benzodiazepines, antidepressants, and beta-blockers. So far, paroxetine (an SSRI) is still the only drug for SAD approved by the Food and Drug Administration (FDA).

Monoamine Oxidase Inhibitors (MAOIs)

The results of four double-blind placebo controlled trials show evidence for the efficacy of phenelzine in SAD (Gelernter et al., 1991; Heimberg et al., 1998; Liebowitz et al., 1992; Versiani et al., 1992). In the study by Liebowitz et al. (1992), 64% of patients receiving phenelzine, 30% of patients receiving atenolol, and 23% of those receiving placebo were classified as responders based on Clinical Global Improvement (CGI) ratings (Guy, 1976). Similar results were reported by Versiani et al. (1992) who compared the efficacy of phenelzine, the reversible MAO (moclobemide), and placebo for treating SAD. After 8 weeks, both active drugs were more effective than placebo. Based on the LSAS, phenelzine was superior to moclobemide. At week 16, 82% of the moclobemide and 91% of the phenelzine-treated patients were markedly improved. However, moclobemide ultimately failed to win FDA approval in the United States.

Two studies included cognitive-behavioral intervention in the study design (Gelernter et al., 1991; Heimberg et al., 1998). Gelernter et al. (1991) randomized 65 patients to one of four groups, each lasting for 12 weeks: phenelzine, alprazolam, placebo, or Heimberg's CGBT. The results showed no significant difference between the active treatments. However, all patients receiving pharmacotherapy also received exposure instructions. More recently, Heimberg et al. (1998) recruited 133 patients for a study comparing phenelzine, CBGT, educational-supportive group therapy (the psychologial placebo), and pill placebo. Approximately two thirds of the patients (20 of the 31 phenelzine patients and 21 of the 36 CBGT patients) were classified as responders after 12 weeks of acute treatment. These findings demonstrate the short-term efficacy of phenelzine and CBGT for the treatment of SAD. However, the use of irreversible MAOIs is limited by the risk of hypertensive crisis if dietary restrictions are not followed and their adverse effects profiled. Newly available is a patch version of MAOIs (i.e., selegiline) which, due to direct absorption through the skin and into the bloodstream, bypasses processing in the stomach and intestines and hence bypasses the potential for significant blockade of tyromine in the gut, at least at its lowest strength. By avoiding blockade of tyromine in foods in the gut, selegiline can be used without the dietary restrictions needed for other MAOIs. Selegiline is currently FDA approved for the treatment of major depression, and, to our knowledge, it has not yet been tested in a trial in patients with SAD.

Selective Serotonin Reuptake Inhibitors

The FDA-approved Paxil (paroxetine HCL) for the treatment of SAD is the first (and so far only) medication approved for this disorder in the

United States. This approval was partly supported by findings by Stein et al. (1998). The authors tested the efficacy of paroxetine in a 12-week, placebo-controlled, double-blind, and flexible dose design that included 187 patients. The results showed that 55% of patients receiving paroxetine and 23.9% of those receiving placebo were classified as responders based on CGI ratings. On the average, the reduction from baseline on the LSAS total score was more than twice as large in the paroxetine group (39.1%) as in the placebo group (17.4%). In addition, various smaller studies have used other SSRIs with promising results, including fluvoxamine (van Vliet, Den Boer, & Westenberg, 1994), sertraline (Katzelnick et al., 1995), and fluoxetine (Black, Uhde, & Tancer, 1992; Schneier et al., 1992; Sternbach, 1990; van Ameringen, Mancini, & Streiner, 1993).

## Benzodiazepines

To date, only two studies have tested the efficacy of benzodiazepines (e.g., clonazepam and alprazolam) for SAD under double-blind conditions (Davidson et al., 1993; Gelernter et al., 1991). The study by Davidson et al. (1993) investigated the efficacy of clonazepam for the treatment of SAD in a 10-week double-blind study including 75 patients. The results showed that 78% of the patients using clonazepam were classified as responders as compared with 20% of those receiving placebo. In addition, the literature reports a number of open trials supporting the efficacy of clonazepam (Munjack, Baltazar, Bohn, Cabe, & Appleton, 1990; Ontiveros & Fontaine, 1990; Reiter, Pollack, Rosenbaum, & Cohen, 1990), and. in a comparative trial, Otto et al. (2000) found it to be equally effective to CBGT. In contrast, the aforementioned study by Gelernter and colleagues (1991) reported that only 38% of patients receiving alprazolam were classified as responders, as compared with 69% of those who received phenelzine. Two months after discontinuation of alprazolam, most patients experienced a recurrence of their social anxiety symptoms to pretreatment levels.

The major disadvantages of using clonazepam or alprazolam for treating SAD is the physical dependence and relatively high relapse rate after discontinuation. Furthermore, benzodiazepines are contraindicated in patients who drink alcohol to reduce their social anxiety due to the synergistic negative effects of the drug with alcohol.

## Tricyclic Antidepressants

Only limited data exist on the efficacy of antidepressant medications for the treatment of social anxiety, such as imipramine (Benca, Matuzas,

& Al-Sadir, 1986; Emmanuel, Johnson, & Villareal, 1998; Liebowitz et al., 1985; Zitrin, Klein, Woerner, & Ross, 1983) and clomipramine (Beaumont, 1977; Pecknold, McClure, Appeltauer, Allan, & Wrzesinski, 1982; Versiani, Mundim, Nardi, & Liebowitz, 1988). These studies showed disappointing results for treating SAD. For example, Emmanuel et al. (1998) treated 41 patients with imipramine or placebo over a period of 8 weeks using a flexible dose design. Only 2 of the 18 patients who received imipramine and 1 out of 23 patients receiving placebo improved. Similar results were reported by another trial (Simpson et al., 1998) and are consistent with earlier case studies (Liebowitz et al., 1985; Zitrin et al., 1983).

Similar conclusions can be drawn with regard to the use of clomipramine as a treatment for SAD. Although depressive and generalized anxiety symptoms showed some improvement, no positive change was observed in the SAD symptoms. In fact, some patients developed even greater social avoidance due to a tremor that developed as a side effect of the medication.

Other Antidepressants

Buproprion, a relatively novel antidepressant with dopamine agonist properties, has been reported to be effective for treating SAD in a single case (Emmanuel, Lydiard, & Ballenger, 1991). Furthermore, buspirone has been studied in one controlled trial (Clark & Agras, 1991) and two open-label trials (Munjack et al., 1990; Schneier et al., 1993). In the Clark and Agras (1991) study, 29 musicians with performance anxiety (all of whom met DSM–III–R criteria for SAD) were treated with either buspirone, buspirone plus CBT, a pill placebo, or a pill placebo plus CBT. All treatments lasted for 6 weeks. The drug was not any more effective than placebo and less effective than CBT. In contrast, Schneier et al. (1993) reported that patients who tolerated high dosages did experience modest benefit. The treatment phase of this study lasted for 12 weeks and it was based on 22 patients.

Beta-Blockers

Beta-blockers (such as propranolol or atenolol) have been widely used for treating performance anxiety since the 1970s (e.g., Gottschalk, Stone, & Gleser, 1974; Siitonen & Tanne, 1976). However, despite the enthusiasm for beta-blockers to treat social anxiety, their efficacy has not been supported by double-blind studies (Liebowitz et al., 1992; Turner, Beidel, &

Jacob, 1994). For example, Liebowitz et al. (1992) compared the effects of phenelzine, atenolol, and placebo for treating SAD and found no advantage of atenolol over placebo. Only 30% responded to atenolol as compared with 64% of patients receiving phenelzine and 23% of patients taking a pill placebo. Similar results were reported by Turner, Beidel, & Jacob (1994) who found no benefit of atenolol over pill placebo. The authors treated 72 individuals with SAD with behavior therapy (flooding), atenolol, or a pill placebo for a period of 3 months. Flooding was superior to placebo in self-report measures, clinician ratings, behavioral assessment measures, and performance on composite indices, and also superior to atenolol on behavioral measures and composite indices. Subjects who improved during treatment maintained gains at the 6-month follow-up regardless of whether they received flooding or atenolol. These data provide little empirical support for atenolol as a treatment of SAD when used on a standing dose.

In contrast, Pohl, Balon, Chapman, and McBride (1998) reported some promising results after conducting a preliminary double-blind study using beta-blockers or placebo for nongeneralized SAD. The study compared 10 patients who received propranolol (pro re nata) with 8 patients who received placebo for a period of 6 weeks after a 2-week placebo lead-in period. The study used self-report measures and a patient diary as an outcome measure. Participants who received propranolol reported less anxiety after both 4 and 6 weeks of treatment, and they rated their level of impairment as less severe after 6 weeks of treatment than patients on placebo. Furthermore, the propranolol group showed greater improvement in the LSAS than the placebo group. However, there were no differences in self-report measures of social anxiety. These results, albeit preliminary, suggest that beta-blockers, when administered pro re nata, might be clinically useful for treating individuals with a nongeneralized subtype of SAD.

## COMBINED PHARMACOTHERAPY AND CBT

The combination of antidepressant medications and CBT has been associated with few benefits over CBT for the treatment of SAD. As noted, Davidson and associates (2004) investigated the efficacy of the combination of fluoxetine with CBT relative to either treatment alone or pill placebo. Combination treatment was associated with less than a 3% increase in response rates for the addition of fluoxetine to CBT. SAD patients treated with CBT achieved a response rate of 51.7% compared with a response rate of 52.2% when fluoxetine and CBT were combined. Similar limited results were evident for a trial conducted in a primary care setting

(Blomhoff et al., 2001) that provided only limited evidence for an advantage for combined treatment over exposure therapy provided by physicians. This study, however, was marked by much more subtle effects for exposure therapy than are typical in the literature (cf. Gould et al., 1997). Moreover, over a follow-up interval, when many patients discontinued their medication, the combined treatment condition lost its advantage, so that it was no longer distinguishable from CBT alone. There is also evidence from the study of panic disorder that when CBT is offered in the context of combined treatment with pharmacotherapy, some of the gains in CBT appear to be lost when the medication is discontinued, potentially due to context-specific (state dependent) learning (for a review, see Otto, Smits, & Reese, 2005). For this reason, Otto et al. have cautioned against the routine use of combination therapy over provision of CBT alone when available (for further discussion, see chapter 6).

These cautions about combined treatment do not appear to apply to a new strategy for augmenting CBT with medication. This new strategy is an outgrowth of basic research on the neuronal circuits underlying fear extinction that led to intervention studies examining the use of d-cycloserine (DCS) to enhance therapeutic learning from exposure-based CBT (for a review, see Davis, Myers, Ressler, & Rothbaum, 2005). Following the successful application of this strategy to the treatment of acrophobia (Ressler et al., 2004), we successfully applied single doses of d-cycloserine prior to exposure sessions to the enhancement of CBT for SAD (Hofmann, Meuret, et al., 2006). At this writing, these exciting initial findings are in need of replication and extension, but the successful studies to date do encourage the consideration of a new strategy of psychopharmacology, where medication is utilized to enhance therapeutic learning from CBT (for a review, see Otto, Basden, Leyro, McHugh, & Hofmann, 2007).

# CHAPTER 2

# Overall Description of Treatment Strategy

This chapter will give an overview of the treatment model for social anxiety disorder (SAD) based on an accounting of the core maintaining factors for the disorder. The resulting model is fully consistent with the evidence for efficacious treatment packages and elements described in chapter 1. Chapter 3 then provides a session-by-session outline of the treatment strategies discussed here.

## JUST DO IT!

In the most straightforward terms, treatment is designed to provide patients with a systematic set of opportunities to learn that social situations are not as threatening, social errors are not as dire, and social performance deficits are not as unyielding as anticipated. And, session by session, it is the therapist's task to construct these opportunities for learning, while attending to the myriad ways in which patients have difficulties allowing themselves the freedom to learn new patterns. The therapist acts as an expert coach, setting up the opportunities for learning, guiding accurate interpretations of current performance, and joking, prodding, encouraging, and otherwise providing a context for patients to try out new alternatives in the most feared social situations. As treatment progresses, long-term maintenance is promoted by helping patients become their own therapists by understanding and applying treatment strategies on their own. Such independent application of therapy skills is initiated by the therapist providing a model of the disorder. This model provides a guide for the interventions to follow, helping patients see that each component intervention is part of an overall plan to eliminate the maintaining factors for SAD. The model also provides patients with a new accounting of their disorder in a way that may help them unleash

their own problem solving efforts, including a way to understand, cata-
log, and respond differently to the cacophony of symptoms that arise at
moments of fear.

After the informational model has been presented, the main tool
for change is stepwise exposure, where the therapist's task is to help
the patient learn by doing—by staying in the social situation long
enough and logically evaluating what is happening in that situation
to allow fear to dissipate and inaccurate expectations to be corrected.
If stepwise exposure is the main tool of therapeutic learning, then
the art of this learning comes from the therapist's ability to provide
patients with a vision that their social distress can change with a new
kind of social practice that involves successively harder social exposures combined with learning to evaluate the experience more dispassionately and accurately. This vision is provided by informational
and cognitive interventions, providing patients with a sense that this
time, with treatment, social exposures may turn out differently. This
is important, given that most patients have tried their own sort of
social exposures for years and are accordingly hesitant to approach
these situations again.

If patients had a chance to read from the therapists' internal play-
book for treating SAD, they would see something like the following:

- You are going to learn how you do in social situations when you
  do not use anxiety as a barometer of your social performance.
- You are going to have a chance to be in social situations long
  enough to allow anxiety to dissipate naturally.
- You are going to have a chance to get more comfortable with
  anxiety experienced in social situations so that you do not
  define social anxiety as a social disaster in and of itself.
- You are going to have a chance to learn how to coach
  yourself more accurately before, during, and after social
  performance.
- You are going to do all this with repeated practice to show
  yourself that things really can be different when using a step-
  by-step Cognitive Behavioral Theraphy (CBT) approach.

Although this learning unfolds differently across different subgroups
of patients, one predominant cascade of change includes the following: Early in treatment, patients develop an intellectual understanding
of the self-perpetuating patterns that underlie SAD, particularly the
cascade of negative social expectations, avoidant and error-focused
social performances, severe self-evaluations, and escape and avoidance
behavior that characterizes SAD. In an exposure-focused treatment,

patients next learn that it is possible to meet reasonable social goals despite the presence of anxiety. This learning often coincides with or heralds a redefining of the experience of social anxiety itself—from the perception of social anxiety as a hallmark of personal ineptitude to the perception of this anxiety experience as an unpleasant and inconvenient symptom that need not be self-definitive or self-defeating. With this shift come changes in the degree to which attention is focused on perceived social failures or errors, as well as reductions in severe and self-defeating post-event processing. In successful cases, social confidence then blossoms.

For therapists, the importance of understanding the order and nature of these treatment-related changes is to be able to encourage patients and underscore the significance of these events. This is particularly important for the span of time between sessions when patients must enact therapy procedures on their own. At the start of each subsequent session, therapists work to help patients form a model of change based on the home practice results they achieved, and then to complete additional exposure practices in session. By describing some of the "signposts" of beneficial change, patients are better prepared to feel the significance of therapeutic changes as they are achieved.

## THE GENERAL TREATMENT MODEL

Figure 2.1 provides an overview of the maintaining factors of SAD. This model also includes important mediators of treatment change. Briefly stated, the treatment model indicates that social apprehension is associated with unrealistic expectations regarding social standards and a deficiency for selecting specific and attainable social goals. When confronted with challenging social situations, people with SAD typically shift their attention toward the negative aspects of themselves and their social performance. Depending on the individual patient, this then leads to an overestimation of the negative consequences of a social encounter, perception of low emotional control, negative self-perception as a social being, and/or perception of poor social skills. As a consequence of this attentional shift and perception of poor coping strategies in socially challenging situations, individuals with SAD anticipate and attend to social errors and perceive these errors catastrophically. In the face of this deluge of social threat, maladaptive coping strategies abound, most prominently including social escape, avoidance, and safety behaviors, followed by post-event rumination. The rumination, accordingly, feeds social apprehension in the future.

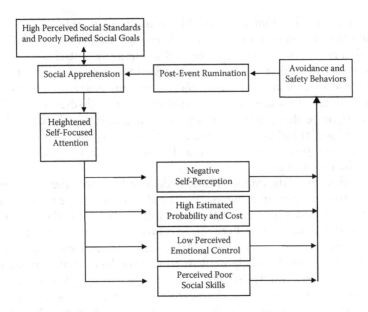

FIGURE 2.1   CBT model of SAD. From: Hofmann, S.G. (2007). Cognitive factors that maintain social anxiety disorder: A comprehensive model and its treatment implications. *Cognitive Behavior Therapy*, Vol. 36:4, pp. 195–209. Taylor & Francis Ltd., http://www.informaworld. com, reprinted by permission of the publisher.

This model of treatment is not only useful to therapists, but also helps patients understand the purpose of the various treatment strategies. Figure 2.1 is provided to patients at Session 1. The treatment techniques that specifically target the various elements of the model are provided next.

## THE ELEMENTS OF THE TREATMENT MODEL

### Targeting Social Standards

Individuals with SAD perceive social standards as high. They typically believe that the expectations of them in a social situation are elevated and that everybody else shares these same lofty social standards. As we will discuss at a later point, research has shown that ambiguous social standards are particularly troublesome for individuals with SAD. Social standards are likely to change slowly. Individual or group discussions and direct behavioral experiments can challenge these beliefs.

## Defining and Selecting Goals

When asked about the goal of a social encounter, individuals with SAD are often unspecific and say things such as "People need to like me," "I have to perform well," or "I have to make a good impression on people." As understandable as these goals are, they do not allow for objective verification. They also illustrate a central feature of goal evaluation for patients; frequently, it demands knowing other people's thoughts. That is, without mind reading, a patient could never validate her or his goals, and this is just one index of the degree to which individuals with SAD are "in the heads" of others, trying to look back upon themselves and make judgments of their own social performance. Indeed, learning to set objective, behavioral, and concrete goals for social performance evaluation is not only important for the immediate goal of helping patients learn about how they actually do in a social situation, it is also an important learning occasion to help patients realize the degree to which they place themselves at the mercy of their subjective guesses about how others feel about them.

The treatment protocol specifically targets this issue by helping patients select the potential goals prior to each exposure practice. Realistic goal setting is aided by clarifying the social standard and perceived expectations of others prior to exposure. Once the goals are clearly defined, they are then used to evaluate the social encounter in terms of the degree of success. (Note: Care has to be taken to help patients identify the degree of success rather than using an all-or-nothing thinking style that attends to the false concepts of complete success or complete failure.)

Once social goals have been identified, care may need to be taken in helping the patient identify and evaluate the best strategy to reach a particular goal. Regardless of how well the goal is defined, it is likely that most patients will organize their behavior around habit—the nonspecific goal of being liked socially, for example—rather than the specified goal. Discussion of how the patient can best meet a goal helps hone attention and behaviors toward some of the actual demands of a social situation, rather than the default fears of humiliation and failure. The selected goals can vary greatly and may include examples such as asking a particular question, showing or not showing a certain behavior, receiving a refund for a particular item that the person just purchased, or being able to arrange a first date with an attractive person. After the exposure, the event is to be evaluated based on whether the goals were reached, regardless of the subjective anxiety encountered in the situation. For example, an exposure task that targets assertiveness may be regarded as relatively successful or unsuccessful, depending on whether the person was able to return an item, irrespective of his/her anxiety in the situation.

## Modifying Self-Focused Attention

Attention is a limited resource. If we focus our attention on ourselves, less attention is available for other things, such as the social performance task. The less attention we have available for the task at hand, the more mistakes we make, which can increase our anxiety. For example, during a social performance task individuals with SAD typically focus on their bodily sensations ("My heart is racing," "I wonder if they can see me sweat"), their appearance ("I should not have worn this dress," "I hope they don't notice my pimple"), or their behaviors ("I am moving around too much," "Why am I stuttering so much?"). In all of these cases, attention is drawn away from the task performance and enhances anxiety.

The treatment program uses instructional techniques to make clients aware of the connection between focus of attention and anxiety, and to retrain the habitual shift of attention during a performance task. As part of this exercise, patients are instructed before a social task to change their attentional focus and to observe their own level of anxiety. More specifically, we ask patients before each social performance situation to direct their attention: (a) inward toward their physiological sensations, (b) toward the physical environment, and (c) toward their speech topic (30 seconds each). After each instruction, patients will be asked to rate their level of anxiety (0–10). This information is used to demonstrate to patients the connection between subjective anxiety and attentional focus.

## Improving Self-Perception

A significant subgroup of individuals with SAD report discomfort when looking at themselves in the mirror. Many also report distress when seeing themselves in pictures or video recordings, or when listening to themselves on an audiotape. In fact, some individuals with SAD feel more distress when watching their own speech on a video than doing the actual performance. When being asked why they feel uncomfortable, they might say: "Oh, I just don't like to look at myself" or "I just don't like hear myself talk." The reason for this distress is obviously related to self-perception. The patient's distress is not only due to their presumed negative evaluation by the audience, but also due to their direct negative evaluation of themselves. Indeed, because the patient is only guessing at evaluations from others, the belief of what others think is of course a reflection of what the person thinks of her/himself. Therefore, changing self-perception will also change the assignment of beliefs to others. This, in turn, will alter the level of discomfort and anxiety in a social situation. This is easier said than done. However, our experience is that treatment can enhance self-perception by specifically targeting self-critical statements.

We have found that reducing the amount of self-criticism (which goes along with self-acceptance) also builds self-confidence and improves self-perception. For many people who undergo this treatment, a core lesson is learned: Instead of trying to improve your social skills and the way you come across, simply accept yourself and your weaknesses, enjoy your strengths, and be content with the way you are while striving to achieve your goals.

In fact, as we will report in chapter 4, changes in self-perception and self-focused attention are closely associated with improvement and appear to mediate treatment change. Different techniques are used to manipulate and modify self-focused attention and self-perception. These include video feedback, audio feedback, mirror exposure, and group feedback.

1. Video feedback. Video feedback can be an effective way of correcting distorted self-perception and manipulating the effect of self-focused attention on subjective anxiety. The therapeutic effect of video feedback can be further enhanced by asking patients prior to viewing their videotaped performance to predict what they expect to see in the video and to form an image of themselves giving the speech, and then to watch the video from an observer's point of view (i.e., as if they were watching a stranger). This technique can be an important tool to challenge distorted self-perception by creating dissonance between perceived and actual performance.

2. Audio feedback. It is our experience that patients primarily focus on the visual information during the video feedback. Furthermore, the sound quality of the videotapes can be poor. Therefore, we recommend also adding an audiotape feedback component to treatment by integrating it into weekly homework assignments. For this purpose, patients are instructed to audiotape a speech and repeatedly listen to the tape between therapy sessions.

3. Mirror exposure. Mirror manipulation is a commonly used method to enhance self-focused attention. We noticed in our earlier work that some patients with SAD experience great discomfort when being asked to look at themselves in the mirror and that repeated mirror exposure seems to be beneficial to correct distorted self-perception. Such mirror exposure exercises seem to be particularly useful for the most severe patients. Therefore, we recommend incorporating this exercise as a

homework assignment to make individuals more comfortable with their self-presentation and to correct distorted and negative self-perception. Specifically, patients are asked to look at themselves in the mirror for 3 minutes and describe what they see while recording their self-statements on an audiotape.

4. Group feedback. Unexpected positive feedback from the other group members can be very effective in challenging the patient's distorted self-perception. It has been our experience that the feedback by group members is considerably more effective than the feedback by the therapists.

## Targeting Estimated Social Probability and Cost

Epictetus, one of the ancient Greek philosophers, once said, "Men are not moved by things but the views which they take of them." In other words, we are only anxious, angry, or sad if we think that we have reason to be anxious, angry, or sad. Aaron T. Beck, professor emeritus at the University of Pennsylvania, has adopted this principle to treat emotional disorders (Beck, 1979, 1985). The resulting technique, cognitive therapy, has become the most influential contemporary treatment approach, next to behavioral interventions and psychodynamic approaches. Today, the most effective (and empirically supported) treatments for anxiety disorders combine cognitive techniques and behavioral interventions.

The goal of cognitive therapy is not to think positively but rather more realistically. If a situation is really very bad and there is good reason to feel bad, then we should feel bad unless we refuse to face reality. For example, the loss of a loved one, a serious personal financial crisis, and serious health problems are all good reasons to feel bad, stressed, anxious, and sad. In contrast, giving a bad and incoherent speech in front of colleagues might be an unpleasant and embarrassing event, but it is not a catastrophe.

Many people have great difficulty identifying these anxious and maladaptive thoughts. These thoughts can be classified into (1) dysfunctional beliefs and (2) negative automatic thoughts. Dysfunctional (or irrational, maladaptive) beliefs are basic assumptions that people have about the world, the future, and themselves. These global overarching beliefs provide a schema, which determines how we interpret a specific situation. For example, Barbara may believe that she should always be entertaining, intelligent, and funny, and thinks that unless everyone likes her, she is worthless. Cognitive therapists call these beliefs dysfunctional beliefs because they lead to a biased and dysfunctional perception of the situation.

Such dysfunctional beliefs can cause the person to be not only very anxious about the specific social situation, but also feel depressed and apprehensive in a number of other social situations. As a result, the person may avoid interpersonal contact due to the anxiety about criticism, disapproval, and rejection, and may feel inferior to others or inhibited in new interpersonal situations because of feelings of inadequacy. Such beliefs can cause problems because they set unrealistic goals. In addition, negative automatic cognitions are thoughts or images that occur in specific situations when the person feels anxious. These thoughts are the specific expressions of these dysfunctional beliefs. For example, Barbara may think: "Other people will think I am boring," "I will embarrass myself," or "Other people will think that I am stupid" when facing the audience. The specific automatic thought "other people will think I am boring" is anxiety provoking if Barbara holds the belief that she will be rejected by other people unless she is entertaining. Cognitive therapists call these thoughts "automatic" because they may occur without (or with little) conscious awareness. These automatic thoughts often lead to distortion of reality because they lead to a misperception or exaggeration of the situation.

Beliefs (schemas) are the driving force behind our thoughts. They are the raw material out of which specific thoughts are made. Beliefs are hard to question and dispute because they are typically taken for fact. They feel part of us (part of our personality) because they include our conviction, our deepest beliefs about what's right and what's wrong; what's good and what's bad; and what's desirable and what's undesirable. Beliefs are the basic assumptions about the world and the future, and we ought to behave and represent the shoulds and shouldn'ts. Many of those beliefs are desirable and help us function in this world. "You should avoid harming other people," "You should be honest," "You should not exploit other people," and so forth are examples of very adaptive and valuable beliefs.

Other beliefs, on the other hand, are irrational, maladaptive, and dysfunctional. They restrict us, inhibit us, and make us prisoners of our own convictions. Many irrational beliefs have to do with perfectionism: "You should not show anxiety or weakness in front of other people," "You shouldn't make any mistakes when performing in social situations," or "Every audience member should love your speech."

SAD is often characterized by two types of irrational beliefs that lead to an overestimation of the probability of social mishaps and an overestimation of the social cost of these mishaps. Our treatment aggressively targets these irrational beliefs in a number of different ways.

1. During the homework review, the therapist will specifically ask questions to identify and challenge the patient's exaggerated probability and cost estimation. Examples of typical questions the therapist may ask are: How likely will a mishap occur? What would be the worst outcome of this situation? Why is this situation such a catastrophic event? How will your life change due to this experience? These discussions are intended to illustrate to participants that social mishaps are normal and that the negative consequences of such mishaps are short lasting. The following is an example of a therapist–patient dialogue that illustrates the cognitive challenge to the patient's tendency to overestimate the probability of negative outcomes.

*Patient:*　When I have to perform in public (such as give a public speech), I won't be able to think of anything to say.

*Therapist:* What exactly do you mean by "I won't be able to think of anything to say"?

*Patient:*　It means that my mind goes blank.

*Therapist:* Does this mean that your mind goes blank *every* single time?

*Patient:*　Well, it might not go blank *every* single time.

*Therapist:* During the last 10 times you had to give a presentation, how often has your mind gone blank?

*Patient:*　I don't remember. Maybe once or twice? Actually, I can only think of one such situation.

*Therapist:* And what kind of situation was that?

*Patient:*　I had to talk about an unfamiliar subject in front of unfamiliar people.

*Therapist:* When using these numbers, the chance that your mind goes blank the next time you have to give a presentation is 10%. In other words, your mind only goes blank sometimes when you don't know the people well or don't know the subject? Isn't that right?

*Patient:*　Yes.

The following is an example of a therapist–patient dialogue that illustrates the technique of challenging catastrophic thinking.

*Patient:*　But what if this unlikely event really does happen? What if I really do lose my train of thought and my mind goes blank?

*Therapist:* Yes, good point. So what if your mind really does go blank? What do you think would happen?

*Patient:*　This would be awful.

*Therapist:* A real catastrophe?

*Patient:*  Yes.

*Therapist:* But what exactly would be so terrible about it?

*Patient:*  It would be embarrassing!

*Therapist:* Why would it be embarrassing?

*Patient:*  Because I will make a fool of myself in front of other people.

*Therapist:* What does "making a fool of yourself in front of other people" exactly mean? What would happen?

*Patient:*  They would laugh about me and think that I am a total loser?

*Therapist:* How do you know what other people think of you?

*Patient:*  What do you mean?

*Therapist:* You are making a number of assumptions here that may or may not be correct. Interestingly, you choose out of many possible alternatives the one that threatens your self the most. For example, you are assuming that if you lose your train of thought, everybody will notice it, laugh at you, and think that you are incompetent. This scenario would then elicit embarrassment in you. If people don't notice that you lost your train of thought or if they do, but are not the least hostile, you wouldn't have any reason to feel embarrassed any more. Isn't that right?

*Patient:*  I guess so.

*Therapist:* Furthermore, while this scenario is not completely impossible, it is not very likely. It assumes that the social world out there is hostile and aggressive, and that people are out to get you. But let's assume for a moment that this scenario actually does happen, and that you happen to speak in front of an audience that consists of some very hostile people, and that you would indeed embarrass yourself. Then what? Have you been in any embarrassing situations before in your life?

*Patient:*  Of course I have.

*Therapist:* How many times?

*Patient:*  Oh, many times. More than I can count.

*Therapist:* And are you still alive?

*Patient:*  (*Laughs.*)

*Therapist:* My point is that even if your mind does go blank, even if people notice that, and even if they are in fact hostile and think that you are an incompetent loser, which causes you a great deal of embarrassment, it is not a catastrophe. You have been embarrassed before, and so has everyone else.

2. During the planning stage of the exposure exercises, the therapist will instruct the patient to specifically create social mishaps in order to examine the actual consequences. For example, the patient may be asked to buy a piece of pastry at a café and "accidentally" drop it on the floor, and then ask for a new one. The specified goal of this situation may be to obtain a new piece of pastry without paying for it. In another example, the patient may be asked to buy and return a book to the same salesperson within a 5-minute span and simply state "I changed my mind." The goal here would be to receive a refund. Table 2.1 shows examples of exposure situations to create social mishaps in order to challenge the patient's rigid social standards. As we will explain in more detail later, the instructions are provided by the therapist in detail in order to avoid the use of any safety behaviors and avoidance strategies.

3. The patient will be instructed to conduct similar and more individually tailored exercises as part of his/her homework assignments. A monitoring form will aid the patient specifically to examine and challenge the perceived social costs and probability associated with these situations (see Appendix D, Handout 4). In all cases, it is important to prepare the patient for his/her negative cognitions prior to the exposure—a cognition that a patient has been prepared for will feel very different from a novel cognition. Nonetheless, regardless of the specific cognitions provoked, the goal of these exposures is to have patients evaluate the perceived social cost of these minor social missteps when the anxiety they provoke *is not used* to define their outcome.

The role of anxiety experiences as part of a cascade of negative thinking and increasing symptoms is worthy of additional note. We would like to direct therapists toward a particular set of negative thoughts that we term *amplifying cognitions* because of the role they have in amplifying social mishaps and/or anxiety symptoms into a sense of catastrophic failure. The goal is to help the patient develop an intuitive sense of the influence of these automatic thoughts and develop an ability to not buy into them. That is, cognitive interventions are not simply directed at helping patients substitute more accurate thoughts in place of dysfunctional ones, but to develop a broader ability of understanding how frequently thinking can become distorted and learning to not take their thoughts too seriously. As noted, exposure is used as a central tool in solidifying this point, but therapists may use a variety of strategies (including those in Table 2.2) to help patients become more vigilant to the self-defeating nature of these thoughts.

TABLE 2.1    Examples of In Vivo Exposure Tasks to Challenge
Estimated Social Cost

- Ask multiple people (e.g., 10 people over a half hour) in a specific and obvious location (e.g., immediately outside Fenway Park) where to find that location. Say: *Excuse me, I am looking for Fenway Park.*
- Order a sandwich at a takeout restaurant and then tell the cashier you cannot buy it because you do not have enough money. Say without apologizing: *I just realized that I forgot my wallet,* then walk out.
- Order a coffee at a coffee bar and when it is handed to you, say: *Is this decaf?* Add without apologizing: *I would like to have mine decaf.*
- Order a bagel, "accidentally" drop it on the floor and ask for a new one. Say: *I just dropped the bagel on the floor. Could I please have a new one?*
- Go to a restaurant and sit at the bar. When asked if you would like to order something, just ask for tap water. Use the bathroom and then leave without saying anything.
- Go to a restaurant and sit at the bar. Ask a fellow patron whether he has seen the movie *When Harry Met Sally* and who the actors were.
- Go to a hotel and book a room. Walk outside and immediately back in and cancel the room because you *changed your mind.*
- Go to a video rental outlet and rent a DVD. Walk out and immediately back in requesting to return it saying: *I forgot I don't have a DVD player.*
- Stand in a subway station (specify location) and sing "God Bless America" for 30 minutes.
- Ask a female pharmacist for some condoms. When she brings them, ask: *Is this the smallest size you have?*
- Go to every man sitting at a table in a crowded restaurant and ask: *Are you Carl Smith?*
- Go to a bookstore and ask a clerk: *Excuse me, where can I find some books on farting.*
- Ask a bookstore clerk for the following two books: *The Karma Sutra* and *The Joy of Sex.* Ask the clerk which one he would recommend.
- Buy a book and immediately return it because you *changed your mind.*
- Ask the book clerk for his/her opinion about a particular best-seller. Ask: *What did you like about this book, and how many copies have you sold.* Don't buy it. Simply say: *Thank you. I will think about it* and leave.
- Ask a book clerk for a book for a 1-year-old. Find out if and how many children the clerk has, how old they are, what school they attend or attended, and what their favorite color is.
- Go to Store 24, buy a *Playgirl* magazine, and ask the store clerk: *Are there also pictures of naked men in the magazine?* Wait for the answer and put it back on the shelf.
- Wear your shirt backward and inside out and buttoned incorrectly in a crowded store. Goal: Look three people in the eye.
- Walk backward slowly in a crowded street for 3 minutes.

TABLE 2.2   Amplifying Cognitions

---

*Great ways to transform everyday events into a sense of failure*

*Think:*

If I get anxious—I am a loser

If my face flushes—Then I failed

If I flub a word—I am worthless as a speaker

If I act different from others—I am weird

If I lose my train of thought—I am incompetent

---

### Anticipation of Social Mishap and Social Threat

Social situations are fear provoking because individuals with SAD believe that social mishaps are likely and costly. Clark and Wells (1995) formulated this as follows: Individuals with social phobia believe that they are in danger of behaving in an inept and unacceptable fashion and believe that such behavior will have disastrous consequences in terms of loss of status, loss of worth, and rejection. These two cognitive errors have been referred to as probability overestimation (overestimating the likelihood of an unpleasant event) and catastrophic thinking (blowing an unpleasant event out of proportion). Both errors can be effectively identified and challenged with the following questions:

1. What evidence do I have that the belief is true?
2. Based on past experience, how often did this feared outcome actually happen?
3. What is the worst that could happen?
4. If this worst outcome happens, would I be able to cope with it?

The first two questions identify errors in thinking that lead to probability overestimation, and the latter two questions identify catastrophic thinking errors. People commit cognitive errors leading to probability overestimations if they believe that an unlikely and unpleasant event (such as losing a job, losing a friend, getting divorced, etc.) is likely to occur based on ambiguous clues. An example might be the socially phobic employee who worries that a bad speech in front of her co-workers would risk the relationship with them and that her co-workers would think that she is incompetent. She might further worry that as a result, she would be asked to leave her company, unable to find another job because of her bad reputation.

Questions 3 and 4 identify catastrophic thinking errors. These are errors that occur if an unpleasant event is in fact happening, but the negative aspects of this event are greatly exaggerated and blown out of proportion. This thinking error occurs if our employee calls up one of his coworkers to ask her out on a date, but the co-worker can't do it because she has already made other plans. An example of catastrophic thinking is the following response: "This is the worst thing that could have happened to me. I feel so humiliated. How could I have possibly thought that she was interested in me? I am such a loser. This will create an extremely uncomfortable situation at work. I will have to quit my job, end up with no money and no friends. I will be miserable and lonely for the rest of my life" and so forth.

Therapists need to make the patient realize that unpleasant things happen now and then to everybody. It is impossible to prevent this from happening. The trick to living a generally happy life is to not be overly affected by these events. Handouts are helpful to identify and challenge frequently occurring cognitive errors. The worksheet in Table 2.3 shows a patient's (let her name be Barbara) two most distressing thoughts that happened during the previous week. As shown by the worksheet, Barbara was very worried about going to the Parent–Teacher Association meeting. Her most distressing thought was "If I mess things up, they will think I am incompetent." The feared consequence was the feeling of embarrassment. She challenged the error of this thought leading to probability overestimation by analyzing the likelihood of the feared consequence. Based on her previous experience, she concluded that the event was not very likely to happen. Furthermore, she examined the catastrophic aspect of this thought by determining how well she would be able to cope with the feared outcome even if it did happen.

Barbara's second situation was indeed an unpleasant performance situation. She lost her train of thought in the middle of her presentation in front of new sales trainees. She was most concerned that the trainees thought that she was totally incompetent and that people would think badly of her, which would inhibit her career. She was again able to challenge this thought by examining the evidence and her coping capabilities.

## Perception of Emotional Control

According to Barlow's (2002) model of anxiety, perception of low emotional control is a crucial aspect of all anxiety disorders. During treatment, perceived emotional control is elevated through repeated and prolonged exposure to physiological symptoms of anxiety in social situations while encouraging patients to experience and accept the feeling

TABLE 2.3    Worksheet: Barbara's Example of Challenging Her Automatic Thoughts

| Situation | Most disturbing thoughts | What is the feared consequence? | Challenge probability overestimation: What is the evidence? How likely is the worst outcome going to happen? | Challenge catastrophic thinking: What is the worst outcome? Could you cope? Is this a real catastrophe? | What is a more reasonable interpretation of the situation? |
|---|---|---|---|---|---|
| Parent–Teacher Association meeting | If I mess things up, they will think I am incompetent. | I will embarrass myself. | The previous meetings actually went pretty well, and people seem to like me. So based on that, it is not very likely to happen. | I will stutter and have to leave the room. It would be hard, but I have been embarrassed before. I guess it is not a real catastrophe. | I will be very anxious, but I will be able to handle it. It won't be a catastrophe if I stutter at some points during my presentation. |
| Lost my train of thought in the middle of my presentation to new sales trainees | The presentation was a total disaster; people must think that I am totally inadequate. | People will think badly of me, and I won't be able to advance in my career. | I just lost my train of thought. Otherwise the presentation wasn't that bad. It is unlikely that a bad presentation in front of new sales trainees could negatively affect my career. | Even if my career is negatively affected, I would be able to find another job. | I lost my train of thought, but I handled it fairly well, and it's no big deal. Some people might not even have noticed it. |

of anxiety to its fullest. This approach is similar to the acceptance technique in acceptance and commitment therapy, as advocated by Hayes and colleagues (1999). Borrowing from this approach, the treatment introduces the patient to the notion that control can be gained by accepting the emotional experience. Acceptance here is defined as being "experientially open" to the reality of the present moment. Patients who fear panic attacks or certain physical symptoms in the social situation are repeatedly exposed to these sensations through interoceptive exposure practices, which are borrowed from treatment protocols for panic disorder (e.g., Barlow & Craske, 2000). These exposures are important for providing an adequate match between patient's fears ("I fear sweating in front of another, not just being in front of someone else when I don't sweat") and the exposure exercises. Specifically, anxiety symptoms may need to be manipulated in exposure exercises to adequately address a patient's core social fears. In this way, use of anxiety symptoms in exposure is similar to the manipulation of social errors in exposure. If a patient fears imperfect but not perfect social performances or fears blushing while giving a speech versus not blushing, then it is these factors that need to be integrated into the exposure—with programmed social mishaps as exemplified earlier or with induction of symptoms, respectively—in order for true learning of safety in situations ("It is OK even if I make a mistake" or "I can blush while giving a speech but still meet my goals").

Perception of Social Skills

There is little evidence to suggest that individuals with SAD are consistently deficient in their social skills (e.g., Stravynski & Amado, 2001). Rather, the literature seems to suggest that individuals with SAD perceive their social skills as being inadequate to reach their social goals and meet the perceived social standard. The perception of one's social skills is an aspect of one's self-perception and is therefore modified during the treatment with the same strategies as other distorted aspects of self-perception (i.e., via video feedback, audio feedback, mirror exposure, and group feedback).

Safety and Avoidance Behaviors

Starting with the first treatment session, patients are instructed to identify and eventually eliminate any avoidance behaviors. The term *avoidance behavior* is broadly defined as anything the person does or does not do to reduce his/her anxiety in the social situation. Avoidance and safety behaviors maintain fear of social situations, and exposure procedures can eliminate them.

Safety behaviors are conceptualized as frequent and subtle forms of avoidance strategies. In order to identify them, patients are instructed to monitor their social encounters between sessions. Furthermore, the group members are encouraged to be vigilant for signs of any such safety behaviors by participants during in-session exposure practices.

Repeated and prolonged exposure to the feared situation without using any avoidance and/or safety behaviors is one of the single most effective methods to overcome social anxiety. In order to determine which situations are the most fear provoking for a particular patient, it is very useful to establish a fear and avoidance hierarchy. This typically lists the 10 most fear-provoking situations in a hierarchy with rank #1 being the most fear provoking, rank #2 being the second most fear-provoking one, and so forth. Table 2.4 is an example of a fear and avoidance hierarchy. The patient in this example (Barbara) ranks a presentation at her Wednesday morning meeting as the most fear provoking. Although she is very afraid of this situation (she gave it a rating of 100), she can avoid this situation only half of the time (she rates her avoidance as a 50). Her fear of giving a presentation on an unfamiliar subject in front of a large audience is slightly lower (85), but she avoids this situation very often (90). When looking more closely at the various situations that she listed, it becomes clear that the size of the audience, the familiarity of the subject matter, and the formality of the situation contribute to her anxiety. The more unfamiliar the subject matter, the bigger (and more hostile) the audience, and the more formal the speaking engagement is, the greater Barbara rates her anxiety and avoidance tendency. In addition, this hierarchy needs to be considered in relation to the presence of safety cues. For example, Barbara may have a variety of strategies for making it through her Wednesday morning meeting, including preparing notes before the meeting, bringing a cup of water for a potentially dry throat, sitting next to her assistant, and averting her eyes from others while speaking. These safety cues should be considered as additional items for modifying the impact (difficulty as well as ultimate usefulness) of exposure practice. All of these factors provide valuable information for treatment planning.

## Post-Event Rumination

Post-event rumination is a frequently occurring phenomenon after a social encounter, especially after situations that are associated with

TABLE 2.4  Barbara's Fear and Avoidance Hierarchy

| Social Situation | Fear (0–100) | Avoidance (0–100) |
|---|---|---|
| My worst fear: *Giving a presentation in our Wednesday morning meeting (hostile audience)* | 100 | 50 |
| My 2nd worst fear: *Giving a presentation on an unfamiliar subject in front of a large audience* | 85 | 90 |
| My 3rd worst fear: *Same as 2nd, subject matter is familiar* | 80 | 80 |
| My 4th worst fear: *Sitting at big conference table with co-workers and discussing things* | 80 | 60 |
| My 5th worst fear: *Giving a presentation to our sales trainees* | 80 | 60 |
| My 6th worst fear: *Disagreeing with a co-worker during Wednesday morning meeting* | 70 | 70 |
| My 7th worst fear: *Introducing myself to new co-workers* | 70 | 20 |
| My 8th worst fear: *Expressing my opinion at a meeting of the Parent–Teacher Association* | 50 | 60 |
| My 9th worst fear: *Leading a conference call* | 50 | 10 |
| My 10th worst fear: *Assigning unpleasant tasks to sales trainees* | 30 | 10 |

high perceived social costs and negative self-perception because of the assumed catastrophic outcome of a social situation. Post-event rumination might serve the purpose of reexamining the situation to evaluate the potential threat involved. Post-event rumination often decreases as changes in negative self-perception and estimated social cost occur.

In addition, post-event rumination is targeted specifically by helping patients to process negative social events more adaptively through guided questions. The goal is to help patients consolidate useful information from their exposure. In most cases, this will be achieved by reviewing how the exposure led to changes in beliefs about social situations and the emotional or social costs of social errors or anxiety symptoms in the context of social performances. Such post-event processing is rehearsed in session after each of the programmed exposures and rehearsed weekly when home practice between sessions is reviewed.

## PUTTING IT ALL TOGETHER: DESIGNING EXPOSURES

To maximize learning of true safety in social situations, patients need to have exposure experiences that are unambiguous with respect to feared outcomes. This means that patients should not just learn that social situations are survivable with the right combination of safety cues and luck, but that the situation is truly safe regardless of the presence of safety cues, anxiety, luck, or perfect performance. This means that social exposures must be arranged to provide evidence to violate the patient's assumptions that the social situation is socially or emotionally dangerous. This is achieved by helping patients think through, define, and discover what constitutes adequate social performance, while having adequate practice in social situations to allow anxiety to dissipate. Elements of exposure also help patients realize how their anxiety changes as their attentional focus shifts (in response to therapist questioning and self-ratings) and as they persist in once-avoided social situations.

Using a combination of instruction, guided discovery, and exposure, the therapist's job is to construct opportunities for this learning. Prior to exposure, therapists help patients define objective goals and consider the elements of the exposure that will lead to useful learning. To avoid overwhelming the patient and to provide her or him with sequential experiences of success, exposures progress along a hierarchy. For this hierarchy, the therapist has a wide range of variables to manipulate to provide sequentially more useful practice (where usefulness is defined by the degree to which exposure violates the patient's expectations of social danger, leaving him or her to conclude that social situations and interactions are safer than he or she had assumed). Appendix I summarizes some of the variables that should be assessed at pretreatment to aid in the construction of subsequent exposure exercises. In all cases, exposure is arranged such that patients: (1) expect initial anxiety, (2) expect imperfect performances and focus on the pursuit of well-defined goals for the social situations, (3) are oriented toward noticing what actually happens in the social situation (vis-à-vis social goals), (4) are prepared for the sort of self-defeating biases they will bring to their evaluation of their own performance, and (5) have clear predictions of their performance so that deviations from this level of performance can be made explicit.

With this information in hand, the therapist is better prepared to understand which elements of social interactions, safety cues, social errors, and anxiety symptoms should be best combined for initial and subsequent exposure procedures. The ordering of interventions to achieve these ends, and the use of standardized and specialized exposure procedures, is described in detail in the next chapter.

# CHAPTER 3

# Session-by-Session Outline

With a conceptual model and elements described in previous chapters, this chapter provides a session-by-session accounting of treatment. A standard course of treatment is targeted weekly for 12 to 16 sessions. The treatment can be delivered in either 1-hour individual sessions or 2.5-hour group sessions (with two therapists and four to six individuals per group). Group treatment has a number of advantages over individual therapy, but it also presents a number of unique challenges. Advantages include a ready-made social group for exposure practices. The group provides an audience, a forum for feedback, and an opportunity for supportive discussions. Yet, although the group provides ample opportunities to learn from others (and understand the global nature of negative thoughts and self-defeating social expectations and interpretive biases), it also diffuses the intensity of focus from what can be provided in individual therapy. As is explicated later, individual therapy also requires the use of other confederates (others who can provide a social exposure audience) or the sort of public exposures (e.g., buying then returning a CD) that do not require confederates but do require a trip from the therapist's office. In this chapter, we provide a primary focus on providing treatment in the context of a group, but the treatment protocol can also be delivered as an individual treatment with relatively minor modifications.

Because of the focus on the provision of objective feedback and the use of objective goals for the exposure, we recommend the use of a white board in treatment offices. This white board can be used for presentation of aspects of the model of the disorder and treatment, writing out specific dysfunctional thoughts for consideration, operationalizing a goal for exposure (in a way that allows verification after exposure), or drawing out the pattern of anxiety symptoms experienced by a patient. In individual sessions, a pad of paper can be substituted, but we have found a large, white board to be uniformly useful and efficient for group work.

## GENERAL OUTLINE

The first two sessions of treatment are especially important for establishing a conceptual model to guide subsequent interventions. During these sessions, patients are introduced to the treatment rationale, with particular attention to the structure of exposure practice. It is in these sessions that the therapist is most directive, providing patients with a model and directly structuring the elements of exposure exercises and interactions between group members. As treatment progresses, the therapist shifts this responsibility to the group members; feedback on exposures, coaching around cognitive biases, and comments regarding social skills increasingly become the responsibility of the group members.

After the first session, which introduces the patient to the treatment, the therapist administers a fear and avoidance hierarchy that lists the most feared and avoided social situations. During Sessions 2 through 6, every group member will be asked to complete exposures, receive feedback from other group members, and watch the videotaped recording of his or her exposure. In most group settings, brief speeches are used for exposure. Speeches are generally toward the top of most patients' hierarchies and, hence, are an excellent method to provide a forum for learning for all group members. The group members have an important dual function in these exposures: (1) They provide emotional support and give positive feedback to the person doing the exposure, and (2) they are at the same time the reason for the person's distress because they serve as the audience during the first half of the treatment. Therefore, positive feedback from group members is very important. In most cases, the therapist should let the group members "do the talking" when support is needed. The therapist's role is then to redirect, focus, and clarify certain points relating to maintaining factors of social anxiety as discussed in the model. Sufficient time should be designated for group discussions.

The therapists and patients have a large degree of flexibility with the topics the patients choose for the videotaped speeches. Examples for speech topics may range from black holes and cloning for patients who are most uncomfortable when speaking about an unfamiliar and complicated subject to social rules of dating and what makes dating fearful, in case they want to target their fear of rejection. Furthermore, the treatment includes modeling (the therapist should not give perfect presentations; little mistakes are desirable), instructions and coaching, and self-monitoring as additional ingredients.

By the beginning of Session 7, participants shift from these speeches to in vivo exposure tasks individually tailored to the person to modify specific cognitive biases. These exposures continue to the end of treatment, where strategies for relapse prevention are covered. In Session 7, exposures are chosen that involve simple interpersonal interactions (e.g., asking for directions). Beginning with Session 8, the patient will be asked to perform challenging in vivo exposure exercises that involve a component of social error or challenge (e.g., "accidentally" dropping on the floor a pastry that was just purchased at a cafe and requesting to get a new one, or returning to the same salesperson a book that it was just purchased from 5 minutes earlier) to ensure that fears of doing something "socially wrong" are fully addressed by treatment. The fear and avoidance hierarchy should be used to construct these exposures.

Across all of these sessions, assignment of regular home practice is essential for learning. Home practice helps ensure that therapy skills are learned independently of the safety cues inherent in the clinic and that skills are learned independently from the direct mentoring of the therapist. By reviewing home practice at the beginning of each session, therapists maintain a consistent focus on the importance of this work outside the session.

## SESSION 1

### General Introduction

The most important goals of the first session are to establish rapport, make group members comfortable with a socially challenging situation, and provide a general introduction to the treatment model with a specific emphasis on exposure strategies. An example for initiating the first group session follows:

> Thanks to everyone for coming tonight. This is the first of 12 to 16 weekly group sessions. Each session will last approximately 2 hours, and the goal is to overcome social anxiety. Welcome and congratulations. Each one of you is here because you feel uncomfortable in social situations. And here you are, sitting in a group of people and willing to confront your anxiety. Coming here is therefore a very courageous act, and courage is one the most important conditions needed to overcome your anxiety. The fact that you are here despite your discomfort tells me that your desire and motivation to overcome your fear is stronger than your desire to avoid dealing with your anxiety. This is very good. You are on the right track. Before we begin, let me introduce myself to you. My name is Beverly. I am a postdoctoral fellow in clinical psychology and I am especially interested in

anxiety disorders. I have done many groups like this, and I have had intensive training in various empirically supported treatments for anxiety disorder, and I am looking forward to working with you for the next three months. And this is John (turn to cotherapist and let him introduce himself).

After John introduces himself, he may turn to the group member sitting next to him and say: "And what is your name and what do you do?" Each group member is encouraged to say as little or as much as desired. If a person is unable to say anything, the therapists should gently and empathetically introduce the person to everyone and mention something they know about the person. Humor helps to break the ice but should never ridicule or embarrass any group member. Following the general introduction, the therapist should discuss issues concerning confidentiality. An example is as follows:

> Before we begin, I have one more important issue. We as therapists are bound by ethics and legal requirements that protect your privacy. For example, all identifying information that we have from you is kept in locked file cabinets and only staff members working at the center have access to this information. Furthermore, we cannot talk about anyone in this group to any outsiders in a way that any group member may be identified without your written permission [exceptions to this general rule—impending harm to self or others, insurance disclosures, and so forth—were discussed individually with patients]. We also ask each one of you to protect the privacy of everyone else. We call this confidentiality. So please don't mention the name of any group member to people outside the group.

### Sharing of Individual Problems/Goals and Drawing Out Similarities

After the general introduction, patients are encouraged to speak briefly on their reasons for being in the group, that is, what are the concerns for which they have sought treatment, how the fear of speaking or other social fears affect their lives, what other fears they have, and what their goals are in the group. The purpose of this discussion is to demonstrate the similarity among patients and to build group cohesion. Each participant should be called on, in turn, by the therapists. The order should be different from the order in which group members originally introduced themselves.

Therapists should liberally provide prompts to help patients express themselves. The patients may be quite anxious and therefore find it difficult to organize their thoughts and should be freely assisted. Any patient who is too anxious to speak at length should be given ample room to decline. Although patients may show a diversity of symptoms and eliciting situations, and although they may differ considerably in the amount of impairment of functioning they experience, all individuals will share at least the fear of public speaking and they may also have additional commonalities with other group members. It is important to point these out and make the point that the similarities outweigh the differences. Differences should not be ignored, but similarities should be highlighted as a means of bringing the group closer together. Specifically, therapists should point out

- Similarities among pairs of patients in the presenting problem, that is, that they wish to overcome their social anxiety
- Similarities among patients regarding bodily reactions they have during speech situations and other social situations
- Similarities among patients regarding how they think other people perceive them in social situations

### Introducing and Discussing the Treatment Model

This is the single most important piece of the initial sessions. It is crucially important that group members understand and adopt a working model for treatment. For this purpose, therapists should distribute Handout 1: CBT model of SAD (Appendix A; see also Figure 3.1) to illustrate the treatment model. The therapist should spend as much time explaining this model as necessary. Furthermore, the therapist should refer back to the model as often as possible. An example for presenting the model follows:

> After our discussion, we now have a common knowledge of what everyone is concerned about and what we all wish to accomplish. Next, we want to talk about the nature of social anxiety. Social anxiety, the fear of social situations, is something really interesting. You are all constantly confronted with social situations in your daily life. Just think about how often you interact with people during your day. And yet, in the absence of treatment, social anxiety can persist for many years or decades. What keeps this anxiety going? Why don't people get used to it? The figure in the handout will illustrate the reasons why.
>
> Please take a few minutes to look at this figure. It is important because this provides an overview of the model of treatment we have adopted. I will go over it in detail. But please take a few moments to study it for yourself first.

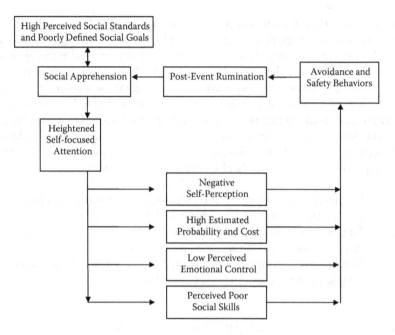

FIGURE 3.1   Handout 1: CBT model of SAD.

What you can see here is a big feedback loop that starts at social apprehensions and leads back via avoidance. Treatment will target all parts of this feedback loop. The figure shows that a social situation is in part anxiety provoking because the goals that you want to achieve in the situation are high or because you assume that the social standard is high. If nobody expected anything from you or if everybody performed very poorly, you would feel considerably less social apprehension than if everybody expected a lot from you and your goals were very high. During this treatment, you will realize that in general people do not expect as much from you as you think they do. Furthermore, you will learn how to define clear goals for yourself during a social situation and how to use this information to determine whether the situation was successful.

Once an individual experiences initial social apprehension, attention is typically directed inwardly—toward self-evaluation and toward sensations of anxiety. We know that this shift in attention makes the problem worse. You are now spending your mental resources scanning your body and examining yourself as well as trying to handle the situation. As part of this treatment, you will learn strategies to direct your attention away from your anxious feelings and toward the situation in order to success-fully complete the social task.

Some of you may focus your attention inwardly and notice aspects about yourself that you don't like when being in a social situation. In other words, you perceive yourself negatively and you believe that everybody else shares the same negative beliefs with you. "I am such an inhibited idiot" is an example of a self-state-ment that reflects negative self-perception. It is important that you become comfortable with the way you are (including your imper-fections in social performance situations). You will learn strategies for how to change this negative view of yourself and become com-fortable with the way you are. You will further realize that other people do not share the same negative view with you.

Major social mishaps with serious consequences are rare. Minor social mishaps are normal and happen all the time. But what makes people different is the degree to which these mishaps affect a person's life. Some of you believe that social mishaps have disastrous consequences for you. As part of this treatment, you will realize that even if a social encounter objectively did not go well, it is just no big deal.

Some of you notice the bodily symptoms of your anxiety a lot when you are in a socially threatening situation, and some of you may even feel paniclike anxiety that appears to get out of your control any second and that everybody else around you can see and sense your racing heart, dry mouth, sweaty palms, and so forth. You will realize that you have more control over your anxious feelings than you think. You will also realize that you overestimate how much other people can see what's going on in your body. Your feeling of anxiety is a very private experience; other people cannot see your racing heart, your sweaty palms, or your shaky knees.

Some of you may further believe that your social skills are inadequate to deal with a social situation. For example, some of you might believe that you are a naturally bad speaker and, therefore, feel very uncomfortable in most public speaking situ-ations. During this treatment, you will realize that your actual social performance is not nearly as bad as you think it is and that poor skills are not the reason for your discomfort in social situations. In fact, there are plenty of people in this world whose social skills are much more limited than yours but who are not socially anxious.

As a result of these processes, you use avoidance strategies. Some of you avoid the situation, some of you escape, and some of you use strategies that make you less uncomfortable. All of these activities (or lack thereof) are intended to avoid the feeling of anxiety. You will learn that using avoidance strategies (either active or passive) is part of the reason social anxiety is so persistent because you never know what would happen if you did not avoid.

But the problem is not over, even after the situation has passed. Some of you tend to ruminate a lot about a social situation after it is over. You might not only focus on the negative aspects but also on ambiguous things (things that could be interpreted as negative or positive), and some of you tend to reinterpret these things negatively. Again, this does not help and makes the situation much worse. You will realize that ruminating about past situations is a bad idea. What happened, happened; time to move on. Ruminating only make things worse and makes you more anxious and avoidant about future situations.

Some of this information is rather complex. But so is your anxiety. It is very important that you understand all aspects of your anxiety and what the maintaining factors are.

At this point, it is advisable to distribute Handout 2: Learning Objectives (Appendix B), which summarizes the points that were discussed, and Handout 3: Approach to Social Situations Scale (Appendix C). Handout 3 is intended to provide feedback to the therapist that can be used to tailor the intervention strategies to the individual patient. Handouts 1 and 2 are kept by the patients, and Handout 3 is returned to the therapist. The items of Handout 3 measure the degree to which an individual matches a particular component of the treatment model. Specifically, the instrument measures perceived social standards (Item 1), goal setting skills (Item 2), degree of self-focused attention (Item 3), self-perception (Item 4), estimated social cost (Item 5), probability estimation of social mishaps (Item 6), perception of emotional control (Item 7), perception of social skills (Item 8), overt avoidance tendencies (Item 9), post-event rumination (Item 10), and safety behaviors (Items 11 and 12). The patient's ratings can give the therapist an idea regarding how much weight needs to be placed on the various components of the model during treatment.

The Role of Avoidance for Maintaining Social Anxiety

The exposure model is the core element of the therapy. The therapist should repeatedly refer back to the basic concepts. Any alternative

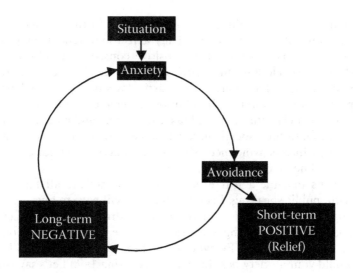

FIGURE 3.2    The vicious cycle model of avoidance.

biological or psychodynamic explanations offered by the patient should
be discussed within the framework of the treatment model. Even if a
patient does not agree with the model, the therapist should try to explain
the model in such a way that it can be incorporated into the patient's
personal beliefs about the etiological or maintaining factors of social
phobia. In order to exemplify the contribution of avoidance to the maintenance of anxiety, show Figure 3.2 with the following explanation:

> Let's say a colleague asks you to give a speech for him about
> a subject you don't know well in front of a lot of people. How
> would this make you feel? (Elicit physiological sensations.)
> When you are anxious and feeling this way, what do you typi-
> cally do then? (Elicit examples.) Right, so you behave in some
> way to make yourself feel a little less uncomfortable. For exam-
> ple, you may tell him that you won't be able to do the speech
> for him, or you may give a very brief speech, or your may take
> medication or even alcohol to make yourself feel a little better.
> (Elicit further examples.) Or in other social situations you may
> not be calling someone for a date, not starting a conversation,
> or maybe choosing a job that won't put you into one of those
> situations. This is called avoidance. We define avoidance as any-
> thing that you do or don't do that prevents you from facing your
> anxiety. This includes not entering the feared situation, escap-
> ing out of the feared situation, taking medications, distracting

yourself, using breathing techniques, and so forth. This has two consequences. The first one is that you feel some relief from your anxiety. This is a short-term positive consequence. However, there is also a long-term negative consequence of avoidance: You will always feel anxious in this particular situation. Avoidance preserves your anxiety. In addition, avoidance tends to spread to other social situations and takes over more and more areas in your life. In sum, social anxiety is so persistent because of a bad habit, which is avoidance. Moreover, anxiety could not exist if you did not avoid. Let me explain this.

Let's imagine a fearful social situation we are all familiar with: public speaking. Let's assume you will have to give a very important presentation in front of hundreds of people. Let's imagine the following scenario: You are entering the room. People stop talking. Everybody has been expecting you. What would your anxiety be? (Elicit anxiety rating 1–9.) Let's say you are now standing in front of all these people; everybody is looking at you, waiting for you to start with your speech. You can feel your heart pounding, your palms sweating, and so forth. (Elicit anxiety rating 1–9.) What will you do if you can get out of the situation? You get out … you avoid (Figure 3.3).

Now, what would happen if you did not avoid? Let's just assume that, just like pressing pause on your remote control button of your video equipment, you could remain in that situation for a while. So let's press the pause button on our imaginary remote control. What would your anxiety be after 2 minutes

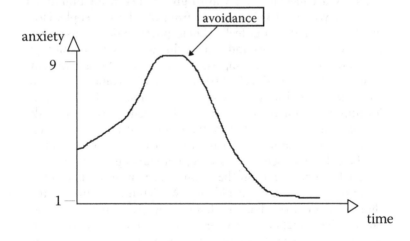

FIGURE 3.3   Anxiety episode with avoidance.

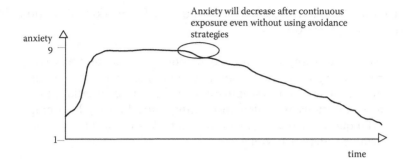

FIGURE 3.4   Anxiety episode without avoidance.

(10 minutes, 60 minutes, 2 hours, etc.)? Eventually, anxiety will
go down just by itself if the person does not avoid. This is how
your body works ... anxiety doesn't kill you (Figure 3.4).

What would your anxiety be if we repeated the same situation over and over again? That is, we rewind the tape of our
imaginary video equipment and do the scene over and over
again (Figure 3.5)?

The therapist should make the following points (in layman's
terms) that after repeated exposure:

1. Anticipatory anxiety will decrease.
2. Maximum anxiety will decrease.
3. The time the maximum anxiety stays on a plateau will
   decrease.
4. Recovery will be faster.
5. This is how the body works.

The conclusion of this discussion is that anxiety can be effectively
overcome with repeated and prolonged exposure to fearful social

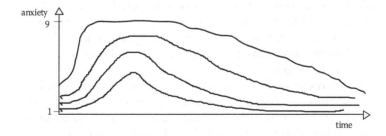

FIGURE 3.5   Anxiety after repeated exposure to the same situation.

situations without using avoidance strategies. The working definition of avoidance is, therefore,

> Avoidance is anything you do or don't do that prevents you from facing your fear of anxiety. This includes not entering the feared situation, escaping out of the feared situation, taking medications as needed, distracting yourself, using breathing techniques, or behaving in a way that makes you feel more comfortable (safety behaviors).

## Importance of Exposure

Exposure situations serve a number of different purposes.

1. Exposures provide an opportunity to practice goal settings and reevaluate social standards. For this purpose, the therapist should discuss with the patient what the social expectations (standards) of a given situation might be and should help the patient to state at least one clear (e.g., behavioral, quantifiable) goal (e.g., asking a particular question). At the beginning, it is important to provide very clear instructions as to what the exposure task should look like. The therapists' role during these early exposures is similar to that of a movie director who provides the patient with a clear script of his or her expected behavior. If the situation requires a complex social interaction (e.g., returning an item to the same salesperson minutes after it was purchased), the therapist should clearly specify when a particular action should be shown. For example, rather than simply instructing the patients to "return a book minutes after you buy it," the therapist should instruct the client to "purchase the newest Harry Potter book, walk with it toward the exit door, and when reaching the exit doors, turn around, find the same salesperson again, and ask for a refund for this book by saying: 'I want to exchange this book that I just bought because I changed my mind.'" The goal of this task may be to say this particular sentence and not to apologize.

2. Exposures provide an opportunity to demonstrate the effects of attentional focus on subjective anxiety. Before every exposure situation, the therapist asks the patient to focus his or her attention toward the self and the anxiety symptoms and to give an anxiety rating (0–10). The therapist

should then ask the patient to direct his or her attention to his or her physical sensations, to describe the feelings, and to rate his or her anxiety. Finally, the patient should be instructed to direct his or her attention to the task (e.g., speech topic, script of exposure task) and to rate his or her anxiety again.

3. Exposures provide an opportunity for the patient to reevaluate his or her social self-presentation. For this purpose, video feedback will be used to reexamine the patient's prediction of his or her performance. Specifically, this technique includes a cognitive preparation prior to viewing the video during which patients are asked to predict in detail what they would see in the video. They will then be instructed to form an image of themselves giving the speech. In order to compare the imagined/perceived self-presentation with the actual self-presentation, individuals will then be asked to watch the video from an observer's point of view (i.e., as if they were watching a stranger). Additional strategies to target self-perception include mirror exposure exercises and listening to their own audiotaped speech. During the mirror exposure, patients are asked to objectively describe the appearance of their mirror image and to audiotape this description. This audiotaped description will then be assigned to independent clinicians to listen to. In addition, patients will be asked to audiotape an impromptu speech about the same topic from the group session and to listen to this speech daily. The reason for these exercises is to correct the person's distorted self-perceptions and to become used to one's own appearance.

4. Asking patients to watch their own videotaped speech performances will provide them with the opportunity to reexamine their social performance. By adding a cognitive preparation prior to watching the videotaped speech, the cognitive dissonance between actual and perceived performance is further increased.

5. In vivo exposure situations that model social mishaps (e.g., dropping a pastry on the floor) provide an ideal opportunity to test distorted assumptions about the social cost of situations.

6. Exposure situations without the use of any avoidance strategies create a high level of emotional arousal, which provide the patient with the opportunity to use acceptance strategies to cope with anxiety.

Nature of Exposure Situations

Effective situations for individuals with SAD differ from exposure situations to treat other phobic disorders. First, they often require performance of complicated chains of interpersonal behavior during exposure. Second, the social phobic patient's specific anxiety-eliciting situations are not always available. For example, an agoraphobic individual may go for a walk away from home at almost any time, but the social phobic may confront that feared staff meeting only once weekly. Other situations may occur only sporadically and be beyond the individual's realistic control. Therefore, the treatment at the beginning will use public speaking situations in the group. This provides the therapist with a maximum degree of control over the situation (e.g., by choosing different speech topics or modifying the situation by bringing in additional audience members or instructing the audience to behave in a certain way). At the beginning of treatment, the therapist should state the following three reasons why the focus will be on public speaking:

1. Public speaking anxiety is often very severe and is the most commonly feared social situation among people with social phobia. It is also one of the most common fears in general. Therefore, all group members share the same type of social fear.
2. A reduction of anxiety related to public speaking (one of the most challenging social tasks) also leads to a reduction of other social fears. This generalization effect can also be seen when treating other fears. For example, a child who is afraid of dogs can overcome his or her fear of dogs if he or she becomes comfortable with the neighbor's dog, especially if the neighbor's dog is friendly but very big and scary looking.
3. In contrast to many other social situations (e.g., dating, maintaining or initiating a conversation), it is fairly easy to create a realistic and uncomfortable public-speaking exposure situation in session.

Later in treatment, exposure tasks will involve more challenging in vivo situations to encourage generalization of treatment gains. This can be achieved first by making the performance situations in group more challenging via changing situational conditions (e.g., adding new audience members, instructing expositing members to act in a disapproving manner) or nature of the task (e.g., interrupting patients at various points or asking them to talk about a sensitive topic, such as their most embarrassing situation). Later in treatment, patients will be asked to engage in a number of challenging social tasks outside of the group setting that create some actual social mishaps or that involve social behaviors that are inconsistent with the patient's perceived social standard.

The fear and avoidance hierarchy (Appendix H) handed out during the first session should serve as a basis to construct the exposure practices for individuals. Later exposure tasks should be designed to specifically create undesirable social mishaps, which provide the patient with the opportunity to examine their actual consequences. Examples were provided in chapter 2 (Table 2.1; see also Appendix K). When conducting these exposures, it is important to discourage patients from using any safety behaviors or other forms of avoidance strategies.

## Practical Issues and Goals

In addition to establishing rapport with the patient and discussing the treatment model, the first session also has an important motivational goal. Discussing the treatment model, the role of avoidance for the maintenance of SAD, and the importance of exposure practices can generate a great degree of distress and increase the likelihood of avoidance tendencies and even treatment drop out. Therefore, it is important to inoculate the patient for avoidance behaviors.

Specifically, the therapist should explain that not doing exposure practices in sessions and home practice assignments (i.e., tasks to be completed between sessions every week after the second session) and missing sessions are all forms of avoidance behavior. For example, the therapist might introduce this issue as follows:

> Before we end this session, I would like to say something very important. Come to every session, be on time, and do your home practice out of fairness to yourself and other members. Let me tell you why. Avoidance has many faces. And sometimes it might be difficult to recognize a behavior as avoidance behavior. This is partly because avoidance has developed into a habit, and habits occur on a subconscious level. Avoidance behaviors are particularly hard to identify if you can give yourself other reasons why you avoided. That way, you can avoid doing something unpleasant and at the same time tell yourself that you didn't do it, not because of your anxiety but because your car broke down, you had a deadline at work, or your dog had really bad diarrhea. Your avoidance is as intelligent as you are and will always find reasons why you can't do it; some might be more convincible to yourself and other people than others. But the bottom line is you are avoiding. Period. Every time you avoid, you are making

a decision against an independent and anxiety-free life and for a life that is controlled by your anxiety. And every time you don't avoid, you are courageous and choose the hard way with the goal to free yourself from your anxiety. I want you to be fully aware of this. So get your priorities straight for the upcoming weeks. Nothing should be more important than coming to these sessions and practicing the home practice exercises. Nothing. Not even your dog's diarrhea.

One more thing: This treatment is not just to make you feel more comfortable in social situations, such as speaking situations. It is much more than that; it entails a change in lifestyle. Clearly saying no to avoidance also means choosing the hard way with the goal to live a better life, a life without anxiety. This applies to virtually all areas in your life.

So when you find yourself debating whether you should go to the next session or clean your house, I want you to be fully aware that at the same time you are making a decision for or against an anxiety-free life. It is your life and you can do what you want. But if you really want to free yourself from your anxiety, I strongly recommend you don't avoid, come to every session, come on time, and do your home practice. Your avoidance may soon whisper in your ear, "Don't go to these sessions anymore; don't do the exposure exercises; it is not going to work." In this case, tell your avoidance that you will do it anyway because you never know unless you try it. Give it a shot and get your priorities straight. You don't have anything to lose but your avoidance and your anxiety.

## Home Practice

Home practice assignments will be given at the end of each treatment session to consolidate new skills, attitudes, and emotional responses. As part of these home practice assignments, patients may be asked to perform behaviors or place themselves in situations that were previously avoided or tolerated only with excessive anxiety. In accordance with the treatment model, patients will be instructed to enter a variety of challenging social situations with the goal to reevaluate a number of assumptions (as outlined earlier) while experiencing a maximum level of anxiety without the use of any avoidance strategies. Before and after each exposure situation, the patient will be asked to fill out a monitoring form to aid the reevaluation process. Patients should be told that home practice is a very important element of this treatment and that not doing the home practice is a form of avoidance.

After each successful exposure, patients are instructed to reward themselves by doing something special or buying something. Discussion of the home practice is an opportunity to reinforce successful behavior and for the therapists to identify the parameters of the patients' feared situations. In addition, it provides an opportunity for the therapists to reinforce the model.

## Flexibility for Dealing With Problems

The exposure assignments should be designed to be challenging for all patients. With group support and motivation by the therapist, most patients should be able to perform the assigned exposure tasks. Some patients, however, may feel unable to conduct the exposures. In these cases, the therapist should show an adequate degree of flexibility and modify the tasks accordingly. People severely anxious about public speaking, for example, might answer simple questions that the therapist or audience members ask rather than giving an impromptu speech, or they may be asked simply to read a paragraph in front of the audience. Conversely, the situation should be made more challenging if the patient does not experience enough anxiety or discomfort. For example, the patient may be asked to give a presentation about a negative personality characteristic rather than a speech about hobbies. Simple physical exercises prior to the exposure task (e.g., push-ups) that induce intense physical sensations and sweatiness can further heighten the anxiety during an exposure exercise (see chapter 6). The optimal level of anxiety during the anticipation phase of a social task is between 5 and 7 on a scale from 0 (no anxiety) to 10 (extreme anxiety), and the therapist should feel free to alter the social topic, interaction, symptom level, or degree of social error of the exposure in order to provide initial practices within this range.

## SESSION 2

### Review of Home Practice From the Past Week

The therapist should start every week with a brief review of the past week using the weekly worksheet (Handout 4, Appendix D).

The figures (Figures 3.1–3.5) that were created during the previous session should be used to illustrate the maintaining variables of social anxiety. The home practice review for each patient should be as brief as possible and focus on only the most anxiety-provoking situation in order to have sufficient time for the more therapeutic in-session exposure practices. Patients should be discouraged from giving long and elaborate descriptions of the situation. Instead, the situation should be summarized succinctly followed by specific and guided questions with the following purposes:

1. Identify anxiety-provoking aspects of the situation. Summarize what exactly made the situation so anxiety provoking.
2. What was the main goal the patient wanted to achieve, and what did the patient think other people's expectations were?
3. What kind of social mishap was the patient afraid of, and what would have been the social consequences?
4. Examine perceptions of control over anxiety: How visible was anxiety to other people? Examine perceptions of social skills: How was the patient's performance?
5. Examine self-focus and self-perception in the situation: Did the patient focus on self and anxiety? What impact did the situation have on his or her self-perception?
6. Identify safety behaviors and other avoidance strategies. Conduct a cost (maintenance of vicious cycle) and benefit (short-term relief) analysis of avoidance. Use simple phrases to illustrate this point, such as "avoidance is your anxiety's best friend" and "anxiety cannot exist without avoidance."
7. Explore post-event rumination: How long did the situation and its feared consequences "linger"? To what extent will this situation change the patient's future life?

Group members who exposed themselves to a fearful situation should be rewarded warmly. If the patient used any safety behaviors or avoidance strategies, the therapist should encourage the patient to repeatedly expose him/herself during the following week while fading these behaviors/strategies (but if the patient does not feel ready to do that yet, the therapist should not push any further). To maximize self-efficacy, the patient should have a maximum degree of control over the nature of the exposure exercise as part of the home practice assignment. However, avoidance strategies should be clearly acknowledged and the negative impact discussed. If the patient shows repeated avoidance behaviors during her or his home practice assignment, the therapist may ask questions such as:

How did you feel after you avoided X?
How do you think you would have felt if you had not avoided X?
Doesn't it bother you that you avoided X?

The therapist should help the patient to perform a cost–benefit analysis after he/she avoided the situation. It should become very clear that the benefit of avoidance (short-term relief) does not outweigh the costs (maintenance of the vicious cycle of social anxiety). Phrases such as "avoidance is your anxiety's best friend" and "anxiety could not exist without avoidance" often help patients to fully understand this principle. Often patients claim that they avoided for some other (seemingly rational) reasons. The therapist may then point out that "avoidance is as intelligent as you are" (meaning that there are always reasons why the patient could not expose himself or herself); but whatever the reason, the anxiety won at this point. The therapist may compare this to a soccer match: Whenever the patient avoids, anxiety scores a goal, and the more often the patient avoids, the more difficult it then becomes to win the match. Social anxiety may be portrayed as a wild and vicious beast that, when examined in more detail, is only a harmless kitten. But one can only realize this if the patient stops running away from it. Using such phrases and figurative examples often helps patients to understand and better consolidate the exposure rationale.

If most participants have not done their home practice, discuss why not and point out the importance of home practice assignments for the therapy outcomes. If possible, refer again to the model (vicious cycle, Figure 3.2) and point out the short- and long-term effects. Socially reward group members who exposed themselves to a fearful situation and analyze the situation in detail (what was the situation, how did you feel at the beginning, what did you do, how did other people react, how did you feel at the end, etc.). Give positive feedback and refer again to the model (vicious cycle).

### Review of Treatment Model

Before the exposure practices, ask group members to explain the treatment rationale by using the figures (Figures 3.1–3.5) from Session 1. These figures should already be on the board prior to the beginning of the session. This should be done with minimal therapist involvement. The therapist will ask guided questions (e.g., what are the components of social anxiety and why is it maintained; what are examples of avoidance and safety behaviors and what are the consequences?). The following messages need to be conveyed:

- The more you think other people expect from you, the greater your anxiety. These expectations may not be correct.
- It is important to clearly define the goals of a social situation. Otherwise, we don't know whether we have reached them and whether the social situation has been a success.
- The more you focus on yourself in a social situation, the more anxious you feel.

- People cannot feel anxious if they feel comfortable the way that they are in social situations.
- Social mishaps are normal; it is no big deal if they do happen.
- Other people can't see how anxious you are, and you're more in control of your anxiety than you think you are.
- Your social skills are most likely better than you think they are. If not, then adjust your standards.
- Safety behaviors and other avoidance lead to the maintenance and worsening of anxiety.

### In-Session Exposures: Explaining the Treatment Model and Rationale

Each member of the group should be asked to give a videotaped talk in front of the rest of the group about what he or she learned in the previous session (i.e., the anxiety model, the role of avoidance for the maintenance of social anxiety, the importance of exposure practices) and how this applies to his or her own anxiety. The therapist needs to be aware that the very first exposure is the worst. Therefore, the therapist should select a group member who is neither the most severe nor the least severe case in the group. If the first speaker is too anxious the situation may be traumatizing to the speaker and the other group members, and if the speaker is too comfortable, other group members might feel intimidated. In both cases, patients are then likely to drop out of group. This issue may be directly discussed with the group members in case a "traumatizing" situation occurs during the first exposure task.

The therapist should give very clear instructions, such as:

> Please give a 3-minute talk about what you learned about social anxiety and on what aspects a successful treatment has to focus. Please illustrate these points by referring to the model and offering concrete personal examples.

Before the speech, patients are asked to specify their personal goals (e.g., maintaining eye contact with at least three people for at least 2 seconds). These goals should be clearly quantifiable, and group members should be recruited to determine whether the goals were reached based on these criteria (e.g., count number and length of eye contacts).

Before and after the speech performance, therapists should ask the subjects to rate their subjective anxiety (0–10). Furthermore, the therapist should ask the patients to (1) focus on and describe anxiety symptoms and self (30 seconds); (2) focus on and describe the environment (30 seconds); and (3) focus on and summarize the speech (30 seconds). After each attentional shift, elicit anxiety ratings. This exercise is designed to illustrate how changes in attentional focus influence the level of anxiety.

If the patient's anxiety is very high at the beginning (>6), the therapist may ask the patient to just stand quietly in front of the audience and let the therapist know when his/her anxiety decreases. Each and every speech should be followed by applause from the therapists and the group members, by immediate positive reinforcement (i.e., telling the speaker what the audience liked about the talk), by asking the speaker about his/her experience during the speech, and by asking the group members to give their feedback. Negative feedback from any of the group members (which happens very rarely) should be restated and modified by the therapists with the support of other group members.

Following the initial discussion, the therapist should play the videotape for the group. This videotape should be saved. It will be watched again during Session 12. Prior to watching the videotaped speech, patients will undergo a cognitive preparation period, which consists of (1) a prediction of social performance (3 minutes per performance); (2) imagining of social performance (2 minutes); and (3) identifying and challenging incorrect predictions (2 minutes). Handout 5: Cognitive Preparation for Video Feedback (Appendix E) provides some examples for instructions for each of these phases (see also Harvey et al., 2000).

When doing cognitive preparation, choose three of the most extreme performance indicators to discuss with the patient (see also chapter 5). For example:

> You gave yourself an 8 for trembling. What part of your body was trembling? (If hands) How much did you tremble ... this much (demonstrate exaggerated hand tremble) ... this much (demonstrate again). Or: You gave yourself a 9 for boring. What are the behaviors that go along with it? Did you speak really slowly? Did you repeat yourself over and over again?

If blushing was one of the patient's concerns in the past, make sure that there is something red and pink in the frame of the video picture. Then if the patient gives an extreme score on blushing, ask: How blushed were you ... as red as that ... or more pinkish like that? Write the patient's specific predictions next to the performance ratings.

### Home Practice

Patients should be asked to prepare a speech about what they do for living. In addition, patients should be asked to give a speech with the same topic they gave during session (i.e., treatment rationale) in front of the mirror every day and to record the speech on an audiotape. Patients are told that this tape may be given to one of the staff members who will listen to it (ensure confidentiality).

## SESSIONS 3–6

The structure of Sessions 3–6 are very similar to Session 2. At times, it can be difficult to induce sufficient anxiety for the exposure tasks, especially after numerous trials of speech exposures. Anxiety can be raised by:

1. Asking the person to talk about a very personal topic (e.g., their most embarrassing situations)
2. Asking the person to talk about a topic he/she knows little about (e.g., black holes, cloning)
3. Bringing in new audience members
4. Interrupting the presenter at various points
5. Asking the presenter to do push-ups, rapid breathing, or stair climbing before the speech to induce intense physical sensations and make the person sweat (see chapter 6)
6. Having the patient sing a children's song or play an instrument

For earlier sessions, the therapists should choose easier topics, such as a presentation about the patient's profession (what do you do for a living?) in order to break the ice. Other topics (in the order of increasing difficulty) are: hobbies (with visual aids such as golf iron, fishing poles, etc.), local politics (e.g., Boston's Big Dig), highly controversial political issues (the war in Iraq), and highly sensitive personal issues (opportunities I passed up because of my social anxiety).

The exact topics should be adapted flexibly to each individual. The important point is to raise the individual's anxiety/discomfort level. For example, if a person is very uncomfortable in a dating situation, he/she may choose to give a speech about dating. The patient should have a maximum level of flexibility for choosing his/her speech topic.

For all home practice assignments, patients should be asked to speak in front of a mirror about a random topic of interest every day and to audiotape one of the speeches. The therapist should ensure on a regular basis whether the practices were being performed and elicit feedback on their efficacy.

It is critically important that patients are supported and encouraged in their home practice exposures. It is equally important that their success is acknowledged and their failures be interpreted in a reasonable way. Thus, the discussion of home practice assignments is very important. Patients should be briefly questioned about what they did and how it went. Home practice assignments that were attempted but did not work out very well should be framed as providing valuable information that will allow us to work all the more effectively on that patient's problems in the future. This latter statement should be followed up by inquiring about the specific problems that arose and giving the patient the opportunity to work on such situations again.

## SESSION 7–END

Beginning with Session 7, the therapist should introduce in vivo exposure situations outside of the group environment. Before each exercise, patients should be asked to give the following predictions:

1. What will be the maximum and average level of anxiety during the exposure task?
2. What will be the outcome of the situation (i.e., what will the interaction partner say, how will she/he behave)?
3. How long will consequences persist (e.g., in case of a social mishap)?

These situations should be individually tailored to the patient and created based on the fear and avoidance hierarchy. They can be relatively simple and straightforward at the beginning (e.g., asking for directions, returning an item to a store after a week, etc). However, beginning with Session 8, the therapists should "push" patients to do situations that would be uncomfortable to most people and/or that create social mishaps. Examples of these situations can be found in chapter 2 (Table 2.1; also see Appendix K).

Toward the end of treatment, it is recommended to include a session that addresses relapse prevention. As part of the home practice review, the therapist should introduce the relapse prevention component as follows:

You have all made great improvement, and I am very proud of you (go around the group and give some examples for everybody). However, since the treatment is almost over, I need to tell you one very important thing. For some of you, there might be times when your anxiety comes back and the avoidance sneaks up on you again, sometimes for no apparent reason. But for others, this might not happen. But if it does, don't be discouraged.

Improvement never follows a straight line. It always has its ups and downs, and some days are better than others. Rather, the improvement curve looks like the Dow Jones on Wall Street. Although there are ups and downs, the tendency goes upward. The important point is not to confuse a lapse (a temporary slip or blip; the recurrence of symptoms after a period of improvement) and a relapse ("I am back at square one," "all my gains are lost," "all my efforts were for nothing"). Anxiety symptoms can reappear, and that is just no big deal. It will depend on the person's response to the lapse whether or not it turns into a relapse. A relapse can be prevented if you use effective coping strategies. Get back on the horse, and come up with a list of exposure situations to help you beat the disorder.

## LAST SESSION

In general, the last session is a low-key way to close the group. When summarizing the progress of each group member, emphasis should be placed on independent functioning and the positive skills each patient has learned. Each person should say something constructive to anyone else in the room (therapists or group members). In a group format, the discussion of what has been learned should be a rather informal affair and should be dominated by the patients. Topics may include what anxieties have been overcome, what anxieties remain, and what patients intend to do on their own to combat any remaining anxieties. Remember that the job of the therapist is to teach patients the model of the disorder and the model of treatment. Not all patients will have completed the full course of treatment by the end of this course of 12–16 sessions (see chapter 6), but the therapist will have succeeded if he or she has helped patients become their own CBT therapists, so they can guide treatment individually from this point forward. Chapter 7 provides a more comprehensive accounting of final session strategies and booster sessions, should they be needed.

# CHAPTER 4

# Research Basis for the Treatment Model

According to the model presented in chapter 2, individuals with social anxiety disorder (SAD) are apprehensive in social situations in part because they perceive the social standard (i.e., expectations and social goals) as being high. They desire to make a particular impression on others while doubting that they will be able to do so (Leary, 2001), partly because they are unable to define goals and select specific achievable behavioral strategies to reach these goals (Hiemisch, Ehlers, & Westermann, 2002). This leads to a further increase in social apprehension and also to increased self-focused attention (Heinrichs & Hofmann, 2001; Woody, 1996), which triggers a number of closely interrelated cognitive responses. Specifically, vulnerable individuals exaggerate the likelihood of social mishaps and the potential social costs involved in social situations (Foa, Franklin, Perry, & Herbert, 1996; Hofmann, 2004). Individuals with SAD assume that they are in danger of behaving in an inept and unacceptable fashion and believe that this will result in disastrous consequences (Clark & Wells, 1995). They further perceive little control over their anxiety response in social situations (Hofmann & Barlow, 2002) and exaggerate the visibility of their anxiety response to other people. These responses are closely associated with one another and with a tendency to perceive oneself negatively in social situations (Clark & Wells, 1995). The activation of these factors leads to an exacerbation of social anxiety. As a result, the person engages in avoidance and/or safety behaviors (Wells et al., 1995), followed by post-event rumination (Mellings & Alden, 2000; Rachmann, Grüter-Andrew, & Shafran 2000). This cycle feeds on itself, ultimately leading to the maintenance and further exacerbation of the problem. The remainder of this chapter will present in more detail the research basis of this model. A more detailed description can be found in Hofmann (2007) and Hofmann and Scepkowski (2006).

## SOCIAL STANDARDS

Several models of social anxiety assume that anxiety arises in social situations when individuals wish to convey a desired impression but are unsure about their ability to do so (Clark & Wells, 1995; Leary, 2001; Trower & Gilbert, 1989). In fact, social anxiety is closely tied to the social norms of a culture (Heinrichs et al., 2006). Studies have further demonstrated that individuals with SAD show a discrepancy between perceived social standards and their perceived social abilities (Alden, Bieling, & Wallace, 1994; Alden & Wallace, 1991, 1995; Wallace & Alden, 1991, 1995). This discrepancy was found to be largely due to the individuals' underestimation of their ability level in relation to the perceived social standards and desired goals.

A recent study by Moscovitch, Hofmann, Suvak, and In-Albon (2005) provided individuals with generalized SAD with cues indicating that standards for their performance were high, low, or ambiguous. Individuals with SAD rated their performance as being worse only in the high and ambiguous conditions as compared to nonanxious controls. The results suggest that information about social standards moderates retrospective self-appraisals of social performance. Emotions may also shift these standards (affect-as-information model; Cervone, Kopp, Schaumann, & Scott, 1994), with the notion that experiencing negative affects can implicitly influence people to set higher minimal standards for their performance (Scott & Cervone, 2002).

Accordingly, one target for intervention involves clarification of actual standards for performance. In the treatment, social standards are questioned in cognitive interventions and receive direct attention in discussions of appropriate exposure goals. Moreover, dire interpretations of the consequences of imperfect social performances are directly challenged by the social mishap exposures, where patients are provided with direct evidence that (1) the likelihood of social mishaps are small and (even more importantly) that (2) the consequences of social mishaps (social costs) are neither catastrophic nor unmanageable.

## GOAL SETTING

Leary and colleagues (Leary & Kowalski, 1995; Schlenker & Leary, 1982) offer that social anxiety occurs if individuals doubt that they are able to make a desired impression on other people and if they feel that they are unable to attain their goals in a social situation. The effects of goal setting on information processing have been well researched by action theorists (e.g., Gollwitzer & Moskowitz, 1996). Action theory emphasizes cognitive processes relevant for successful goal attainment. The goal a person is trying to achieve not only determines the demands of a situation, but it also influences cognition, affect, and behavior in a specific way. In the case of SAD, individuals engage in information processing that interferes with successful goal attainment when approaching social situations.

Interventions designed to help patients set objective and attainable goals for social situations are designed to intervene for both elevated social standards and diffuse unrealistic or subjective goals. In treatment, attention is devoted to ensuring that goals are objective; in particular, to ensure that goals do not involve the "mind reading" of others' judgments of social adequacy. In this way, goal setting interventions provide the dual benefits of: (1) helping patients "get out of the heads" of others and define what is truly needed from a social interaction or performance, while (2) defining an adequate level of performance relative to a specified situation.

## SELF-FOCUSED ATTENTION

The cognitive model assumes that when confronted with social threat, socially anxious individuals shift their attention inward and engage in a process of detailed monitoring and observation of themselves, which is consistent with some of the information processing literature (e.g., Heinrichs & Hofmann, 2001). Recent studies show that under conditions of high self-focused attention, individuals with SAD experience spontaneous, recurrent, and excessively negative self-images, which they believe to be accurate at the time they occur (Hackmann, Clark, & McManus, 2000; Hackmann, Surawy, & Clark, 1998; Hofmann & Heinrichs, 2003). These negative self-images are causally related to social anxiety (Hirsch, Clark, Matthews, & Williams, 2003). Compared to nonanxious controls, individuals with SAD are more likely to "see" themselves in social situations as if from an observer's perspective (Hackmann et al., 1998). When instructed to focus their attention on aspects of the external environment, individuals with SAD report less anxiety and fewer negative beliefs (Wells & Papageorgiou, 1998). Moreover, individuals with SAD have a tendency to miss important positive cues during a social encounter and lack the type of positive inferential bias that characterizes the cognitive processes of nonanxious controls (Hirsch & Matthews, 2000).

As part of this treatment program, patients get active practice performing under different attentional conditions. These procedures are designed to not only help patients notice the differential impact of these attentional perspectives on the experience of anxiety, but also ensure that patients rehearse the active shifting of perspectives in relevant social situations. Changes in anxiety from this exercise help inform patients that social anxiety is not an inviolate response to social situations, but rather is a function of subjective and modifiable attentional factors.

## SELF-PERCEPTION

Cognitive models of SAD have placed a particular emphasis on self-perception as an important maintaining factor of the disorder (Beck & Emery, 1985; Clark, 2001; Clark & Wells, 1995; Leary, 2001; Rapee & Heimberg, 1997). Social anxiety is thought to arise from the perception that one is unable to convey a desired impression of oneself to important others (Leary, 2001; Schlenker & Leary, 1982). This conceptualization of social anxiety has received support from research on self-discrepancy theory (e.g., Higgins, 1987; Strauman, 1989; Strauman & Higgins, 1987), which distinguishes between beliefs individuals hold about their *actual* self (the attributes people believe someone, self or other, feels they actually possess), their *ideal* self (the attributes people would like to possess), and their *ought* self (the attributes people believe they ought to possess). Studies have consistently found that patients with social phobia experience significant *actual:ought/other* trait self-discrepancies, indicating that they perceive their self attributes to fall short of the characteristics they believe others expect them to possess (e.g., Strauman, 1989; Weilage & Hope, 1999).

Socially anxious or phobic individuals under social threat experience self-discrepancies that are characterized by an underestimation of their abilities relative to others' standards (Alden, Bieling, & Wallace, 1994; Wallace & Alden, 1991). Although, surprisingly, patients' estimations of others' standards do not typically exceed those of nonanxious controls (Alden, Bieling, & Wallace, 1994; Wallace & Alden, 1991). Research does suggest that individuals with social phobia are concerned that others may hold high standards for their performance in social situations and that this concern may significantly influence their emotions and behavior. For example, patients who receive feedback that they performed well during a social encounter have been found to react with *increased* anxiety when anticipating a subsequent encounter due to their perception that their initial success may have led evaluators to raise expected performance standards (Wallace & Alden, 1995, 1997). Similarly, when individuals with social anxiety perceive expected standards to be unreachable, they may employ the self-presentational strategy of purposeful failure in order to influence potential evaluators to lower their performance expectations to a level they can more confidently match (e.g., Baumgardner & Brownlee, 1987). In addition, studies have generally shown that patients with social phobia form negative mental self-representations based not on how they view themselves but on how they believe potential "audience" evaluators view them at any given moment (Hackmann et al., 1998; Wells, Clark, & Ahmad, 1998; Wells & Papageorgiou, 1998; also see Rapee & Heimberg, 1997).

Negative self-perception plays a central role in the development and maintenance of social phobia (e.g., Hook & Valentiner, 2002). Cognitive theories (e.g., Beck & Emery, 1985; Clark & Wells, 1995; Rapee & Heimberg, 1997) posit that on the basis of early learning experiences, individuals with social phobia develop a number of distorted, negative assumptions about themselves (e.g., "I'm stupid," "I'm unattractive"; Clark & Wells, 1995) that become reinforced over time by selective information processing errors that occur both within and between social encounters (see Bögels & Mansell, 2004; Clark & McManus, 2002; Heinrichs & Hofmann, 2001; Hirsch & Clark, 2004). When faced with social threat, socially phobic individuals shift their attention inward and engage in a process of detailed self-monitoring (see Spurr & Stopa, 2002), during which they experience spontaneous, recurrent, and excessively negative self-images that they perceive as being accurate (Hackmann et al., 1998, 2000).

It has been argued that biased, negative self-appraisals are "a general feature" (Alden & Wallace, 1995, p. 503) of social phobia that occur irrespective of social context. In support of this view, individuals with social phobia have been found to appraise their own behavior in a manner that greatly minimizes their performance accomplishments (Norton & Hope, 2001; Rapee & Lim, 1992; Stopa & Clark, 1993), regardless of their level of skill or the degree of warmth and friendliness exhibited by their interaction partners (Alden & Wallace, 1995). In contrast, other evidence suggests that for highly self-conscious individuals, negative self-appraisals are actually context-specific and activated only by social cues that trigger memories and expectancies of social rejection and failure (Baldwin & Main, 2001).

Recent studies further suggest that changes in self-perception directly mediate treatment change (Hofmann, 2000a; Hofmann, Moscovitch, Kim, & Taylor, 2004). Video feedback has been shown to be a particularly effective tool to correct negative and distorted self-perception (Rapee & Hayman, 1996), especially when combined with a cognitive preparation period prior to viewing the videotaped performance (Harvey, Clark, Ehlers, & Rapee, 2000; Hirsch, Clark, Matthews, & Williams, 2003; Kim, Lundh, & Harvey, 2002). From the introduction of the treatment model forward, patients are taught about the impact of negative expectations on levels of distress. Cognitive restructuring and goal setting interventions provide additional therapeutic teaching about the nature of common cognitive biases in SAD while introducing the patient to alternative self- and performance evaluations. Exposure with videotaped feedback is then used to solidify these changes, where patients are provided direct opportunities to dispassionately evaluate their own social performance vis-à-vis reasonable social standards and specific social goals.

## ESTIMATED SOCIAL COST

One of the most popular accountings of the crucial change processes in Cognitive Behavioral Theraphy (CBT) is that alternations in cognitive schemata account for therapeutic benefits. This notion has been studied primarily in investigations of major depression (Barber & DeRubeis, 1989; Evans & Hollon, 1988; Hollon, Evans, & DeRubeis, 1990; Whisman, 1993). Likewise, researchers of anxiety disorders believe that effective psychotherapy either directly modifies the patient's irrational beliefs or deactivates them while making other schemata available.

Clark and Wells (1995) argue that individuals with SAD believe that "(1) they are in danger of behaving in an inept and unacceptable fashion, and (2) that such behavior will have disastrous consequences in terms of loss of status, loss of worth, and rejection" (pp. 69–70). Consistent with this model are the results from studies showing that socially anxious individuals believe that negative social events are more likely to occur than positive social events (Luckock & Salkovskis, 1988), and that most people are inherently critical of others and are likely to evaluate them negatively (Leary, Kowalski, & Campbell, 2001). Furthermore, the belief system of socially anxious individuals appears to magnify the competitive aspects of interpersonal relationships, but minimizes the cooperative, supportive aspects of them (Trower & Gilbert, 1989).

Direct evidence for the role of estimated social cost as a treatment mediator comes from a study by Foa et al. (1996). The authors found that patients evidenced socially relevant judgmental biases prior to treatment, which were attenuated following treatment. Similar results were reported by McManus, Clark, and Hackmann (2000) and Hofmann (2004). The latter study showed that direct cognitive intervention leads to better maintenance of treatment gains, and this effect appears to be mediated via changes in estimated social cost during treatment. Estimated social cost is a specific expression of the dysfunctional beliefs about the potential outcome of a social encounter. As other dysfunctional social beliefs, this maladaptive thought should therefore be responsive to cognitive intervention.

According to this model, therapeutic mediation occurs by changing patients' mental representation of the self in a more positive direction (Rapee & Heimberg, 1997), and by changing their beliefs that behaving in an inept and unacceptable fashion in a social situation will have disastrous consequences in terms of loss of status, loss of worth, and rejection (Clark & Wells, 1995).

Similarly, a model proposed by Foa and Kozak (1986) suggests that treatment change is mediated by a reduction in the exaggerated probabilities and cost associated with the feared consequences. The model further states that if the individual's fear structure is completely activated, exposure in the absence of negative consequences would alter the exaggerated probability estimates of harm typical to anxiety patients. Habituation of anxiety during exposure would then reduce inflated estimated cost if the person attributes the decline of his/her anxiety to characteristics of the social situation (e.g., "If I am not anxious, the situation cannot be so bad"). If during repeated role play mild criticism ceases to evoke physiological arousal, then being criticized is no longer perceived by the patient as disastrous. The model predicts that exaggerated cost would be more likely to underlie social anxiety than elevated probability estimation for negative events.

In an attempt to test Foa and Kozak's (1986) mediation hypothesis of change in the treatment of SAD, Foa, Franklin, Perry, and Herbert (1996) treated 15 generalized social phobic individuals with a modified version of Heimberg's cognitive-behavioral group therapy (CBGT; Heimberg, Dodge, et al., 1990). Before and after treatment, all patients and 15 nonanxious controls filled out the experimenter-developed Probability/Cost Questionnaire (PCQ). The results were consistent with Foa and Kozak's hypothesis that social phobic subjects would exhibit specific judgmental biases for the costs of negative social events. Patients evidenced socially relevant judgmental biases prior to treatment, which were attenuated following treatment. A decrease in both estimated costs and overestimation of the probability of negative social events was highly associated with posttreatment levels of symptom severity. The relationship between estimated costs and posttreatment scores remained strong after controlling for change in estimated probabilities ($r = .76$). However, the partial correlation between social probability and posttreatment scores was considerably smaller when controlling for estimated costs ($r = .27$). Furthermore, appraisals of cost and probability of negative social events were highly correlated ($r = .74$), suggesting that estimated costs, as measured with the PCQ, were the best single predictors for treatment outcome based on Foa and Kozak's mediation model.

This mediation model further predicts that cognitive therapy plus exposure should be superior to pure exposure therapy because cognitive interventions are aimed at changing dysfunctional cognitions directly and systematically (Butler, 1985; Butler, Cullington, Munby, Amies, & Gelder, 1984; Clark & Wells, 1995; Heimberg & Juster, 1995; Stopa & Clark, 1993).

Although certain cognitive strategies in traditional CBT approaches address this issue to some degree, the present protocol aggressively targets estimated social cost in a number of different ways. During the homework review, the therapist specifically asks questions to identify and challenge the patient's exaggerated cost estimation (e.g., "What would be the worst outcome of this situation? Why is this situation such a catastrophic event? How will your life change as a result of this event?"). These discussions are intended to illustrate to participants that social mishaps are normal and that the negative consequences of such mishaps are short lasting. Furthermore, during the planning stage of the exposure exercises, the therapist instructs the patient specifically to create social mishaps in order to examine the actual consequences. These exposures are designed to help patients realize that perfect performance need never be the standard for social acceptability or safety, and to help patients realize, through repeated and vivid experiences of committing social mishaps, that these mishaps need not and should not be interpreted catastrophically. We believe these interventions may have specific value for relapse prevention; treatment establishes not only new patterns of social attention, goal setting, and performance evaluations, but sets a standard for the notable distinction between social failure and social mishaps. The latter can occur with no important social consequences.

## PERCEPTION OF EMOTIONAL CONTROL

Emotional disorders are frequently associated with a perception of a lack of control over aversive events (Alloy, Abramson, & Viscusi, 1981; Barlow, 2002; Lang, 1985), which can result in subjective, behavioral, and physiological distress (Geer, Davison, & Gatchel, 1970; Glass & Singer, 1970; Sanderson, Rapee, & Barlow, 1989). Furthermore, it has been demonstrated that repeated experience with uncontrollable aversive events can lead to pathological emotional states, such as anxiety and depression (Abramson, Seligman, & Teasdale, 1978; Barlow, 2002; Mineka, 1985). Therefore, it has been suggested that the degree to which people view events as within their control may be a fundamental mediator of psychopathology and treatment (e.g., Rotter, 1966, 1975). Similarly, Barlow (2002) suggested that the unexpected experience of bursts of emotions may lead to anxiety disorders in vulnerable individuals because they view their own emotions or bodily reactions as out of control. In the case of panic disorder, for example, vulnerable individuals may unexpectedly experience a brief and intense burst of fear and subsequently develop anxiety over the possibility of the reoccurrence of this response in an uncontrollable manner. Moreover, Barlow (2001) hypothesized that all anxiety disorders share a lack of perceived control over negative emotional and bodily reactions.

Consistent with this hypothesis are the findings from studies suggesting that patients with SAD perceive a lack of internal control (Leung & Heimberg, 1996) and believe that events are controllable only by people other than themselves (Cloitre, Heimberg, Liebowitz, & Gitow, 1992). Furthermore, panic attacks seem to play an important role in phobic individuals, including those suffering from specific phobias and SAD (Craske, 1991; Ehlers, Hofmann, Herda, & Roth, 1994; Himle, Crystal, Curtis, & Fluent, 1991; Hofmann, Ehlers, & Roth, 1995; McNally & Steketee, 1985). For example, Hofmann, Ehlers, and Roth (1995) showed that people who are afraid of public speaking attributed their fear more often to "panic attacks" (defined as a sudden rush of intense fear without apparent reason) than to traumatic events or indirect conditioning events. Although all subjects of this study met diagnostic criteria for SAD, they regarded panic attacks as more important for their speech anxiety than their fear of negative evaluation by others (which is considered the core feature of SAD). Similarly, a more recent study (Hofmann, 2005) employed structural equation modeling procedures in a large and representative sample of social phobics, and suggested that "costly" social situations are anxiety provoking in part because social phobic individuals perceive their anxiety symptoms as being out of control.

In sum, the literature suggests that individuals with SAD not only believe that their anxiety response is out of control in social situations, but also that it can be easily noticed by other people, which increases their level of public self-consciousness and self-focused attention (e.g., Bögels, Alberts, & De Jong, 1996; Hofmann & Heinrichs, 2003; Mansell & Clark, 1999; Mellings & Alden, 2000; Norton & Hope, 2001; Wells & Papageorgiou, 2001). Based on these studies, it can be hypothesized that the perception of control over one's anxiety response associated with threatening events may be an important mediator of treatment gains in SAD. Our treatment targets this potential mediator by ensuring that social exposures include emotional inductions when relevant to a patient's core social fears. These exposures (combining external social cue exposure with exposure to feared anxiety sensations) are designed to redefine the "safety" of these anxiety sensations, helping patients learn that these sensations (1) are readily tolerable, (2) need not impair social performance, and (3) certainly should not be used to define social failure experiences.

## PERCEIVED SOCIAL SKILLS

It has been suggested that increasing one's sense of competence in mastering a feared situation (i.e., perceived self-efficacy) is the single result of all successful anxiety reduction techniques (Bandura, 1977, 1983, 1984). Consistent with the previous section, earlier versions of Bandura's theory assume that performance capabilities can be predicted independently from the person's anxiety state. For example, Bandura (1984) wrote:

> Perceived self-efficacy does not include anxiety in either the definition or the measuring device. Self-efficacy scales ask people to judge their performance capabilities and not if they can perform nonanxiously. (p. 238)

This narrow definition of the self-efficacy theory has been criticized for a number of reasons. Borkovec (1977), for example, pointed out that self-efficacy is more likely to be a reflection of a behavioral change mechanism than to be the mediator of such change. Furthermore, performance capabilities alone often play little or no role in many anxiety disorders (Barlow, 2001). In fact, most social phobic people seem to possess adequate social skills but are inhibited when it comes to applying them in social situations (Juster, Heimberg, & Holt, 1996). As a result of these and other criticisms, subsequent versions of the theory conceptualized self-efficacy more generally as a perceived ability to manage potential threats, which also increases the sense of predictability and controllability of anxiety-provoking events (Bandura, 1986).

Numerous studies have provided some evidence for perceived self-efficacy (in its broader definition) as a correlate and potential mediator of exposure therapy. For example, Williams and colleagues (Williams, Dooseman, & Kleifield, 1984; Williams, Kinney, & Falbo, 1989; Williams, Turner, & Peer, 1985) presented data suggesting that perceived self-efficacy predicts therapeutic outcome more accurately than arousal during treatment, anticipated danger, or perceived danger in specific phobia and agoraphobia. In addition, Williams et al. (1989) found that perceived self-efficacy was the most accurate predictor of therapeutic change regardless of whether the phobia was targeted. Williams et al. (1989) interpreted their findings as supporting evidence for the view that agoraphobia is maintained by low perceptions of self-efficacy, and agoraphobic dysfunctions are alleviated by raising people's perception of self-efficacy.

The perception of one's social skills and abilities appears to be an important component of perceived self-efficacy in SAD. Although it remains uncertain whether socially anxious individuals are in fact deficient in any of their social skills (Clark & Arkowitz, 1975; Glasgow & Arkowitz, 1975; Halford & Foddy, 1982; Hofmann, Gerlach, Wender, & Roth, 1997; Rapee & Lim, 1992; Stopa & Clark, 1993), they do tend to appraise their own performance in social situations more negatively than nonanxious individuals, even when actual differences in performance are accounted for (Alden & Wallace, 1995; Glasgow & Arkowitz, 1975; Rapee & Lim, 1992; Stopa & Clark, 1993). Possibly as a result of this tendency, socially anxious individuals frequently doubt their ability to create desired impressions on others (Wallace & Alden, 1995), and they expect their performance to fall short of other people's expectations of them (Alden & Wallace, 1991; Wallace & Alden, 1991, 1995). Therefore, it has been suggested that social anxiety arises in social situations when people desire to make a particular impression on others but doubt that they will be able to do so (Leary & Kowalski, 1995). If, as a result of treatment, patients perceive their social skills as improved or as better than they originally thought, social situations would then appear less threatening and dangerous due to an increased sense of control over the situation. Consequently, patients become more confident and less fearful of future social situations following psychosocial intervention if treatment enhances the patient's perceived social skills to manage social threat. This would explain findings showing that after exposure, therapy patients showed less anxiety and rated themselves as better speakers, although they did not objectively show better social performance than individuals from a waitlist control group (Newman, Hofmann, Trabert, Roth, & Taylor, 1994).

Although these studies provide some indirect evidence for the validity of perceived self-efficacy, and in particular for perceived social skills, as a potential mediator of treatment change, no attempt has been made to directly test the predictions of this model. Strong corroborating data for this model would come from well-controlled studies showing that treatment changes in perceived social skills are related to changes in social anxiety independent of the person's actual social skills or any other variables. In addition, it still remains uncertain whether there are, in fact, subgroups of social phobic individuals who lack social skills. Although social skills training seems to be effective in reducing social anxiety (Stravynski, Grey, & Elie, 1987; Stravynski, Marks, & Yule, 1982), there is no clear evidence to suggest that it is more effective than exposure therapy or cognitive behavioral therapy for any SAD subgroup, including those who were judged to have poor social skills (Mersch, Emmelkamp, Bögels, & van der Sleen, 1989; Mersch, Emmelkamp, & Lips, 1991; Wlazlo, Schroeder-Hartwig, Hand, Kaiser, & Münchau, 1990).

In sum, socially anxious individuals appraise their own performance in social situations more negatively than nonanxious individuals, even when accounting for differences in actual performance (Alden & Wallace, 1995; Glasgow & Arkowitz, 1975; Norton & Hope, 2002; Rapee & Lim, 1992; Stopa & Clark, 1993). Although social skills training is often beneficial (most likely due to the exposure part of therapy), it does not seem to be a necessary treatment component. However, effective treatments typically lead to an improvement in the perception of the patient's social skills (e.g., Newman et al., 1994). There is little evidence to suggest that individuals with SAD are consistently deficient in their social skills (e.g., Stravynski & Amado, 2001). Rather, the literature seems to suggest that individuals with SAD perceive their social skills as being inadequate to reach their social goals and meet the perceived social standards. The perception of one's social skills is an aspect of a person's self-perception and is therefore modified during treatment with the same strategies as other distorted aspects of self-perception (i.e., via video feedback, audio feedback, mirror exposure, and group feedback). Accordingly, we don't conceptualize self-efficacy as a target of treatment—it is defined without reference to the cognitive and behavior changes that likely underlie the concept—but as a potentially relevant higher-order measure of the shifts in attention, goal setting and monitoring, performance interpretation, and skill levels that are targeted most directly by treatment.


## SAFETY AND AVOIDANCE BEHAVIORS

A study by Alden and Bieling (1998) found that high socially anxious students who participated in a getting-acquainted task used more safety behaviors and elicited more negative responses from others when they were led to believe that others were particularly likely to appraise them negatively, compared with individuals who engaged in positive appraisal. Wells et al. (1995) further demonstrated that exposure interventions, with specific instructions to abandon safety behaviors, are more effective than exposure therapy without instructions to refrain from such behaviors. Similar results were reported by Morgan and Raffle (1999). In this study, individuals with SAD were assigned to either a standard CBT program or to a CBT program that also included instructions to refrain from any safety behaviors. As expected, individuals showed greater improvement if they were instructed to abandon their safety behaviors. These studies provide support for the notion that safety behaviors are important maintaining factors, similar to withdrawal, escape, and other avoidance behaviors (e.g., Battersby, 2000).

As mentioned earlier, safety behaviors are conceptualized as subtle forms of avoidance strategies. In order to identify them, patients are instructed to monitor their social encounters between sessions. Furthermore, group members are encouraged to be vigilant for signs of any such safety behaviors by participants during in-session exposure practices. Starting with the first treatment session, patients are instructed to identify and eventually eliminate any avoidance behaviors. The term *avoidance behavior* is very broadly defined as anything the person does or does not do to reduce his or her anxiety in the social situation. Avoidance behaviors are conceptualized as important maintaining factors of SAD. As depicted in Figure 3.1 in chapter 3, avoidance behaviors establish the positive feedback loop leading to high anxiety in social situations despite repeated and often successful social encounters.

In our treatment, the presence and need to eliminate safety behaviors receives attention as part of exposure planning (e.g., see the exposure worksheet, Appendix I). In every case, we conceptualize exposure as a forum for learning that social situations are safe. Planning for exposures involves creating the situations where beliefs about the "dangerousness" of social situations are directly challenged. Use of exposures involving social mishaps, induction of anxiety-like symptoms, and multiple contexts involving the elimination of safety cues and behaviors helps ensure that social situations will be redefined as "safe," independent of the use of specific cues for conditional safety (e.g., "Who knows what would have happened if I did not have my [safety cue or behavior] to rely on?").

## POST-EVENT RUMINATION

According to the cognitive model by Clark and colleagues (e.g., Clark, 2001; Clark & Wells, 1995), individuals with SAD engage in post-event processing during which they mentally review the social interaction in detail. This processing typically centers on anxious feelings and negative self-perceptions, in which the individual recalls the interaction as being more negative than it actually was. As a result, the social phobic individual engages in anticipatory processing in which his or her thoughts are dominated by the recollections of past failures, leading to the maintenance of the problem. Recent empirical studies found a high degree of association between post-event processing of negative evaluative events and social anxiety in student samples (Lundh & Sperling, 2002; Mellings & Alden, 2000; Rachmann et al., 2000). A study by Rachmann et al. (2000) found that post-event rumination was associated with avoidance of similar social situations in the future. Post-event rumination may be closely associated with exaggerated social cost in SAD if individuals with SAD engage in ruminative thinking about a social encounter because they believe that an inadequate social performance leads to disastrous consequences.

Post-event rumination is a frequently occurring phenomenon after an unsuccessful or ambiguously successful social encounter, especially after situations that are associated with high-perceived social costs and negative self-perception because of the assumed catastrophic outcome of a social situation. Post-event rumination is targeted specifically by helping patients process negative social events more adaptively through guided questions (e.g., "How will your life change as a result of a particular social mishap?"). This is done through group discussions during the homework review, or through Socratic questioning in relation to well-defined social goals and accurate performance standards in the case of individual treatment.

## SUMMARY

Our treatment model has elements of treatment designed to address each of the empirically supported maintaining factors for SAD listed earlier. We do not believe that any one-to-one relationship need exist between a particular intervention and a change mechanism. For example, it is clear from the literature that exposure-based interventions change cognitive factors in SAD as readily as cognitive interventions. Rather, the treatment is designed to provide a broad and converging set of interventions to provide learning through experiential, cognitive, and direct informational interventions. Also, the use of cognitive, attentional, and postprocessing interventions in the context of repeated exposures helps ensure that these cognitive skills are rehearsed in the situations where they are needed—in the midst of social situations involving varying social tasks and including (for at least some exposures) programmed inclusion of social mishaps and anxiety symptoms.

# CHAPTER 5

# Treatment in Action
## *Clinical Examples*

Susan is a 42-year-old, married, white female with two young children. She has worked as a homemaker since the birth of her children, but in the last two years she has returned to outside employment as a part-time accountant. She describes herself as being socially anxious since grade school. She reports that her time alone with her children was a respite from the worst of her social anxiety, but now that she has more time at hand, she realizes that she finally needs to attend to her social anxiety disorder (SAD). In seeking treatment, she stated that she needs to be less anxious at work and at social gatherings, but that she also wants to be less anxious so that she provides a better role model for her children.

In the first group session, Susan easily presented herself as warm and supportive as she introduced herself and enthusiastically stated her eagerness to change this "lifelong disorder." At the same time, she stated that she believed she was much worse than other group members because they all looked and acted like "normal people." The therapist capitalized on this statement to lead a brief discussion of how individuals with SAD tend to believe all their anxieties and symptoms show, and almost every other group member said they felt similarly to Susan—that they were the only oddball in group and the others had a much less severe disorder than they had. This discussion provided Susan (and other group members) with an initial chance to challenge her assumptions that (1) others see her degree of social anxiety, (2) she routinely appears much less competent than others, (3) she believes that others expect her to be more competent, and (4) individuals with her disorder (SAD) are oddballs. She described herself as being "utterly incompetent" and a "social loser." Susan further stated that when confronted with certain social evaluative situations, such as public speeches, she feels panicky. She described this feeling as a state of strong bodily symptoms characterized by heart

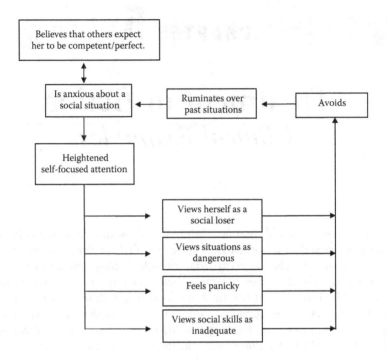

FIGURE 5.1   Maintenance factors of Susan's social anxiety.

racing, being flushed, trembling, and dry mouth. She stated that the only way to stop these symptoms is by leaving the situation.

She feels a great deal of sadness and frustration because she had a number of "missed opportunities" because of her social anxiety (e.g., she turned down a number of attractive career options). At the same time, Susan continuously avoids social situations because the consequences can often be humiliating and embarrassing. As a result, she keeps avoiding them. If she cannot avoid them, she endures them with extreme discomfort and tends to ruminate about them long after the event has passed. Figure 5.1 is an adaptation of the model to Susan's case.

Following the first session, Susan gained an intellectual understanding of the treatment model but was still hesitant to believe she could achieve many gains from exposure given that she had been trying for years to "be better" in social situations. She also found herself doubting that others did not expect a lot from her in social situations, stating that "my husband and my boss would hate it if I screwed up in public." These expectations are readily apparent after her assessment, which was remarkable for the predominance of her fears of social errors (saying something stupid or being quieter than she thinks she should be). Her worksheet, a brief semistructured interview, is also notable for her strong negative post-event processing, where she honed in on core beliefs of her essential flawed nature.

**What sorts of situations best characterize the patient's fears of humiliation or embarrassment? Are they individual interactions, small groups, or large groups; informal or formal; structured or unstructured; work or socially related; dependent on topic, etc.?**

*Ask:* Describe for me some of your most feared social scenarios.

*(1) Giving a presentation at work would be really hard—I hate the idea of people staring at me waiting for me to say something smart. (2) I also have trouble with parties. I always feel like I am going to say something stupid or that I will have nothing to say —you know, freeze up.*

**What are the actual fears of humiliation? Do they center on social errors, emergence of symptoms, beliefs of incompetence, etc?**

*Ask:* Many times, individuals with social anxiety fear they will make certain social errors. Can you tell me about some of the things you fear will happen in a social situation?

*(1) Saying something stupid. People can really go after you for that.*

*(2) Also just being quiet like a bump on a log. People think you are an idiot if you do that.*

**Are social fears richly dependent on the emergence of symptoms (heart rate, sweating, flushing, dry throat, etc.)?**

*Ask:* Are there any symptoms that intensify your fears of embarrassment when present (blushing, sweating, dry throat, etc.)? Why are these symptoms bothersome?

*I just get sweaty and feel really bad on the inside. After these social events, I could just die of embarrassment. I hate how I come across.*

**What are common safety cues used by the patient?**

*Ask:* What are those things you do, or keep with you, that help you feel less anxious in social situations?

*I stay close to my husband and I don't say much at parties. Sometimes I look down so that I don't freeze up. It is hard for me to make eye contact.*

**What are the usual ways in which the patient nullifies adequate performances or self-criticizes after a social performance?**

*Ask:* What do you typically say to yourself after a social situation?

*I am an idiot. I blew that one. I am a failure.*

*Ask:* How would you fill in the following statements?

I can't believe I did that (in a social situation), I always ...

*Look like an idiot ... just standing there saying nothing.*

I blew it, I am such a ...

*Idiot, loser, just stupid.*

I should have ...

*Said something smart, contributed more to the party or the meeting.*

And when you prepare for your next social situation, what are some of the things you worry about or pay attention to?

*I just wait to be a stupid cow again ... just standing there frozen like an idiot.*

The answers to these questions suggest that Susan holds a very negative perception of herself. The most effective way to target self-perception is through videotape feedback. Other strategies to target self-perception include mirror exposures, audiotape feedback, and, to some extent, feedback from other group members. In all of these cases, the feedback creates a state of dissonance between expected outcome and actual outcome. An example of videotape feedback instruction is given in Appendix E. Similarly, patients may be asked to expose themselves to their audiotaped speeches or mirror images. In addition to creating a state of dissonance between expected and actual feedback, the purpose of these exercises is to help patients become comfortable with their self-image, including all their imperfections and problems.

Susan also appears to believe that her social skills are inadequate to deal with challenging social situations. As with other aspects of self-perception, the perception of social skills is modified by creating a discrepancy between expected negative outcome and actual outcome. As a rule, we tend to focus on changing a patient's sense of high social standards and negative self-evaluation of abilities. We use videotaped feedback to illustrate to patients that their social skills are actually not as bad as expected. In the majority of the cases, this becomes obvious to patients.

## PREPARATION FOR EXPOSURES

Based on careful questioning, it became apparent that Susan shows a number of typical behaviors that maintain her social anxiety. She displays obvious overt avoidance and also more subtle avoidance behaviors, such as avoiding eye contact. In preparing Susan for exposure, this issue is emphasized.

*Susan:* How is it that getting into our anxiety is going to help us when we've been suffering for a long time?

*Therapist:* Because anxiety could not exist without avoidance. Do you know what I mean by that?

*Susan:* Yes, but what would I do if I was not trying to make it go away? How would I act when I am feeling anxious? Would I just psyche myself into an attitude where I say, "Great, I am feeling anxious! This is wonderful; my mouth is really dry, I can't think of what I want to talk about, I'm shaking, I'm blushing, I feel horrible, and I want to run away." How can this help?

*Therapist:* Good point. Why does repeated and prolonged exposure to fearful situations decrease anxiety in those situations? Do you remember our chart?

*Susan:* I remember it can decrease with exposure.

*Therapist:* Can you explain this a little more?

*Susan:* Anxiety goes down automatically after a while.

*Therapist:* Right. As long as you avoid, you will continue to have this anxiety in this particular situation. And this is not only true for anxiety—as soon as you are trying to control your emotion, your emotion will control you. The way to get rid of your anxiety is by accepting it—embrace it, welcome your anxiety, let it stay there if it wants to stay there, and let it go if it wants to go. Eventually, it will go away. And the more often and the longer and the more intense you experience this in a particular situation, the less anxious you will feel in the future. And there is nothing that you need to do. Just experience your anxiety to its fullest, don't do anything to make it go away or diminish it. I am not saying that you need to learn how to enjoy the feeling of anxiety. What I am saying is that you need to learn to accept it and let it stay with you without trying to do anything to bring it down. Anxiety is a normal but a very unpleasant experience. No one likes to feel anxious. But anxiety is a temporary state. Eventually it will go down. So the best way to deal with your anxiety is to experience anxiety to its fullest, without you trying to bring it down by avoidance strategies. Do you understand?

*Susan:* (Nods.)

*Therapist:* What kind of avoidance strategies have you been using?

*Susan:*     A therapist before told me to use breathing techniques, and I have been using them. But these are also avoidance strategies, right?

*Therapist:* Yes, avoidance is anything that you do or don't do to bring your anxiety down. What else have been doing?

*Susan:*     I would take beta-blockers or have a drink before going to a party.

*Therapist:* Very good. These are very typical avoidance behaviors. So would you please tell me now in your own words how avoidance and social anxiety are related and what this means for handling socially anxious situations in the future?

## EARLY IN-SESSION EXPOSURES WITH ATTENTION TRAINING

Susan reported that she is particularly fearful of social performance situations. When she is unable to avoid them, she reported that she feels sweaty and "really bad on the inside." This reflects her tendency to focus her attention toward herself and her anxiety. The effects of self-focused attention on the subjective feeling of anxiety can be easily demonstrated by instructing her just prior to an in-session exposure task to focus her attention toward the anxiety-related and unrelated stimuli and aspects of the situation. This can be done by asking Susan to anticipate a fearful (exposure) task and to (1) focus on and describe anxiety symptoms and self (30 seconds); (2) focus on and describe the environment (30 seconds); and (3) focus on and summarize the speech (30 seconds). After each attentional shift, Susan's anxiety is recorded with the goal to demonstrate the link between voluntarily directing attention on fear-relevant and fear-irrelevant cues and changes in subjective anxiety. Even if this link cannot be easily demonstrated (which is not at all uncommon), the exercise demonstrates that attentional focus is under voluntary control and contributes to anxiety. The attention exercise begins by asking Susan to stand in front of the recoding video camera, facing an audience created for the benefit of the patient from members of the clinic staff.

*Therapist:* What is your anxiety right now on a scale from 0 (no anxiety) to 10 (extreme anxiety)?

*Susan:*     It is high ... maybe an 8?

[If Susan's anxiety had been lower than 7, the therapist would have elicited the reasons why her anxiety was not as high as usual and modified the situation based on this information. This would require some creativity and instinct on the part of the therapist. In our experience, patients respond well (i.e., with more anxiety) by bringing new members into an audience, by asking some audience members to act bored or hostile, by choosing a topic that is more challenging or personal, by choosing a topic the patient did not prepare for, by interrupting the patient at random points with questions so that the patient looses his/her train of thought, etc.]

*Therapist:* I am very glad that you have the courage to stand in front of us to give a speech. This must feel very uncomfortable. But remember, the more anxiety you experience during our treatment sessions, the better. What does an anxiety of 8 feel like? Please move your attention inwardly and tell me what is going on in your body.

*Susan:* I feel like my heart is racing, my palms are sweating, and my mouth is dry.

*Therapist:* Thanks. What else do you notice inside of yourself? What kinds of thoughts are going through your mind?

*Susan:* I feel that everybody is staring at me. I am about to make a fool of myself because I don't really know much about the topic.

*Therapist:* OK. What is your anxiety now on a scale from 0 to 10?

*Susan:* It has not changed. Maybe it even went up a little. Maybe a 9?

*Therapist:* OK. Now please look around. What are the things in the environment that make you anxious?

*Susan:* Obviously, the people starting at me. The video camera in the back is recording every single move I make. This makes me feel very uncomfortable.

*Therapist:* Great. And what is your anxiety now?

*Susan:* The same; about an 8 or 9.

*Therapist:* Now please tell me what else you see in the environment that does not increase your anxiety.

*Susan:* I see a picture on each wall. I see the plant.

*Therapist:* Anything else?

*Susan:* The carpet. And I see the papers on the desk in the back and the books on the shelves. The lamp looks nice.

*Therapist:* Great work! What is your anxiety at this very moment on a scale from 0 to 10.

*Susan:* Not much different. But maybe a little bit down because I was distracting myself. Maybe at a 7 and a half.

*Therapist:* Thanks. Now please focus on your talk you are about to give. Focus on the topic at hand and give me a one- to two-sentence summary of your talk.

*Susan:*     I want to tell people about global warming.
*Therapist:* Excellent. What is your anxiety now?
*Susan:*     It just went up. 8.
*Therapist:* Thanks. Please tell me what goals you would like to meet. Without referring to your anxiety, what would make this situation a success? Are there any behaviors or other things you could do that would make the situation a success?
*Susan:*     Just being able to speak for 3 minutes would be a success.
*Therapist:* I agree. What else? Are there any behaviors—gestures, eye contact, and so forth—that would make it a success?
*Susan:*     I guess having eye contact with people.
*Therapist:* Great. So the goal is to speak for 3 minutes and to make eye contact with at least three people?
*Susan:*     OK.
*Therapist:* Ready to start?
*Susan:*     Yes.

## POSTEXPOSURE DISCUSSION

Almost as important as the actual exposure tasks are the discussions that occur immediately following the exposures when the patient and therapist (and other group members if done in a group setting) process the event. These discussions often provide the patient with information that generates a state of dissonance between the perception she holds of herself and the perception that other people have of her. For example, upon completing one of her brief, typically 3-minute, exposures, Susan almost begrudgingly reported meeting her goals, "Well I guess that I was able to speak for 3 minutes and look at people in the eye ... but wasn't I so stupid?" In response to this statement, one of the group members exclaimed, "You really are hard on yourself. The talk was fine." Susan took this comment as reproach, leading to the following interchange:

*Susan:*     Sorry, sometimes I say stupid things.
*Therapist:* I think what [the other group member] was getting at isn't that you say stupid things but that you always seem at the ready to label what you said as stupid. This is a habit that you may want to take a good look at. How did you come to be so critical of yourself?
*Susan:*     If you think I am critical, you should hear what my mother has to say.
*Therapist:* Ah, so you have had some training from others in being critical?

*Susan:* Yeah, I don't want to be nasty to my mother or anything, but it seems like she always had a correction for me, no matter what I said.

*Therapist:* And somehow you started talking to yourself in that way. Tell me, how did it feel when your mom talked with you that way?

*Susan:* Well, I think she was just trying to make me better at things, but it always made me feel kind of lousy.

*Therapist:* And when you say it, how does it make you feel?

*Susan:* Well, I feel lousy much of the time, but you don't want to go around pretending like you are better than you are do you?

*Therapist (to the group):* What does everyone think? How should we talk to ourselves?

*Member 2:* I don't know, I don't think it is good to always criticize yourself; it just makes you feel like dirt all the time.

*Member 3:* But what about people like [the successful football] Coach Lombardi? Wasn't he hard on his players to make them better? He had winning teams.

*Therapist:* Coach Lombardi had a reputation for yelling at players at times. He also had a reputation for rewarding them for wins. But more importantly, would any one of you choose to live with a Coach Lombardi all the time, to take him home with you?

*Member 2:* No ... it would be bad enough in a game ... I always hated coaches that yelled ... At a game it might be OK, but no way at home.

*Therapist:* This is what happens to us when we take on the job of out criticizing ourselves (criticizing ourselves worse than our worst coaches); we are stuck with someone yelling at us from our own heads. That can't be right.

From this point on, the therapist moved on to additional feedback for Susan and then moved on to the exposure for the next group member. But the idea of a hostile coach stuck in the therapist's mind sufficiently well that at the end of the next week's session, the therapist decided to strengthen this model by telling a cognitive restructuring "story" described elsewhere (Otto, 2000). The idea of using a story in group is to provide a memorable and compelling example to all group members by which to conceptualize how they talk to themselves. This example is based on coaching, this time in relation to a child playing little league baseball. Although the use of any story or metaphor in therapy requires careful evaluation of how the story content will strike different group members, the previous week's spontaneous discussion of coaching style made this story an easy fit (adapted with permission from Otto, 2000).

> This is a story about little league baseball. I talk about little league baseball because of the amazing parents and coaches involved. And by "amazing" I don't mean good. I mean extreme.
>
> But this story doesn't start with the coaches or the parents; it starts with Johnny, who is a little league player in the outfield. His job is to catch "fly balls" and return them to the infield players. On the day of our story, Johnny is in the outfield and "crack!"—one of the players on the other team hits a fly ball. The ball is coming to Johnny. Johnny raises his glove. The ball is coming to him, coming to him ... and it goes over his head. Johnny misses the ball, and the other team scores a run.
>
> Now there are a number of ways a coach can respond to this situation. Let's take Coach A first. Coach A is the type of coach who will come out on the field and shout: "I can't believe you missed that ball! Anyone could have caught it! My dog could have caught it! You screw up like that again and you'll be sitting on the bench! That was lousy!"
>
> Coach A then storms off the field.
>
> At this point, Johnny is standing in the outfield and, if he is at all similar to me, he is tense, tight, trying not to cry, and hoping that another ball is not hit to him. If a ball does come to him, Johnny will probably miss it. After all, he is tense, tight, and may see four balls coming at him because of the tears in his eyes.
>
> If we are Johnny's parents, we may see more profound changes after the game. Johnny, who typically places his baseball glove on the mantel, now throws it under his bed. And before the next game, he may complain that his stomach hurts, that perhaps he should not go to the game. This is the scenario with Coach A.
>
> Now let's go back to the original event and play it differently. Johnny has just missed the ball, and now Coach B comes out on the field. Coach B says: "Well, you missed that one. Here is what I want you to remember: High balls look like they are farther away than they really are. Also, it is much easier to run forward than to back up. Because of this, I want you to prepare for the ball by taking a few extra steps backward. As the ball gets closer you can step into it if you need to. Also, try to catch it at chest level, so you can adjust your hand if you misjudge the ball. Let's see how you do next time." Coach B then leaves the field.
>
> How does Johnny feel? Well, he is not happy. After all, he missed the ball; but there are a number of important differences

from the way he felt with Coach A. He is not as tense or tight, and if a fly ball does come to him, he knows what to do differently to catch it. And because he does not have tears in his eyes, he may actually see the ball and catch it.

So, if we were the type of parent who wants Johnny to make the Major Leagues, we would pick Coach B because he teaches Johnny how to be a more effective player. Johnny knows what to do differently, may catch more balls, and may excel in the game.

But if we don't care whether Johnny makes the Major Leagues—because baseball is a game, and one is supposed to be able to enjoy a game—then we would again pick Coach B. We pick Coach B because we care whether Johnny enjoys the game. With Coach B, Johnny knows what to do differently; he is not tight, tense, and ready to cry; he may catch a few balls; and he may enjoy the game. And he may continue to place his glove on the mantel.

Now, while we may all select Coach B for Johnny, we rarely choose the voice of Coach B for the way we talk to ourselves. Think about your last mistake. Did you say, "I can't believe I did that! I am so stupid! What a jerk!"? These are "Coach A" thoughts, and they have many of the same effects on us as Coach A has on Johnny. These thoughts make us feel tense and tight, may make us feel like crying, and rarely help us do better in the future. Remember, even if you are only concerned about productivity (making the Major Leagues) you would still pick Coach B. And if you were concerned with enjoying life, with guiding yourself effectively for both joy and productivity, you certainly would pick Coach B.

During the next week, I would like you to listen to see how you are coaching yourself. If you hear Coach A, remember this story and see if you can replace Coach A thoughts with Coach B thoughts.

## VIEWING VIDEOTAPED EXPOSURES

After each exposure, the patient, therapist, and other group members watch the recording. It is not uncommon that some patients feel more uncomfortable viewing themselves on the videotape than doing the actual exposure. At first glance, it seems surprising that watching oneself giving a speech can be more anxiety provoking than actually giving the speech because the feared stimulus (the audience, the negative evaluative situation, etc.) is no longer present when viewing the videotaped speech.

Obviously, the anxiety-provoking source when viewing the videotape is the negative self-perception, not the social situation per se. Therefore, the use of videotapes is highly therapeutic and should be part of every social phobia treatment program. The effect of videotaped feedback can be even further enhanced by conducting a cognitive preparation phase just before viewing the tape (Harvey et al., 2000). During the cognitive preparation period, Susan was asked to (1) predict her social performance; (2) imagine her social performance; and (3) identify and challenge incorrect predictions.

*Therapist:* The video feedback provides you with the opportunity to thoroughly evaluate your own performance and to examine whether some of your assumptions are correct. In order to do this, I would like you to predict in detail what you think you will see in the video. In order to do this, please rate your speech on a number of dimensions. How well do you think you came across on a scale from 0 (very poorly) to 10 (very well)?

*Susan:* I think a 2.

*Therapist:* And how well do you think you performed during the speech on a scale from 0 (very poorly) to 10 (very well)?

*Susan:* Again a 2.

*Therapist:* In addition, I would like you to tell me how you would rate the presence of each of the following performance indicators on a scale from 0 (not present at all) to 10 (extremely apparent):

| | Not at all present | | | | | | | | | Extremely apparent | |
|---|---|---|---|---|---|---|---|---|---|---|---|
| eye contact | 0 | 1 | 2 | ③ | 4 | 5 | 6 | 7 | 8 | 9 | 10 |
| stuttering | 0 | 1 | ② | 3 | 4 | 5 | 6 | 7 | 8 | 9 | 10 |
| long pauses | 0 | 1 | 2 | 3 | 4 | 5 | 6 | 7 | ⑧ | 9 | 10 |
| fidgeting | 0 | 1 | 2 | 3 | 4 | 5 | 6 | 7 | 8 | ⑨ | 10 |
| ums and ahs | 0 | 1 | 2 | 3 | 4 | 5 | 6 | 7 | 8 | ⑨ | 10 |
| trembling/shaking | 0 | 1 | 2 | 3 | 4 | 5 | 6 | 7 | 8 | ⑨ | 10 |
| sweating | 0 | 1 | 2 | 3 | 4 | 5 | ⑥ | 7 | 8 | 9 | 10 |
| blushing | 0 | 1 | 2 | 3 | 4 | 5 | 6 | 7 | 8 | 9 | ⑩ |
| face twitching | 0 | 1 | 2 | 3 | 4 | 5 | 6 | ⑦ | 8 | 9 | 10 |
| voice quivering | 0 | 1 | 2 | 3 | 4 | 5 | 6 | 7 | 8 | ⑨ | 10 |
| nervous | 0 | 1 | 2 | 3 | 4 | 5 | 6 | 7 | 8 | ⑨ | 10 |

| | Not at all present | | | | | | | | | Extremely apparent |
|---|---|---|---|---|---|---|---|---|---|---|
| boring | 0 | 1 | 2 | 3 | 4 | 5 | 6 | 7 | 8 | (9) | 10 |
| fluent speech | 0 | 1 | (2) | 3 | 4 | 5 | 6 | 7 | 8 | 9 | 10 |
| looking awkward | 0 | 1 | 2 | 3 | 4 | 5 | 6 | 7 | (8) | 9 | 10 |
| looking embarrassed | 0 | 1 | 2 | 3 | 4 | 5 | 6 | 7 | (8) | 9 | 10 |
| were interesting | (0) | 1 | 2 | 3 | 4 | 5 | 6 | 7 | 8 | 9 | 10 |

*Therapist:* You gave yourself a 10 for blushing. How red were you? As red as this sweater? (*Points to one of the group member's sweater.*)

*Susan:* Well, not quite that red.

*Therapist:* Maybe as red as this pen?

*Susan:* Yes, I think so.

*Therapist:* And you rated fidgeting and trembling/shaking as a 9. How much is a severity of 9? Like that? (*Shakes hands vigorously.*)

*Susan:* No, a little less.

*Therapist:* Like that? (*Shakes hands a little less vigorously.*)

*Susan:* Yes, I think I moved it like that at various points.

*Therapist:* Great. Thanks. Now please close your eyes and form a clear image of how you think you came across during the speech. Please construct an internal video of how you think you appeared (after 2 minutes). Thank you. How vividly were you able to see yourself giving the speech on a scale form 0 (not at all) to 10 (extremely)?

*Susan:* Very clear; 9.

*Therapist:* And how was your performance in the image on a scale from 0 (very poor) to 10 (very good)?

*Susan:* Poor; maybe a 1 or 2.

*Therapist:* Thanks. In order for you to watch the video objectively, please only pay attention to how you looked but not how you felt. Please watch the video as if you were watching a stranger. (*Plays video.*)

*Therapist:* So, let me ask you—were you as red as this pencil?

*Susan (laughs):* No.

*Therapist (addressing group):* And how many times did Susan move like that (*shakes hands vigorously*).

*Member 1:* None.

*Therapist:* Susan, what do you think your performance was on the video on a scale from 0 (very poor) to 10 (excellent)?

*Susan:*     Well, maybe not as bad as I thought. Maybe a 3.

*Therapist:* Only a 3? I think this looked much better than a 3. What do other group members think? What rating would you give the person on the video?

This exercise provides information that creates strong dissonance between expected and felt performance; self-perception; and feedback from the therapist, videotaped recording, and other group members. Group members typically provide more accurate and much more positive ratings than the patient. If on rare occasions, a group member is overly critical toward the patient's performance, other group members typically contradict and correct this assessment. Furthermore, critical comments by another group member can be corrected by the therapist with a discussion of the true social cost of whatever issue or foible that was identified ("What would be the worst outcome of this situation? Is there any way that [issue] would change your life?"). Our experience is that the possible benefits of honest group members' feedback far outweigh any possible harm that can be done by rare overcritical comments from another group member (see chapter 6 for additional discussion).

### CLINICAL CHALLENGE: HOW TO PROCESS A "BAD" SOCIAL PERFORMANCE

It is our experience that in only a very small number of cases, patients are disappointed by their performance when viewing themselves from an observer perspective. We do not believe that this creates a therapeutic dilemma because the goal is to gain a realistic, not an overly positive or distorted, view of oneself. Nevertheless, it can be beneficial in some cases to select certain behaviors that can be targeted for change using videotaped feedback.

*Patient:*     I hated myself on the videotape.

*Therapist:* Why? What was so bad about it?

*Patient:*     I looked pathetic, like a complete idiot.

*Therapist:* I disagree. But that aside, what are the behaviors that you showed that you didn't like?

*Patient:*     I stuttered, I looked on the floor the whole time, you could hardly hear my voice, and I just stood there like an idiot.

*Therapist:* The harsh, insulting, and self-deprecating judgment of yourself is a big reason why you are uncomfortable in social situations. Therefore, one very important goal of our treatment is for you to become more comfortable with the way you are. At the same time, I agree that you showed awkward behaviors during the exposure that can be easily changed. You noted a few things. I agree with two of them.

First, you looked at the floor the entire time, and second, you spoke very quietly. I would like you to do the same speech again. This time, I would like you to have eye contact at least once with each audience member and I would like you to speak more loudly, like this (*demonstrates it*).

## HOME PRACTICE EXPOSURES

A key element of treatment is to carry the newly learned approach to dealing with anxiety from session into the real world, outside the protected therapy environment. Home practice exposures should be tailored to the particular patient's idiosyncratic fears. If the patient is only afraid of some very specific situations that do not often occur in his/her daily life, the situations have to be created or approximated. For example, if a patient is primarily nervous about job-related interview situations, the patient may be encouraged to apply for jobs without accepting any of the potential offers; repeated public speaking exposures can be created on a regular basis by joining Toastmasters; dating situations can be generated by joining a dating service; and so forth.

Once the home practice exposures are chosen, a frequently occurring complication is how to concretely define the goal of the exercise. The immediate goal should not be to perform without anxiety. In contrast, the goal is to perform despite the anxiety, and the success of the situation should be measured based on specific behavioral goals. The following example illustrates how such a goal was generated in Susan's case.

*Therapist:* Can you please tell me why you are avoiding initiating a conversation with your new co-worker?

*Susan:* Because I don't know what to say and because I don't want to appear stupid.

*Therapist:* Why would you appear stupid?

*Susan:* For many different reasons, and I usually appear stupid.

*Therapist:* Like not being able to complete your sentence, stuttering, and blushing?

*Susan:* Yes, for example.

*Therapist:* So the goal would be not to show those behaviors that you think the other person would interpret as stupidity.

*Susan:* Yes.

*Therapist:* Let's look at the reverse. When would the situation be a success?

*Susan:*     If I appear intelligent and make a good impression.

*Therapist:* So the goal of a conversation with co-workers is to appear intelligent. This is a pretty vague goal. Can you tell me more specifically what behaviors you will need to show so that you make a good impression and appear intelligent?

*Susan:*     Not stuttering, not showing my anxiety? I don't know.

*Therapist:* This brings us to an important point: It seems to be difficult for you to clearly define the goal of the situation outside of your own experience of anxiety. If the goal is not defined objectively, it will be difficult to organize yourself behind the goals and tell if you met them. After all, you know that trying not to be anxious doesn't work for you; let's help you decide what you do want to do in the social situation. What would be a clear goal you could use to measure the success of the situation?

*Susan:*     Hmmm, maybe if they have a little conversation with me?

*Therapist:* Terrific. I agree. How about if the goal is to have a 2-minute conversation with one of your new co-workers? What person do you want to talk to?

*Susan:*     Mary looks friendly.

*Therapist:* Great. What would you like to choose as a topic?

*Susan:*     I am not sure.

*Therapist:* What do other people talk about?

*Susan:*     Around the water cooler they often talk about their weekend.

*Therapist:* Very good. So the goal of the task for next week is to have a 2-minute water cooler conversation about the weekend with your co-worker Mary. OK?

*Susan:*     OK, I will try.

## CLINICAL CHALLENGE: HOW TO DEAL WITH HOMEWORK NONADHERENCE

Homework nonadherence is a common problem in every treatment that includes the patient as an active participant. Fortunately, there is no clear evidence to suggest that homework nonadherence reliably predicts poor treatment outcome. Nevertheless, homework adherence should be closely monitored and nonadherence should be directly discussed with the patient.

*Therapist:* I am sorry that you did not do your homework. I noticed that you also did not complete the homework assignments in the last two weeks. What do you think the reason is?

*Patient:*     I don't know. I just never get around to it.

*Therapist:*  You mean other things just get in the way?

*Patient:*     Yeah. I am sorry.

*Therapist:*  There is no need to apologize. I am simply trying to understand what I can do to make the treatment work better for
you. The treatment we are doing is very powerful. But it
can only work if you give it a chance to work. Let me give
you an example: If you have an infection and your doctor
prescribes you an antibiotic, it only works if you take a
certain number of pills for a certain amount of time. If you
stop before that time or if you don't take enough of it, you
will not get rid of your infection. This is also true for treating anxiety problems with exposure.

*Patient:*     I understand.

*Therapist:*  I don't want to make you feel bad. I want to make sure
that you get better, and doing the homework assignments
is one important part of it. So let's briefly talk about last
week's exposure. Please tell me, very honestly, if there were
any aspects of the exposure assignment that made you not
want to do it. Let's then change the task so that we can
make sure that you do it next week.

## LATER IN-SESSION EXPOSURE

In the later sessions, Susan transitioned to more challenging in-session
speech exposures. It can require a considerable amount of creativity by
the therapist to create in-session exposure situations that elicit a significant amount of anxiety even in later sessions. Susan might have
become used to the group and may no longer expect negative comments
from the group members. In order to raise Susan's anxiety, the therapist
might have to choose more challenging, controversial, or personal topics. Moreover, the therapist might ask strangers to join the audience,
ask the patient to stand in front of a mirror, interrupt her during her
speech, or ask the other group members to act hostile by displaying their
disapproval to controversial topics. If Susan does not experience sufficient physical anxiety, the therapist might have to ask her to rapidly
climb several flights of stairs or run in place before giving a speech in
order to heighten Susan's physiological arousal. The use of video feedback, again, can effectively demonstrate to the patient that despite experiencing intense physiological symptoms, very little, if anything, can be
noticed from an outsider's perspective. Moreover, Susan learns there is

no need to attempt to control intense physiological symptoms, and the less she tries to control the feelings, the more likely it is that the symptoms will diminish.

In addition to speech exposure, the therapist might also choose in-session role practices. Two exposures seemed to be particularly valuable for Susan. First, in a mock cocktail party exposure she was required to ask another group member questions about herself and to present at least one new topic in the conversation. The list of topics was expressly to be from things she had read in the paper during the previous week. She met these two explicit goals but then continued her negative evaluation that she was too quiet. She was reminded that one of the explicit goals was to ask a group member two questions, which meant she had to listen to the answers. In fact, feedback from other group members was notable for the way in which they found her to be a warm and accepting listener. This feedback directly challenged her self-perception as a dull and overly quiet party member and gave her first glimpses that listening was an acceptable party activity that could be valued.

The second exposure of particular value for Susan was changing her mind about a book purchase and returning it, while also affecting an odd walk while in the store. Both behaviors were targeted toward her concerns about looking odd, indecisive, or stupid. One week after these exposures, in discussing her home practice, she presented the following to group members:

> How does it all get so screwed up, so that we walk around with these voices in our heads. It never occurred to me that I could use my thoughts for my own good. I just mirrored my mom's voice, always criticizing. And my husband just sort of fell in that role himself. The other day, I asked him why he thought I had to be so perfect. He got this confused look on his face and asked me what I meant. I mean, he can be a jerk some of the time, but I think he isn't half as hard on me as I imagine him to be. I just have to get some of these constant criticisms out of my head and realize that I really am not so bad the way I am. I am starting to think that the world is a lot safer than I had assumed.

This spontaneous presentation by Susan provided evidence of ongoing consolidation and adoption of previous cognitive interventions, but it is noteworthy that the cognitive interventions were solidified only after beliefs were challenged by experience during the exposure exercises. In our experience, this is often the ordering of therapeutic change. Although early cognitive interventions may set the stage for change, providing a rationale for approaching exposures differently and providing a framework for alternative evaluation of social performances, it is the experience that is derived from well-planned exposures that provides the actual occasion for cognitive change.

Subsequent exposures continued to focus on the theme that social errors are acceptable. As Susan continued to hone her ability and willingness to, in her words, "make social waves," she stated, "I have spent my whole life trying not to ripple the water, assuming that it will bother or hurt everyone else, and now I realize that I can't move myself without making some ripples. Everyone makes ripples; ripples aren't waves, and it is OK for me to make my own ripples. I have to move just like everyone else."

As Susan moved toward the close of treatment, she was asked what was most helpful to her from group. She stated that she loved the idea of self-coaching and the freedom she felt starting to coach herself in a way that felt useful. She also underscored the value of practice (from exposure) saying, "Without practice, this all would have been a nice idea, but I never would have realized that I really could change, and that it would be OK. I also learned that I don't have to be just like everyone else. I think I am starting to learn that it is OK to be different. Different does not mean bad."

## CLINICAL CHALLENGE: HOW TO INDUCE SUFFICIENT ANXIETY

Surprisingly, one of the most common challenges during the later in-session speech exposures is a suboptimal level of subjective anxiety. We recommend that patients report anxiety levels of 7 or higher during the anticipatory phase of the speech exposure. If the anxiety is too low, the therapist should explore the reason and adjust the situation accordingly.

*Therapist:* What is your anxiety now?

*Patient:* Pretty high. Maybe a 5 or 6.

*Therapist:* Your anxiety was quite a bit higher during the previous exposures. Why is it now at a more moderate level?

*Patient:* I don't know. Maybe the treatment works?

*Therapist:* There is no doubt in my mind that the treatment will help you. But what can we do right now to get your anxiety a bit higher?

*Patient:* I don't know. The talking in front of the same people is not as difficult as it was before; maybe it's because I know them and because they won't judge me negatively?

*Therapist:* So if we brought in somebody new would this help?

*Patient:* Probably. Who will you bring in?

*Therapist:* Which person would create the most anxiety?

*Patient:* My boss.

*Therapist:* I thought so. So I called him, but he sends his apologies; he can't make it tonight.

Patient:     (*Laughs.*)
Therapist:   So I assume that a fairly senior person who is an authority figure and who might judge you negatively will be more anxiety provoking that a young person who you know and who is unlikely to judge you negatively. Correct?
Patient:     Yes.
Therapist:   Great. Please just stand there for a few minutes. I will be right back. I will see if one of our senior clinicians is available. Perhaps I can even get the director of our center. Before I leave, what is your anxiety now?

## IN VIVO SOCIAL MISHAP EXPOSURES

At around midtreatment the patient should begin exposures to actual in vivo social mishaps. This is the single most effective strategy to target exaggerated probability and cost estimates. When generating these exposure tasks, it is important that patients are challenged to violate the perceived social norms. If therapists do not feel comfortable assigning such tasks, we suggest that the therapists themselves should expose themselves to these tasks first to become more comfortable with the assignments. We would like to emphasize that is important to create exposures that go beyond the "normal" social challenges. Mishap exposures are intended to create situations that most people would define as a social mishap, a slip, an embarrassing moment, and so forth, in order to expose the patient to the feared consequences. None of these exposures are, by definition, pleasant. In addition to social anxiety, they typically create feelings of embarrassment and shame, and make the person feel ridiculed. Examples were presented in Table 2.1 of chapter 2 (see also Appendix K).

It is our experience that patients are only *initially* hesitant about engaging in these practices. In the majority of cases, patients begin to enjoy social mishap exposures, in part because the exposures provide such dramatic relief of a "lifetime of trying to avert social disasters." This experience can be enhanced by assigning and discussing the outcome of the mishap exposures in a group setting. In Susan's case, social mishaps were introduced as follows:

Therapist:   Susan, you wrote on your fear and avoidance hierarchy that "being assertive" in one of the most challenging situations for you. Do you mean returning goods to a store and the like?
Susan:       Yes, that's right.

*Therapist:* What are you most concerned about in these situations?

*Susan:* I guess I would be afraid about what people think of me.

*Therapist:* What do you think they might think of you?

*Susan:* That I am a nasty person.

*Therapist:* And what would happen if they think that you are a nasty person?

*Susan:* I don't know. They would think badly of me and not want to talk to me.

*Therapist:* And reject you?

*Susan:* Yes, definitely.

*Therapist:* I see. What are some everyday situations when you could be assertive?

*Susan:* I don't know. I have never been in those situations.

*Therapist:* Right, because you have been avoiding those situations, and you never gave yourself the chance to see what would happen if you were assertive. Remember what we discussed earlier? What does avoidance do to your anxiety?

*Susan:* It keeps it alive.

*Therapist:* Very good; it keeps it alive. You also never gave yourself the opportunity to see what would happen if the worst situation did happen. You don't really know how people would respond if you were assertive. Do you agree?

*Susan:* I guess so (*laughs*).

*Therapist:* Let's pick a random everyday situation. Do you sometimes go to Starbucks?

*Susan:* Oh yes, every morning.

*Therapist:* Every morning? So that's why they make so much money. What do you buy there?

*Susan:* (*laughs*) A latte grande.

*Therapist:* Decaf?

*Susan:* No, regular.

*Therapist:* Great. Let's turn this situation in an experiment to see what people will do if you are assertive. How about you order the latte, wait, and when you get it you ask, "Is this decaf?" When the person says, "No. It is regular," you say, "I would like to have mine decaf. Thanks." Do you think we can try this?

*Susan:* I guess so.

*Therapist:* Great! It is important that you say exactly what I am suggesting; you can only say "Is this decaf?" and "I would like to have mine decaf." Nothing else. Do you notice anything?

*Susan:* You are not apologizing.

*Therapist:* Correct. Very good. So I actually want you to be more assertive than probably most people are. The purpose of this exercise is to push the limits a bit in order to see what the response
of the person will be. What do you think the Starbucks person will do?

*Susan:* He will probably give me decaf.

*Therapist:* And what will he think of you?

*Susan:* I don't know. Probably not much because he has dealt with
this before.

*Therapist:* I agree. What will be your anxiety?

*Susan:* I don't know. Maybe a 4?

*Therapist:* So let's make our assertiveness task a notch more challenging; may I? Why don't you also order a pastry? Ask the person to put it on a plate. After you pay, you pick up the plate
and let the pastry slide down to fall on the floor. Pick it up
and tell the person, "The pastry just fell down on the floor.
Can I have new one?" Then you wait for your latte and ask
for a decaf.

*Susan:* Wow, I am not sure if I can do it.

*Therapist:* Of course you can. What do you think the person will do?

*Susan:* He will think that I am a complete bitch.

*Therapist:* This sounds like a perfect experiment. How will he respond?

*Susan:* He will probably say something like this or will get the manager to throw me out of the store.

*Therapist:* So he might say you are a bitch and will get the manager to
throw out of the store?

*Susan:* Well, maybe he won't say "you're a bitch," but he will say
something nasty to me.

*Therapist:* Great. Let's test it out. Your social anxiety makes you believe
that being overassertive by asking for a new pastry and
another decaf latte will cause the person to say something
nasty. The question is, will it happen, and if it happens, how
bad will it be? Let's do this right now. I will accompany you.
So why don't you summarize the task for me, please.

It is important that the task is very concretely described (i.e., stand
in line, ask for a croissant and a latte grande, tell employee to put croissant on a plate, as soon as you pick up the plate, let the croissant fall
on the floor, pick it up and say, "The pastry just fell down on the floor.
Can I have new one?" Irrespective of employees response, wait for latte
grande. When it is ready ask, "Is this decaf?" and "I would like to have
mine decaf. Thanks."). The more scripted the exposure tasks, the more
difficult it is for the patient to use subtle avoidance strategies (such as

being overly apologetic or otherwise modifying the task in ways to make it less anxiety provoking). The exposure tasks should be viewed similarly to a scene for a movie: The movie director is the therapist, and the actor is the patient. The situation is successful if the patient is able to adhere to the script. Anxiety or the lack thereof does not define success. Therefore, the task should be considered as unsuccessful if the patient was doing the exposure task nonanxiously by deviating slightly from the script.

## CLINICAL CHALLENGE: HOW TO DEAL WITH EXTREMELY CHALLENGING EXPOSURES

Patients typically underestimate themselves with regard to what they think they can do in a social situation. It is our experience that therapists also tend to underestimate what the patient is able to do in a social situation. It is important that the therapist does not openly show these concerns. Instead, the therapist should push the patient as hard as possible without compromising the therapeutic alliance.

*Therapist:* So, let's summarize. I would like you to go downstairs, stand on the street, and sing "God Bless America" for 1 minute, OK?

*Patient:* I am sorry. I can't do this.

*Therapist:* I bet you can. Do you want to bet? Let's see who is right.

*Patient:* I really don't think I can.

*Therapist:* Why?

*Patient:* It is too hard.

*Therapist:* I know it's hard, and I admire your courage and motivation that you have shown so far. As a result of it, you have come a long way, and with a bit more courage, you will go even further. I told you at the beginning that it won't be easy but that it can be very difficult and painful at times. This is one of those times. Should we try it?

*Patient:* I really don't think I can.

*Therapist:* I understand. You should know that if there was anything easier that I could do to take away your anxiety, I would do it. But I know that exposing yourself to your worst fears is the only way we can get rid off it. This is the only way to stop the avoidance/anxiety cycle. The way to get there can be quite painful, but once you get through that, you can finally live a life without social fear and avoidance. Now, having said that, I know that it is hard. My job as a therapist is to push you as hard as you let me push you. At the same time, I can feel your pain and would like to ease it as much as possible. Do you understand where I am coming from?

*Patient:* Yes, I am just so sorry. I don't think that I can do it.

*Therapist:* I know you can, but perhaps you are not quite ready for it yet. Let's modify the task to make it slightly less challenging. How can we do it?

*Patient:* I don't know.

*Therapist:* Is it the singing part?

*Patient:* Yes, definitely. Being the center of attention and making a complete fool out of myself.

*Therapist:* OK, I tell you what. Let's go down there together. I'll show you what I would like you to do. Instead of singing, I will stand there whistling "God Bless America" and hold out this cup for people to throw in some money. You just stand there and observe. Should we try it?

# CHAPTER 6

# Complicating Factors

In this chapter, we provide a number of complementary perspectives on complicating factors in treatment. First, we describe the case of Bob who reported a frequent, intrusive, and obsession-like thought (I am a failure). Lisa, our second case, is an example of a hostile and paranoid patient. These treatment difficulties can arise when patterns of social anxiety are particularly chronic and generalized. The value of these cases is to illustrate the range and application (or frequent reapplication) of the core principles of change for individuals at the severe edge of the continuum of social anxiety disorder (SAD). Following these cases, we discuss responses to the most common complicating factor in SAD, comorbid depression. Although there is some evidence to suggest that Cognitive Behavioral Therapy (CBT) for SAD frequently is resilient to comorbid depression, we devote attention to some commonsense strategies to apply when depression appears to slow treatment response to SAD. We next discuss a general troubleshooting approach for attending to treatment nonresponse, and then we note some of the issues in treating comorbid SAD and substance use disorders. Finally, we close this chapter by considering medication issues relative to CBT for SAD.

## INTRUSIVE AND SELF-DEPRECATING THOUGHTS

We start with the case of Bob who had SAD comorbid with longstanding avoidant personality disorder as well as recurrent major depression. Bob, a 31-year-old white male, had sought psychotherapy the previous year for his chronic feeling of anxiety and alienation from others. With the first therapist he received supportive and psychodynamic therapy and, upon a subsequent referral to CBT, reported a sense of benefit from this first round of treatment that was reflective of his anxiety in front of others: "I learned to sit in a room with another person, and she was nice to me."

Bob's persistent SAD severity was readily evident in his blanket refusal to come to group therapy, asking for another round of individual therapy by which to become comfortable with the process of a more directive treatment. When he said he did not know what to say in group, he meant that he had no intuitive sense of what was demanded as part of social interactions, including the initial social interactions of a structured group therapy. Accordingly, Bob was started in a brief program of individual treatment focused on providing him with a model of the disorder and initial help restructuring his pervasive self-critical and self-defeating thoughts, while also providing him with initial role play rehearsal in completing component social interactions with the therapist. Although he could complete the social rehearsals, he would cringe with each repetition, convinced that the modeled words from his mouth were indeed insipid and evidence of social failure. In Session 2 of this treatment, Bob summarized his sense of his social skills by stating, "Anything I say is, by definition, stupid. I am a social idiot. I don't know how to do anything right, and it is just a matter of time before everyone hates me and knows I am a failure."

Bob had finished college but had never been employed outside the house (but had done computer work for hire). He lived at home along with other siblings and reported a chaotic home life with no effective problem solving. For example, despite adequate monetary resources, he described chronically leaking faucets and a long-broken stove.

His severe interpretation of his social self was resistant to change, in part given the longevity by which he had defined himself as a failure on a daily basis. His self-statement, "I am a failure," served as a strong negative emotional consequence of each role play attempted—in effect, maintaining negative emotional outcomes and perceived failure despite evidence of objective improvement in social skills in session.

When his dysfunctional self-view was challenged with traditional cognitive therapy strategies, Bob stated that any other perspective felt untrue. Rather than asking him to logically dispute a thought that he reports, "Feels true; in fact always has felt true," the therapist adopted a different tactic. In discussions with Bob, the therapist "marveled" at the power of his long-rehearsed self-statement and selected an exposure-based approach to trying to help him find an alternative way of proceeding. Emphasis on exposure was selected to be consistent with the role of exposure in the upcoming group treatment, with the rationale that early success with exposure would help motivate Bob to further engage in this strategy. Following this line of logic, the therapist said:

Given how long you have been rehearsing that line, "I am a failure," I am not going to try to directly break the habit of your saying it. But I do want you to know that it does not serve you well; as long as you buy into that thought, it keeps you stuck in your current position, making it hard for you to learn new ways of interacting socially. So, while respecting the power of your habit in saying "I am a failure" to yourself, I am also going to ask you to help this phrase lose its current meaning. I want it to become a phrase that can no longer push you around emotionally or stand in your way of developing more social comfort. Starting today in session, I am going to ask you to expose yourself to this thought ("I am a failure") by saying it over and over to yourself aloud. I want you to listen to yourself say this statement and, as you hear it, realize that this thought has traditionally pushed you around and made it harder for you to reach your goals. I want you to say it to yourself, and let it lose some of its meaning.

Table 6.1 characterizes one such rehearsal (with the patient's reactive comments in parentheses). The phrase "I am a failure" was written in large block letters on a 3 × 5 card, and Bob was asked to read it repeatedly and to make editorial comments as initially guided by the therapist.

With repeated exposure, Bob reported that his negative thought held less emotional power for him and consequently served as less of a punisher when he spontaneously said it to himself in the context of social role plays. With rudimentary social skills in place and this initial model of exposure encouraging the patient's further attempts at exposure, he was enrolled in group CBT. Bob improved with a standard course of a dozen sessions of group treatment, but due to his severity, remained at a concerning level of SAD. Individual booster sessions were an option, but for cost efficacy, after a several months' break from treatment, he again returned for another dozen sessions of group treatment. This series of sessions nicely illustrates a model of therapy that allows for periods of consolidation of learning in individuals with severe disorders. Use of two courses of group treatment, rather than a chronic treatment approach, served as a balance against relapse from an incompletely treated disorder and the risk of complacency from an uninterrupted series of sessions (for a discussion of sequential therapy outside of a CBT model, see Paris, 2007). It also reflected a belief in the overall model of treatment while recognizing the distance the patient had to travel to social health; the decision was to break that journey into therapy segments over a reasonable time frame.

TABLE 6.1    Exposure Intervention Targeting a Chronic Negative Thought

Assignment—Daily exposure looking at a printed card with the words. The task was defined as follows:

> I have a strong and bad habit of saying really nasty things to myself, and these nasty things sap my motivation for change. I want change, and so I need to be better at ignoring these thoughts while working on developing a more reasonable way to coach myself ...
>
> I AM A FAILURE!

The goal: Repeat the phrase and get bored with it by taking away all the meaning from this old and maladaptive habit. The phrase should be repeated at least 20 times within a minute or so each day.

Below are examples of thoughts that went through Bob's head as he was reading the phrase:

> I am a failure (boy, that is a nasty thought, generally makes a person feel lousy)
> I am a failure (yep, this is what I say to myself to make myself feel bad)
> I am a failure (pretty negative ... this is my habit)
> I am a failure (I will just need to get bored with hearing this)
> I am a failure (yep, this is what I say over and over again)
> I am a failure (getting boring)
> I am a failure
> I am a failure
> I am a failure (yep, I use this thought to really screw myself over)
> I am a failure
> I am a failure (time to really get bored with this)
> I am a failure
> I am a failure (time to take away all meaning from this thought)
> I am a failure
> I am a failure
> I am a failure
> I am a failure (here I go again with this old, negative thought)
> I am a failure
> I am a failure ...

## HOSTILITY AND PARANOIA

Lisa is a white female waitress who suffers from severe SAD. Aside from her social anxiety, the most prominent feature was her hostility and (mild) paranoia evident in the group setting. Her self-blame for her perceived social inadequacies was part of a broad and pervasive sense of shame that left her feeling chronically vulnerable to rejection from others. One of her responses to her chronic feelings of vulnerability and fears of impending rejection was to criticize others. Her fears of impending rejection were also communicated with a paranoid flair. Lisa was sure that others would be talking about her or be planning to exclude her, and with her criticism and hostility, she was planning to ensure that she would reject others well before they did the same to her.

All of these patterns were, of course, a particular problem for group management. Given Lisa's willingness to criticize others (in expectation of being roundly criticized herself), her fears of rejection could easily emerge as a self-fulfilling prophecy, as group members reacted negatively to her hostility and criticism. Likewise, Lisa was not a person who would make a therapist feel good about his or her efforts. Lisa was quick to point out any lack of organization in the running of the group, in part because any seemingly unplanned moment in therapy enhanced her sense of impending humiliation. Accordingly, working well with her demanded considerable empathy on the part of the therapist, not only because the therapist was a direct target of her criticisms, but also because her hostile and critical attitude was a direct threat to group cohesion and accurate feedback during exposure. The therapist needed to remember how much anxiety was underlying and motivating her hostile comments to the therapist and others. Interventions were also made difficult by the degree to which Lisa seemed brittle with her sense of fragility, where direct feedback threatened what little calm and reserve she had during group.

The strategy adopted by the therapist was to complete initial cognitive restructuring in terms of Socratic questioning of all group members about the range of behaviors people adopt when feeling socially threatened, followed by a specific discussion on how both avoidant and aggressive responses can keep cycles of social anxiety active. Once criticism was defined as a response to anxiety, the therapist had a bit more leeway in responding to Lisa's criticisms of other group members. The therapist tried to use this criticism for the benefit of all group members by explicitly including a review of her frequently critical assessments in the post-event processing of the social cost of errors. The therapist would respond to her critical assessment of another group member's performance by saying something like, "Yes, you are absolutely right, it was an imperfect performance. But how perfect does a performance need to be? What would be the worst outcome of a performance like this?" This general Socratic questioning was then followed by a discussion of the patient's thoughts and feelings motivating the criticism, "And notice that it still feels important to you to have a perfect performance. What sort of thoughts do you have about the importance of [specific example]?" The therapist should also model appropriate acknowledgment of his own errors, while at the same time challenging the idea that a perfect performance is required (e.g., "That was an awkward transition, wasn't it? I think we will all survive it though").

The most important intervention for Lisa, however, was the culmination and utilization of this cognitive restructuring in her own in-session exposure assignments, where she was asked to discuss the thoughts and feelings that motivate a person to be critical of others. This assignment obviously asked Lisa to be vulnerable by discussing her defensive responses to her own feelings of shame. During this assignment, she had the explicit goal of providing an imperfect discussion of her own feelings of anxiety. Objectively, her goal was to say three things that made her feel vulnerable while completing a 2-minute discussion of the topic. With the completion of the assignment, Lisa exclaimed, "Now you know how I work, and that I am not so great at stuff, and I guess I have to get used to being that way." The group members warmly accepted her imperfection, and Lisa's social anxiety and critical comments began decreasing across subsequent sessions.

## DEPRESSION AND SAD

Treatment of SAD virtually guarantees therapists will have regular experience with the management of comorbid depression. Among treatment-seeking outpatients, half to two thirds of patients report lifetime major depression, and one out of five will report lifetime dysthymia (Brown, Campbell, Lehman, Grisham, & Mancill, 2001). With the presence of depression, patients are at risk for an intensification of negative self-evaluations. For example, beliefs that social errors will result in negative evaluations from others and herald long-term negative consequences are intensified among SAD patients with comorbid depression (Wilson & Rapee, 2005; see also Ball et al., 1995; Bruch, Mattia, Heimberg, & Holt, 1993), consistent with the general notion that SAD severity is higher among individuals with comorbid depression (Erwin et al., 2002).

Although comorbid depression has been hypothesized to reduce motivation to conduct self-directed exposures (Marks, 1987), slow extinction (Abramowitz & Foa, 2000; Abramowitz, Franklin, Street, Kozak, & Foa, 2000; Foa, 1979; Mills & Salkovskis, 1988), and minimization of therapeutic learning from exposure interventions (Telch, 1988), there is evidence that anxiety treatment effects may be more robust than expected (for a review, see Otto, Powers, Stathopoulou, & Hofmann, in press). For example, early indications that severe depression may interfere with extinction learning in the anxiety disorders (Foa, 1979) have not been noteworthy in subsequent studies (e.g., Abramowitz et al., 2000). Also, in a comparison of SAD studies that did and did not exclude comorbid depression, no difference in efficacy was reported in a meta-analytic review of 30 outcome studies of CBT (Lincoln & Rief, 2004), with near identical estimates of mean pre- to posttreatment effect sizes for studies that did and did not exclude patients with depression.

On the negative side, however, Chambless, Tran, and Glass (1997) found that out of a series of potential predictors—pretreatment depression, personality disorder traits, frequency of negative cognitions, expectations of treatment benefits, clinician-rated breadth and severity of impairment, and frequency of negative thoughts—pretreatment depression was the most consistent predictor of poorer treatment response to group CBT for depression. Similar findings were reported by Scholing and Emmelkamp (1999), although by an 18-month follow-up assessment, depression no longer predicted treatment outcome.

Other research acknowledges that SAD severity scores are higher in those with comorbid depression, but that these individuals achieve similar gains in therapy to patients who are not depressed. Nonetheless, with similar gains in treatment, those who started treatment with greater severity are still left with a greater level of severity after treatment. This effect was effectively illustrated in a large trial ($N = 141$) by Erwin, Heimberg, Juster, and Mindlin (2002). These investigators compared the response to 12 sessions of cognitive-behavioral group therapy (CBGT) in three groups of SAD patients: those with SAD and no comorbidity, those with SAD and a comorbid anxiety disorder, and those with SAD and a comorbid mood disorder. Consistent with the idea that a mood disorder can intensify SAD severity, Erwin et al. (2002) found that those with SAD and comorbid mood, but not anxiety disorders, were more severely impaired than those with no comorbidity. Nonetheless, the *rate* of improvement in therapy was the same in those with and without depression comorbidity.

There is also evidence that improvements in social anxiety in CBGT are linked to subsequent improvements in depression. In particular, Moscovitch, Hofmann, Suvak, and In-Albon (2005) found that improvements in social anxiety mediated 91% of the improvements in depression over time. These findings support the notion that in individuals with SAD, secondary symptoms of depression can be treated by effective interventions for SAD. One mechanism for this effect might be the return of the patients with SAD to pleasant and positive social interactions. Moreover, in our experience, the content of cognitions encountered in depression is similar to many of those encountered in SAD. In both disorders, restructuring efforts are likely to target beliefs about personal inadequacy and unlovability, at times related to self-imposed perfectionistic standards. Hence, because of this shared content of dysfunctional thoughts, cognitive interventions for one disorder may extend to the other as well. Also, stepwise exposure to feared situations and events in the anxiety disorders finds its counterpart in behavioral activation treatments for depression that emphasize step-by-step reemergence into meaningful work, social, and leisure activities (for a review, see Hopko, Lejuez, Ruggiero, & Eifert, 2003; see also Hopko, Lejuez, & Hopko, 2004). Accordingly, depending on the level of depressive symptoms, it might not be necessary to target depression specifically when treating SAD.

There is the issue, nonetheless, of which disorder to target initially when co-occurring depression and SAD are confronted. SAD does appear to impair depression treatment (e.g., Gaynes et al., 1999), and, given the success of SAD treatment in the context of depression, we recommend an initial focus on the SAD when it appears this disorder is the primary source of distress. There are two elements to this assessment of primacy: the patient's report of her or his primary area of distress and the therapist's analysis of the functional relationship between depressive and SAD symptoms. Concerning the former, linking treatment to the patient's identified source of distress has the advantage of providing a match to the patient's treatment expectations that is important for enhancing treatment adherence (e.g., Eisenthal, Emery, Lazare, & Udin, 1979; Schulberg et al., 1996). However, patient's expectations regarding treatment are malleable when presented with a compelling case formulation, and, accordingly, the therapist needs to assess the degree to which depressive symptoms may be dependent on the distress and disability of the SAD. Important questions to consider are whether the situational distress and avoidance of the SAD limits the affective benefit that a patient may derive from a more primary focus on depressed mood, or whether the distress and dysfunction from the SAD are used as evidence for core beliefs underlying depression. On the other hand, depression treatment may be considered first if the depressed mood is profound enough so that the patient's motivation or willingness to complete exposure exercises, or the ability to judge or utilize the success of these exercises, is compromised (Otto et al., in press).

As an additional issue in the ordering of interventions, we also encourage attention to providing patients with early evidence that interventions *can* lead to beneficial change. Research suggests that early gains in treatment boost motivation and alliance (Tang & DeRubeis, 2005; also see Hofmann, Schulz, et al., 2006), and, hence, the most central problem does not always need to be the first treatment target. Attending to the interventions that might offer the earliest palpable benefits to the patient has value, where initial treatment gains are used to boost the patient's momentum in therapy.

Maintaining momentum in therapy is also an issue relative to the weekly distress encountered in treating SAD patients with comorbid depression. Elsewhere, we have cautioned against therapist overattention to in-session weekly depressive distress to the exclusion of out-of-session dysfunctional patterns (Otto et al., in press). In-session depressive symptoms, particularly in-session sadness and tearfulness, are often more salient to clinicians than the anxiety and avoidance that occurs outside the clinician's office. Maintaining momentum in the treatment of the depressed patient with SAD may require clinicians to focus on what is most *useful* to the patient over the interval between sessions instead of what is most *comforting* to the patient within the session. It requires clinicians to direct their empathy to helping patients achieve their broader agenda earlier (relief from the disorders that maintain the distress) rather than to ameliorating their emotional distress of the moment. Continuity in therapy is aided by the therapist's commitment to checking into progress from the previous weeks' assignments and making sure that in-session progress is translated into additional home practice assignments for the next week.

Throughout this process, therapists need to be cognizant of the degree to which strategies used in one problem area (e.g., SAD or depression) can be utilized in the treatment of other areas of distress, while maintaining vigilance to ways in which the combined weight of two areas of distress may slow treatment. In Table 6.2, we have summarized a number of recommendations for trying to minimize the impact of depression on interventions for SAD.

As a final issue in the consideration of co-occurring depression, it is important to note that SAD is frequently comorbid with bipolar disorder, with estimates ranging between 7.8% and 47.2% for SAD among

TABLE 6.2   Challenges and Strategies for Comorbid Depression

| Challenges From Depression Comorbidity | Strategies for Enhancing Change |
| --- | --- |
| Role of depression in intensifying fears of and the perceived consequences of negative evaluations from others | Devote early attention in treatment to discussing the mood-state dependency of anxiogenic thoughts ("When feeling down, your concerns about [set of thoughts] will feel more real to you. I want you to know that this is a common effect of depression, but you need to be careful of buying into these thoughts. When feeling down, I would like you to be extra vigilant in making sure you are coaching yourself accurately in how you are thinking about the world and about your social performance as well as progress in treatment ..."). |

*(continued)*

TABLE 6.2 (CONTINUED)    Challenges and Strategies for Comorbid Depression

| Challenges From Depression Comorbidity | Strategies for Enhancing Change |
|---|---|
| Depressed mood impairs motivation to attempt home exposures | At every stage of treatment, help patients see the link between their efforts in and out of therapy and changes in symptoms and disability. Patients may require additional attention to home practice adherence, perhaps including clearer objective self-monitoring of progress as well as cognitive-restructuring interventions focused on motivation for home practice completion. |
| Enhanced negative postexposure processing and failures to acknowledge progress | Patients should be prepared for the tendency to negatively evaluate progress and practice recognizing and confronting these thoughts. Provide patients with the form and content of thoughts before they are encountered outside the session. Having the negative thought preprinted on a 3 × 5 card (e.g., This isn't working; I am not like other patients that can get better; I am failing) will help neutralize the impact of these thoughts if encountered between sessions. |
| Impaired problem solving and stress buffering due to depression (cf. Otto et al., 1997) | Consider using in-session exposure assignments to demystify this characteristic of depression by asking patients to discuss these issues and generate attempts to cope as part of public speech exposures. |
| A history of self-critical attitudes that have been characteristic of both depression and SAD | Acknowledge the link between classic depressogenic thoughts and those encountered in SAD, with the explicit assignment of using therapy to challenge these long-held assumptions that can maintain both disorders. |
| Few activities that maintain positive mood outside the session | In addition to exposure assignments for SAD, therapists need to attend to assigning a range of activities designed to promote feelings of well-being. Some of these should be explicitly nonsocial, but social exposure assignments should include not only those that directly challenge the patient's social fears but also those that provide an opportunity for fun. Promotion of social well-being is a direct goal for helping prevent both depression and SAD recurrences. |

samples of patients with bipolar disorder. Moreover, there is consistent evidence for a worse course and poorer functioning among bipolar patients with comorbid SAD (e.g., Otto et al., 2007; Simon et al., 2007). For example, Otto et al. (2007) reported that according to regression analyses, comorbid SAD was associated with failing to have recovered from a depressed, manic, or hypomanic episode for an additional 34 days per year. These consistent findings motivate additional attention to treating anxiety disorders among bipolar patients. With the success of psychosocial interventions, such as CBT targeted directly to bipolar depression and the prevention of future episodes (e.g., Lam et al., 2003; Miklowitz et al., 2007), application of CBT to anxiety comorbidity is encouraged as well for bipolar patients.

In summary, we recommend that clinicians approach patients with SAD and comorbid depression with the dual expectations that brief CBT for SAD has a good chance of success despite the presence of depression, and SAD patients with comorbid depression may need a longer or more intensive course of treatment to reach full remission. In this treatment, it is possible the comorbid depression may not be resolved (requiring additional treatment of one disorder once the other has been treated), and it is possible the selected treatment may fail outright. The next section considers troubleshooting options when such nonresponse is apparent.

## SUBSTANCE ABUSE AND SAD

No chapter on complications in the treatment of SAD would be complete without attention to substance abuse comorbidity. In the empirical literature, SAD and substance use disorders have received particular attention, in part due to the prominence of SAD among individuals with these disorders. For example, among samples of individuals with alcohol use disorders, SAD was much more strongly represented than the other anxiety disorders (Kushner, Sher, & Beitman, 1990). Estimates of SAD among polysubstance-dependent patients have been even higher (51%) than among alcohol-dependent patients (34%) according to a survey of individuals in public treatment programs in Norway (Bakken, Landheim, & Vaglum, 2005). Among individuals with substance dependence, SAD often emerges as the first disorder, and, consistent with the idea that substance use in some of these cases is linked with attempts to self-medicate in social situations, individuals with alcohol use disorders and SAD comorbidity were more likely than those without SAD comorbidity to report drinking to improve sociability and enhance functioning, and also tended to be more depressed (Thomas, Thevos, & Randall, 1999).

## CASE REPORT

Phil is a 27-year-old, single, white male who reports onset of regular marijuana and alcohol use during his high school years. His case is nicely representative of the onset of substance use in response to social concerns. Diagnostically, he had a history of social anxiety and worry since early childhood and first met criteria for SAD in his transition from middle school to high school. It was at this time, after a year of feeling extremely socially isolated, that he began using marijuana as a form of both self-medication and social entry. He explains it as follows:

"I was so painfully shy as a freshman. I was kind of a geek, and didn't know how to fit in. I would worry about it all the time. But once someone introduced me to pot in my sophomore year, it was like I had a place to go and had someone to hang out with. It also helped deal with my anxiety. Alcohol use came later, but it was the same thing. It was a way to fit in, a way to have a group of friends. Drinking was my entrance to a social group."

Although his alcohol use was always heavy relative to his peers, Phil did not meet criteria for alcohol dependence until he was 22 years old. He presented for treatment 5 years later. His drinking was bingelike, and he came to treatment after a period of self-withdrawal and self-imposed social isolation. These steps toward initial sobriety allowed his therapist to work collaboratively with him to institute rules against a return to drinking while treatment of SAD was initiated. With the patient's self-imposed social isolation, he was relatively safe from his primary cue of high alcohol use—trying to be sociable in bars. As treatment focused on relieving his social anxiety and establishing nondrinking social interactions, the patient decided to try Alcoholics Anonymous (AA) meetings. Exposure assignments incorporated the interactions common to these meetings, but effort was placed in therapy to ensure that his socializing occurred outside AA meetings as well. Over time, as the patient became more confident in his social abilities—specifically, his ability to interact with others successfully without alcohol—he increasingly substituted other social activities (e.g., playing regular basketball with postgame socializing) for AA and eventually discontinued AA while maintaining sobriety.

Clinical care of patients dually diagnosed with SAD and substance dependence needs to take into account the phase and severity of the substance use, in particular the need for detoxification as a first step in treatment. However, once initial stabilization has been achieved, there is little empirical guidance other than encouragement to treat both disorders vigorously. Distinct from clinical lore, there is evidence that interventions for SAD can be applied effectively to those also in treatment for substance dependence. Specifically, a study of men with comorbid alcohol dependence and anxiety disorder (SAD or agoraphobia) in the Netherlands indicated that the anxiety disorders improved with CBT regardless of the severity of alcohol dependence, thereby encouraging vigorous attention to anxiety comorbidity despite the presence of the substance dependence (Schadé et al., 2007). However, this research group also found that successful treatment of the anxiety disorder did not have an effect on acute alcohol relapse rates (Schadé et al., 2005; see also Terra et al., 2006), indicating that alcohol dependence requires an ongoing focus in its own right and is not simply dependent on the success of anxiety treatment. Also, clinicians need to be aware that substance dependence is a predictor of poor recovery from anxiety disorders over time (Bruce et al., 2005), and hence these patients may require additional booster sessions over time to help them maintain their treatment gains for anxiety, while they also focus on achieving and maintaining abstinence in substance-dependence treatment. Finally, during the treatment of SAD comorbid with substance dependence, therapists should pay particular attention to the establishment and maintenance of social relationships with alcohol- and drug-free individuals because the ability to elicit and receive social support appears to be important in the long-term recovery from alcohol dependence (e.g., Gordon & Zrull, 1991).

## TROUBLESHOOTING: NONRESPONSE

Perhaps the most relevant first step in troubleshooting nonresponse to CBT for SAD is to reassess the core fear(s) and associated avoidance patterns that define the patient's difficulties. In some cases, misdiagnosis may be discovered, where apparent social concerns appear to be (better or additionally) linked to other disorders such as chronic worry patterns underlying generalized anxiety disorder, or fears involving the meaning of symptoms that may characterize panic disorder or agoraphobia. Clarification of the role of additional diagnoses is just one instance in the demand on the clinician to continue to assess and hone attention to the core fears underlying the patient's distress and disability. Additional examples include other factors that may make the fear conditional on a context (the absence of a significant other or the presence of a specific cluster of somatic symptoms) for full amplification of social concerns. In any of these cases, the clinician may need to titrate the elements of exposure to ensure that core fears are being addressed, in part by making sure that exposure encompasses the most common "what if" thoughts reported by patients in considering their fears of social situations.

One common conditional factor underlying exposure success is often the presence of a specific symptom or set of symptoms (e.g., dry mouth, sweating, blushing, trembling) that define the social threat for a patient when present (e.g., "I can talk to a group just fine, until I start to sweat; then I fear I am going to blow it and they are going to think I am a fool."). For these individuals, learning of social safety must involve social performances while the feared symptom is present. To achieve these ends, interoceptive (internal cue) exposure is helpful. Table 6.3 presents a number of interoceptive exposure procedures that can be used to induce feared symptoms prior to a social performance exposure. The aim is to help the patient learn that social goals can be met regardless of the presence of the symptom. As a procedural point, we try to induce the symptom without knowledge of other group members (e.g., the patient steps out of the group to complete the symptom induction, and the patient is not to explain the source of the symptom until well after the social exposure had been completed).

We extend this general point for patients with comorbid panic disorder. For this comorbid condition, treatment should involve a fuller protocol of interoceptive exposure exercises designed to eliminate the fear of somatic symptoms of anxiety (the core fear associated with panic disorder) regardless of whether these fears occur in the context of a social situation. A variety of protocols can help guide this work (e.g., Barlow & Craske, 2000).

Another source of poor response to exposure is the patient's use of nonobjective standards for judging exposure success. Some patients, for example, will try to define exposure success in terms of a single symptom ("But my heart still beat rapidly; I failed"). Accordingly, it is crucial to objectively define an exposure success prior to an exposure exercise (clinicians may need to write out these criteria to help keep the patient focused on these goals) and to faithfully check in with these evaluation criteria after exposure, especially if the affect of the patient does not match the clinician's expectation. Socratic questioning with appropriate cognitive restructuring and refocusing on appropriate exposure goals is a suitable response to the sometimes fluid shift in exposure expectations among patients. Furthermore, as part of the attention to goals, patients should be asked to attend to what is actually going on with others during the social exposure. As indicated by an elegant study by Wells and Papageorgiou (1998), asking patients to attend to what is going on (e.g., what other people are doing) in social situations can aid fear reduction during exposure, perhaps by reducing self-focused attention and overinterpretations of one's own affective experience during exposure.

A third issue in arranging effective exposure is the step-by-step elimination of safety cues. Safety cues received direct attention in chapters 2 and 3, but they should always be a consideration should nonresponse be encountered. A functional analysis of which cues help the person feel

TABLE 6.3    Interoceptive Exposure Exercises to Enhance Social
Exposures

| Symptom Induction Exercise | Goal and Strategies |
|---|---|
| Hyperventilation— rapid once-per-second breathing | As long as the patient works to "blow off air" with each breath, a dry throat is achieved within a few seconds. This procedure alone is useful for individuals fearing a dry throat/mouth during a speech. It requires patients to have to cope through this symptom at the beginning of a speech, focusing on meeting their goals despite this difficulty. With longer inductions (30–60 seconds), a fuller panoply of symptoms can be induced (lightheadedness, flushing, numbness, and tingling) as is useful for individuals with concerns about paniclike responses to their social stressors. |
| Running up stairs (several flights) or running in place for 30 seconds | This procedure will produce the out-of-breath and "heavy legs" sensations that some patients fear will prevent a coherent speech or discussion. Again, performance despite this symptom is the goal. This procedure is also very useful for the subtype of individuals who fail to pause and breathe at the natural pauses in a discussion (i.e., at the commas and periods in a presentation). Without these pauses, patients may drive increasing amounts of breathlessness. Inducing breathlessness, but also instructing patients to allow pauses between sentences in their presentations, can help them develop a natural cadence of speaking despite the presence of symptoms. |
| Sitting with head between the knees (be mindful of orthostatic hypotension if patients rise from this position too quickly) | Due to the blood rushing to the head, this procedure can produce sensations of or actual flushing responses. With physician approval, a more prolonged flushing response can also be induced with 200 mg of niacin (vitamin B3) taken on a full stomach. |
| Staring into a mirror into one's own eyes (hand mirror held 6 inches away) | This procedure can produce sensations of derealization and disorientation, which can be useful for individuals with fears of losing one's train of thought in a social setting (speech or conversation). |

"safe" during exposure, plus in-session rehearsal aimed at altering any recurrent patterns (placement of hands, adjustment to the voice, eye contact) which the patient may be using to avoid more straightforward and useful exposure experiences.

Recent research has documented that safety behavior *availability* (such as the perceived ability to escape a situation should symptoms increase) interfered with fear reduction during exposure on par with the actual use of safety behaviors (Powers, Smits, & Telch, 2004). These findings suggest that subtle behaviors, such as carrying in a pocket a "rescue medication" such as a benzodiazepine, may compromise exposures. Moreover, the fading of safety behaviors across exposure sessions appears to facilitate exposure efficacy (Wells et al., 1995). Accordingly, part of a full analysis of treatment resistance should include an informed hunt for safety behaviors that may compromise treatment efficacy.

## TROUBLESHOOTING: POOR ADHERENCE

If in-session exposures are designed to provide patients with initial real-world practice (and show them a new way of approaching their phobic experiences), then home practice is where patients truly set their new learning in stone. Accordingly, avoidance of home practice can directly prevent adequate consolidation and application of therapeutic learning. Reasons for avoidance of home social exposures can be multifaceted and are deserving of a full analysis of apparent controlling factors.

As noted in chapter 2, we believe that at each session it is the therapist's job to examine, with the patient, whether the learning from the last session and home practice assignments led to an incremental value in distress reduction. That is, it is up to the therapist to underscore, on a session-by-session basis, the expectation that principles from each week's therapy session should be applied during the subsequent interval between sessions, with feedback the next week on what was useful and what was not useful about the week's learning. Use of this strategy will provide consistent encouragement and responsibility to the patient for completing each week's assignments and underscores the notion that change occurs not because of session material, but because of the application of session material during relevant moments in the patient's life. If this is not happening, then adherence troubleshooting should be implemented

We recommend first reviewing the patient's assumptions about treatment, and the link between methods being applied and the patient's goals. Has the therapist drifted from the patient's goals, or has the therapist failed to provide an adequate link between goals and methods to be applied in therapy to help achieve those goals? Anxiety treatment, by its nature, represents an investment in willingness to reapproach phobic stimuli with the hope of achieving a different response than has been achieved during the years of previous disability and distress. It is by sequential successes that patients increase willingness to engage in exposures that will truly bring about change. As such, in the face of non-adherence, therapists should also reassess whether therapy assignments represent too large a conceptual jump from the last successful assignment. Repetition of past successful exposures with greater attention to post-event processing of the meaning of the exposure success (and how patients can better cognitively coach themselves given this experience) can aid in helping patients better progress to the next level of exposure. In addition, therapists should assess whether home practice is being compromised by other life issues, scheduling problems, or motivational lapses. As a matter of course, we recommend in-session troubleshooting of out-of-session assignments. A first step is to discuss the day and time when the patient next plans to practice therapy material, taking time to discuss where the patient will be and what may make it difficult to initiate the practice, including motivation-sapping cognitions (e.g., "I am too busy now; I can wait until later in the week" or "I should wait until I am feeling more confident"). Second, therapists should complete problem solving around any true blocks to scheduling of home practice, and then rehearse successful application of home practice and overcoming obstacles to practice by asking the patient to discuss (1) what will be hardest about completing the practice, (2) what will be most useful about completing the practice, and (3) how the patient wants to think about the experience after completing the home practice. In addition, the therapist may want to send home a written cue (e.g., 3 × 5 card) summarizing this discussion and clarifying time, place, and motivations for out-of-session practices. An example of troubleshooting the scheduling of home practice follows.

*Therapist:* OK, Dina, we have agreed that your home practice will include three social mishap exposures. We know that you are nervous about doing these, so let's go over your plan for home practice. When during the week do you think you might do the first one?

*Dina:* Well, I guess I could do it right after work tomorrow.

*Therapist:* What do you usually do after work?

*Dina:* I like to get right home, change my clothes, and just take a break for a while with the TV.

*Therapist:* So right after work is your break time; you feel like you deserve a little down time.

*Dina:* Yes.

*Therapist:* Hmmm, that doesn't sound like a great time for you to expect yourself to do some home practice.

*Dina:* Yeah, you're right. I really like my break.

*Therapist:* So thinking about it a bit more, what might be a better time? When does your break end (and remember, you need to be in the right setting for the exposure); when might you be close to the bookstore for your first exposure?

*Dina:* I do sometimes go out for a bite in the early evening, and there is a bookstore not far from this takeout place I like.

*Therapist:* OK, do you want to do the exposure before or after you order your food?

*Dina:* Before.

*Therapist:* And about what time might that be tomorrow evening?

*Dina:* I could do it about 7:00; the bookstore is open till 8:00.

*Therapist:* OK, and what thoughts do you think you are going to have as you think about going to the bookstore?

*Dina:* Oh gosh, I am going to think it will be a disaster and wonder whether I really have to do it.

*Therapist:* I think you're right. When you go to do your home practice, you can expect all the old thoughts to come rushing in, and your urges to avoid will be strong. How do you want to coach yourself at that moment?

*Dina:* I might use part of what we used today, that "there go those thoughts again, do I really want to buy into them" phrase.

*Therapist:* Great, and how about the urges to avoid?

*Dina:* I have got to tell myself that I feel better after the exposures and that across these weeks of treatment, I have been feeling more confident. I guess that if I want to get the benefit, I should just get the exposure going so that I can see how it works.

*Therapist:* Nicely said. I like how you are approaching this. The goal of the exposure is to see what you can learn when you don't avoid and when you don't assume the social cost of a mishap is an automatic "disaster."

*Dina:* Right.

*Therapist:* Let's do a brief rehearsal. I want you to picture yourself during tomorrow evening. You have had your break at home after work and watched a little TV. Now you are realizing it is time to go out and do your exposure. Your natural thoughts are, "This will be as disaster. I don't want to do that. Maybe I can wait until Thursday to do it." What will you say to yourself at that moment?

As a final issue in considering factors influencing treatment adherence, clinicians need to be attentive to the role changes that treatment may bring in the patient's family. With changes in social goals, assertion, and abilities, the spouses and families of patients may be unprepared for the new social agendas emergent in the patient. Informational interventions, and specific consideration of how treatment changes might affect family members, can be helpful. If the SAD patient is in a relationship, it is often useful to hold a couple's session where the process of change is discussed. We recommend asking the question: How might changes in social patterns be beneficial and difficult for the patient? In addition, once social comfort increases, the newfound assertive behavior on the part of the patient may be experienced as a challenge by the patient's significant other. Prepare the patient's spouse or significant other for this change, and notify both the patient and significant other that it may take some time to develop new and successful patterns of communication once the patient is more attuned to his or her social agenda and needs. Early attention to these factors can help prevent spousal resistance of change that may otherwise slow treatment efforts.

## COMBINATION TREATMENT WITH MEDICATION AND CBT

The wish that one powerful modality of treatment (CBT) can be combined effectively with another modality (medications) has been one of the elusive hopes of psychiatry for quite some time. Although there have been limited successes in the treatment of mood disorders, combination treatment strategies have long been met by disappointment in the anxiety disorders (for a review, see Foa, Franklin, & Moser, 2002; Otto et al., 2005). In the treatment of SAD, for example, a two-site randomized trial of the individual and combined effects of CBT and the antidepressant fluoxetine revealed no significant benefit for combination treatment; the combination treatment condition was associated with a response rate of 54.2% relative to a response rate of 51.7% for CBT alone and a response rate of 50.8% for fluoxetine alone (Davidson et al., 2004). Also, even in trials where clinicians relatively new to CBT offered exposure therapy, there is evidence that combined treatment does not have an advantage over CBT alone over long-term intervals (Haug et al., 2003).

These disappointing results do not indicate that an individual who has failed to respond to one modality of treatment cannot be crossed over and succeed with the other modality of treatment. Instead, we believe these results indicate that for the average patient, combination treatment is not likely to achieve significantly better results than CBT alone. For any individual patient who has not responded to an adequate course of CBT, a medication referral should be considered. Likewise, CBT should always be considered for patients who have failed to respond to pharmacotherapy. Indeed, there is emerging evidence from the treatment of major depression that CBT offers a more efficacious alternative than medications for patients with a history of multiple antidepressant exposures (perhaps reflecting failure to respond consistently to antidepressant pharmacotherapy over time). The evidence that pharmacotherapy nonresponse is not a contraindication to CBT success is also indicated by a number of open studies in panic disorder (Heldt et al., 2006; Otto, Pollack, Penava, & Zucker, 1999). Accordingly, nonresponse to pharmacotherapy should never discourage expectations of a full response to CBT.

Nonetheless, the application of CBT to patients taking medications does introduce some treatment complications. In such combined treatments, there are reasons to be concerned about state dependent learning effects, where some of the benefits of what is learned in CBT while on medications may be lost upon medication discontinuation (for a review, see Otto et al., 2005; Powers, Smits, Leyro, & Otto, 2006). However, there is evidence from the treatment of panic disorder that reinstatement of CBT during and after medication discontinuation aids the maintenance and expansion of treatment gains (see Otto et al., 2005). Hence, for patients who are taking medications, we see no contraindications to offering a full program of CBT, but routinely ask patients to achieve a stable dose of medication before starting CBT and to maintain this dose during treatment, so that treatment gains from CBT can be appropriately attributed to the patient's efforts rather than medication. Such attributions appear to be important for the maintenance of treatment gains, particularly after discontinuing medication (Basoğlu, Marks, Kilic, Brewin, & Swinson, 1994).

Also, it is important to note that these concerns about the limits of combination treatment approaches are specific to current anxiolytic and antidepressant medications. In contrast to these agents, we are cautiously optimistic about the efficacy of putative memory enhancers used to enhance the efficacy of exposure-based CBT. Specifically, three studies have now shown that d-cycloserine (DCS), a partial agonist at the N-methyl-D-aspartate receptor, is capable of enhancing exposure-based CBT for anxiety disorders (Hofmann, Meuret, et al., 2006; Kushner et al., 2007; Ressler et al., 2004). Relevant to the treatment of SAD, in a randomized placebo-controlled trial, we showed that the efficacy of brief CBT (five sessions) was enhanced by the use of DCS. Most of the SAD patients had the generalized subtype of SAD, and in the trial, DCS or placebo was administered one hour before each of the final four sessions of CBT. Patients who received DCS achieved significantly better outcomes at posttreatment and at a one-month follow-up assessment. Consistent with evidence from animal models (Davis, Ressler, Rothbaum, & Richardson, 2006), we believe DCS aids in the consolidation of therapeutic learning from exposure, helping patients remember their in-session successes, thereby motivating more out-of-session application of initial learning (see Hofmann, 2007, for a review). At this writing, new trials of the efficacy of DCS for augmenting CBT are underway, and we are hopeful that DCS, as well as related agents now under study, will emerge as a reliable strategy to help patients who otherwise may have difficulty responding to CBT alone.

# CHAPTER 7

# Maintenance and Follow-Up Strategies

This chapter addresses the fading of regular treatment sessions and the application, if needed, of booster sessions. Therapeutic techniques to consolidate improvements are discussed along with a review of general relapse prevention strategies. The goal is to help patients generalize their knowledge of treatment strategies so they can act as their own therapists once regular treatment sessions end.

We believe the task of ensuring long-term maintenance of treatment gains is a function of (1) an adequate breadth and depth of the initial treatment such that core maintaining factors for social anxiety disorder (SAD) are altered, and (2) teaching the patient how to reapply treatment principles as needed around future symptoms. Concerning the former goal, our treatment protocol emphasizes multiple strategies to aid in the learning of safety that are consistently applied in relation to a wide range of phobic cues, including the characteristics of the social situation, the presence of anxiety symptoms, and the presence of social mishaps. Considering the adequacy of these interventions, we want to caution therapists against unwittingly collaborating with patients in providing low-level exposures. Elsewhere, this habit has been termed "leaving well enough alone" (Otto, Jones, Craske, & Barlow, 1996) and is assumed to be most prominent in patients who have ridden a wave of early success in treatment (e.g., low anxiety in initial exposures) and then became cautious in subsequent exposures to not upset their new sense of control. Our belief is that the relapse potential is high with these cases because the patient did not have adequate opportunities to learn true social comfort and resilience with the full range of social fear cues. In every case, therapists should be sure to include exposures with social mishaps, exposures where anxiety symptoms are provoked by interoceptive exposure, and exposures where safety cues are systematically identified and faded to help protect against this tendency toward subtle avoidance of some of the most important cues of social anxiety.

As an associated caution, therapists need to make sure that social exposures are practiced in a wide range of contexts. Exposure practice in group is useful, but it is the exposure in more realistic settings that helps lock in useful therapeutic learning. Likewise, exposures completed when the patient is confident are useful, but it is the exposures completed when the patient is tired, worried, sad, or otherwise feeling less than optimal that help the patient know she or he can be socially comfortable under a range of internal and external conditions. Therapists should think of exposure in these varied cues and contexts as strategies to help reduce the potential for relapse (see Powers et al., 2006).

Concerning our other goal for relapse prevention—teaching patients how to reapply treatment principles in the future—this training begins at Session 1 when patients are provided with a clear model of the disorder and an overview of treatment elements. This teaching is enhanced with realistic rehearsals of all skills, applied not in abstract but applied in situations of high emotion (realistic social exposures)—the very situations where these skills will be needed. Independence in the application of these skills is further strengthened by the therapist's fading role across the treatment sessions, where in the case of group treatment, group members take on a more direct role in discussing home practice outcomes and problem solving patients' concerns, distresses, and remaining disabilities. In other words, in the protocol, patients have increasing practice in acting as their own therapist as treatment progresses. As a final task in helping patients develop stronger skills in acting as one's own therapist, effort is made in final sessions to help patients abstract the principles behind their treatment successes. This is done not just in the context of SAD, but, more generally, with attention to therapy skills that may aid the patients' functioning across a number of affective domains.


## GENERALIZING TREATMENT SKILLS

As noted in chapter 2, the goal of cognitive interventions in this protocol was not simply to replace specific dysfunctional thoughts with more accurate alternatives, but to help patients develop a general skill of understanding that thoughts are frequently distorted and should not be viewed as necessarily valid reflections of reality. Indeed, research on the application of cognitive therapy to depression suggests that it is this ability to distance oneself from the content of thoughts (treating them as behaviors rather than necessarily accurate statements of reality) that may underlie the strong relapse prevention effects of cognitive therapy (Teasdale et al., 2002). As such, we believe therapists should make efforts in the final sessions to underscore the importance of understanding the degree to which thoughts may be distorted and to develop skills for evaluating situations in terms of objective criteria related to the patient's goals. An example of this process in a group format follows.

*Therapist:* What is your general sense of what you have learned in therapy about your thoughts and how well you guide yourself with your thoughts?

*Barbara:* I was really surprised, as we started looking at my thoughts, at how dire my predictions were. All of my thoughts were about failure and embarrassment and disasters. I never realized what a downer these thoughts were.

*Therapist:* Can you describe the nature of these thoughts a bit more?

*Barbara:* They were so "what if" and "watch out" and "I told you so."

*Therapist:* So, if you had to give advice to someone else about the nature of thoughts, what would you say?

*Barbara:* That you can really think some stupid and harmful stuff. I really have an appreciation for how off track my thinking can be.

*Therapist:* I think that is an accurate and important statement, to caution others not to trust their thoughts ... to caution them that one's thoughts can get off track, particularly in high-emotion situations. But what is a person to do; how should we treat our thoughts?

*Barbara:* I think people should know that thoughts can get off track and not to take them too seriously, but to realize they can be on track as well.

*Therapist:* How do you know which thoughts to attend to?

*Barbara:* Well, thoughts are only part of the picture. You really need to look at what is going on too, to try to see what is going on when your scary thoughts are not the only source of information.

*Therapist:* Was it easier not to pay so much attention to your thoughts after you realized how habitual your thoughts were, that you tended to scare yourselves in social situations with the same sort of phrases over and over again?

*Barbara:* Yeah, I was so "on automatic" with some of my thinking, it took a while to notice that what was going on was not fitting what I was saying to myself. I really liked getting the form of the thought "what if ...." When I heard myself saying "what if," I was probably trying to get into someone else's head to guess whether they liked me or thought I was smart or stupid.

*Therapist:* This is a terrific skill you are developing, and I hope you continue to hone this skill of not taking your thoughts too seriously, to realize that there are lots of different sources for what you may be thinking—sometimes a dispassionate appraisal of what is going on, sometimes an "old habit" thought that represents some of your historical fears about yourself, and sometimes more random concerns kicked off by characteristics of the situation.

It is further helpful to patients to remind them of the degree to which a more considered approach to their own cognitions is aided by the appropriate organization of well-defined goals for high-emotion situations. In treatment, objective goal setting was emphasized, as were practical examples of the impact of attentional sets on emotion. Accordingly, the therapist may continue his review of useful interventions by saying:

And please remember the value of keeping your own goals clear. When your goals were clear, it seemed easier for you to examine a situation to see if you were on track with the outcomes you wanted. Clear, *and reasonable*, goals make it easier to hone your attention and actions in the situation, and not to get too lost in all your thoughts. As you go forward acting as your own therapist, please remember the value of asking yourself, "What outcomes do I want in this situation, and how can I be specific enough and realistic enough in defining these goals so that I can see if I actually achieve my goals."

In addition to helping patients to abstract broader principles about the nature of cognitions from treatment, we believe it is important to also review the value of resilience in the face of emotions and everyday negative outcomes. The repeated exposure exercises were designed to give patients unambiguous opportunities to learn that negative emotions do not have to portend negative outcomes. Indeed, the ability to persist with goal-directed behaviors in the face of high emotion may be one of the general factors underlying therapy success in the treatment of affective disorders (for a discussion, see Barlow, Allen, & Choate, 2004). In our treatment, patients have the ability to learn that they meet their social goals despite anxiety, despite programmed errors, and despite programmed symptoms. They also learn that chronic avoidance patterns take their toll in terms of both distress and disability. As part of relapse prevention efforts, we encourage therapists to help patients abstract the full importance of these principles.

*Therapist:* If you were going to give advice to others who may pursue treatment for their SAD in the future, what would you say regarding avoidance?

*Barbara:* Oh man, when I think of the years that I spent hoping my social phobia would go away, while I continued to give myself breaks from social demands. I will tell you what I think of avoidance; I think it is a great way to lose control of your life. It feels good, it makes sense, but then it sucks your life away.

*Therapist:* But you know how hard it is not to avoid when your anxiety is high. What sort of advice would you give about how to persist despite anxiety?

*Barbara:* Well, anxiety is a lousy feeling, but I learned over time that it was just that—a feeling. And I never realized how much of my life I was organizing around this feeling. Once I had a chance to understand how my anxiety worked, how it did not always remain high, and that how I approached a situation made a difference, it was so much easier to keep my anxiety in perspective.

*Therapist:* And do you think you will be able to apply this skill to other emotions in the future?

*Barbara:* Huh! I had not thought of that. You mean like sadness?

## ADDITIONAL RELAPSE PREVENTION SKILLS

As applied across a wide range of additional disorders, relapse prevention interventions generally refer to the identification of higher risk situations for relapse, followed by review and rehearsal of appropriate ways to cope with these situations. In this way, these high-risk situations become a cue not just for old, maladaptive patterns, but for active coping as well. As part of this review, the return of SAD symptoms themselves should be considered. Anxiety in social situations could act as a cue to patients that "it is all coming back, treatment did not work." Active review of this process, including review of this specific cognition can help patients achieve one of the other classic goals of relapse prevention—the ability to interpret a downturn as a lapse rather than a relapse. A lapse can be defined as a temporary slip from a higher to a lower state of functioning or a temporary failure to apply skills. On the other had, a relapse refers to a true return to the previous maladaptive state of functioning. The goal of relapse prevention efforts is to help patients anticipate that lapses

TABLE 7.1    Relapse Prevention Checklist

A. Discuss and acknowledge improvement
  1. Identify areas in which the patient made improvement
  2. Discuss strategies that led to the improvement
  3. Emphasize the importance of continuously practicing the newly acquired skills
B. Work to expand therapy strategies for application to other problem areas
  1. Review the nature of cognitions and the importance of a considered perspective on the content of one's own thoughts
  2. Review the importance of goal setting to focus attention and cognitive interpretations on desired outcomes
  3. Review the importance of goal persistence in the presence of negative emotions
  4. Review the cost of chronic avoidance patterns to functioning
C. Identify and challenge unrealistic expectations
  1. Identify unrealistic expectations (e.g., "I will never have panic in a social situation again")
  2. Explain that it is less likely to experience social anxiety and avoidance if strategies are practiced in the future
  3. Explain that improvement has its ups and downs (e.g., due to stress); therefore, a person may reexperience periods of anxiety in the future
  4. Explain that effective coping strategies can lower the risk of experiencing downs (lapses)
D. Decatastrophize a lapse
  1. Explain that a person with a catastrophic way of thinking may view a lapse as a relapse; review countering strategies of catastrophic thoughts, such as "it is all coming back"
  2. Alternatively, a lapse can be viewed as an opportunity to practice or modify the skills that the patient learned during the treatment
E. Home practice
  1. Ask the patient to develop a list of potentially problematic situations, stressors, and risk situations that might cause a lapse and ask the patient to list possible coping strategies. A written record of these situations and alternatives can provide patients with an important reminder of coping strategies in the future.

may occur and to use these moments as occasions to review therapy skills and apply them. Helping patients to construct a written record of treatment benefits and strategies, as well as the high-risk situations where these strategies may be needed, provides a useful written record and reminder for patients to use at a point in the future when memory of session content may have faded (for the value of an approach such as this, see Öst, 1989). Table 7.1 provides an overview of some relapse prevention skills.

A clinical example of a sample therapist–patient dialogue around these relapse prevention strategies follows.

*Therapist:* I am very happy about your progress. You came a long way.

*Barbara:* I never would have thought in a million years that I would ever do the things you asked me to do (*laughs*). I can also clearly notice a change in how I am dealing with my anxiety and especially with my avoidance.

*Therapist:* Yes, you really changed tremendously. No doubt. I am very happy for you. But what would happen if one day your anxiety returns? What if you wake up one day and you felt for some odd reason anxious again in situations you felt totally comfortable before.

*Barbara:* Is this possible?

*Therapist:* I wouldn't say that it is impossible. I don't think it is very likely if you keep following our strategies. But it is not impossible. You have had your social anxiety for many decades and have been well engaged in some of the things that maintain social anxiety for all these years. We are comparing this to a few weeks of practicing new ways of dealing with your anxiety and avoidance. It is therefore possible that the old way of dealing with your anxiety and avoidance can sneak in again and you might feel that your social anxiety is back. How would this make you feel?

*Barbara:* I would never want to go back to the point where I was before.

*Therapist:* I completely understand why. What you just said points to an important distinction: having a little lapse when your anxiety is a bit worse again, and having a complete relapse where everything you had gained is lost and when you start at square one again. A lapse does not equal a relapse. You have made an amazing amount of gains and you will improve even further. However, improvement is never a straight line. Instead, it looks more like a stock that is doing really well. The improvement curve will show ups and downs, sometimes little blips, sometimes even bigger drops, but the general trend still goes in the positive direction toward further improvement. This is something you will have to keep in mind for the future. So when you wake up one day and you feel for some odd reason more anxious than the day or week before, it does not mean that you are back at square one and that all that you had gained is lost. Instead, you know what to do. What will you do?

*Barbara:* Exposing myself to whatever made me nervous again and making sure I don't think any stupid things again.

*Therapist:* Yes, you got the essence ... you will think back to what we have discussed. You will take a look at our model of social anxiety again that shows which thoughts, behaviors, and perceptions can maintain your anxiety and you will start thinking about the exercises, including exposure practices, to correct your faulty beliefs. And in case this does not seem to work and you think you might need a few refresher sessions, you will give me a call again. OK?

## CLOSING TREATMENT: ATTENDING TO WELL-BEING

Phobic disorders, by their nature, provide patients with chronic training in avoidance and vigilance to negative outcomes. Whereas the treatment program we described is designed to dismantle the factors that maintain SAD, this process is not necessarily commiserate with increasing joy. We believe that at the end of treatment, patients generally need help in recalibrating their social agendas to attend to potential joy and well-being in social situations. The following provides a sample of how the therapist might introduce this topic in group:

> As you are well aware, social anxiety disorder is often a long-standing condition. You have had the disorder for a very long time. This means that you have had years of training in being apprehensive about social situations, in planning on how to *get through* them, and in being vigilant to negative outcomes. In treatment, you have had a chance to dismantle these patterns and learned how to meet your goals for social situations and events. But this is only part of the picture. You have not had a chance in years to think about how social situations may actually bring you joy. Now is the time to restart this thinking, to help yourself think about what sort of goals you have for social pleasure, to have some time to daydream about nice social moments you might have and why they are valuable for you. This is the final part of the change away from social anxiety patterns; you develop the ability to focus on social pleasure. And just as you used to spend some time thinking about upcoming social situations with dread, it seems only right for you to start the process of thinking ahead about social situations that might provide you with pleasure. Take a moment to think about what moments you think you would like to have.

These sorts of interventions, aimed at helping patients focus on increasing well-being rather than reducing distress, are becoming more common in the empirical literature. Research to date suggests that interventions focused on enhancing well-being are associated with reductions in residual symptoms and protection from relapse (e.g., Fava, Rafanelli, Cazzaro, Conti, & Grandi, 1998; Fava et al., 2001, 2005).

## BOOSTER SESSIONS

If needed, patients can be provided booster sessions to help them reorganize skills and reorient themselves toward core interventions. Booster sessions should be organized around the two themes of understanding: what is going poorly and what is going well. We want to emphasize the importance of focusing the patient's attention on achievements to strengthen rather than just deficit areas for amelioration. In particular, the final session of regular treatment and booster sessions provide an excellent opportunity to continue well-being interventions, while also working to evaluate and intervene with recurring phobic issues. For this intervention, an assessment of areas of returning fear can be aided by using a modification of the exposure worksheet to identify areas of distress and avoidance (see Appendix L). Booster sessions can then be organized around an exposure practice in session, with follow-up self-exposures as indicated by the analysis of the patient's current patterns.

# References

Abramowitz, J. S., & Foa, E. B. (2000). Does comorbid major depressive disorder influence outcome of exposure and response prevention for OCD? *Behavior Therapy, 31,* 795–800.

Abramowitz, J. S., Franklin, M. E., Street, G. P., Kozak, M. J., & Foa, E. B. (2000). Effects of comorbid depression on response to treatment for obsessive-compulsive disorder. *Behavior Therapy, 31,* 517–528.

Abramson, L. Y., Seligman, M. E., & Teasdale, J. D. (1978). Learned helplessness in humans: Critique and reformulation. *Journal of Abnormal Psychology, 87,* 49–74.

Albano, A. M., & DiBartolo, P. M. (2007). *Cognitive-behavioral therapy for social phobia in adolescents: Stand up, speak out therapist guide (Treatments that work).* Oxford, UK: Oxford University Press.

Alden, L. E., & Bieling P. J. (1998). Interpersonal consequences of the pursuit of safety. *Behaviour Research and Therapy, 36,* 53–65.

Alden, L. E., Bieling, P. J., & Wallace, S. T. (1994). Perfectionism in an interpersonal context: A self-regulation analysis of dysphoria and social anxiety. *Cognitive Therapy and Research, 18,* 297–316.

Alden, L. E., & Capreol, M. J. (1993). Avoidant personality disorder: Interpersonal problems as predictors of treatment response. *Behavior Therapy, 24,* 357–376.

Alden, L. E., & Wallace, S. T. (1991). Social standards and social withdrawal. *Cognitive Therapy and Research, 15,* 85–100.

Alden, L. E., & Wallace, S. T. (1995). Social phobia and social appraisal in successful and unsuccessful social interactions. *Behaviour Research and Therapy, 33,* 497–505.

Alloy, L. B., Abramson, L. Y., & Viscusi, D. (1981). Induced mood and the illusion of control. *Journal of Personality and Social Psychology, 41,* 1129–1140.

American Psychiatric Association. (1980). *Diagnostic and statistical manual for mental disorders* (3rd ed.). Washington, D.C.: Author.

American Psychiatric Association. (1987). *Diagnostic and statistical manual for mental disorders* (3rd ed., rev.). Washington, D.C.: Author.

American Psychiatric Association. (1994). *Diagnostic and statistical manual for mental disorders* (4th ed.). Washington, D.C.: Author.

Amir, N., Foa, E. B. & Coles, M. E. (1998). Automatic activation and strategic avoidance of threat-relevant information in social phobia. *Journal of Abnormal Psychology, 107,* 285–290.

Baker, S. L., Heinrichs, N., Kim, H.-J., Hofmann, S. G. (2002). The Liebowitz Social Anxiety Scale as a self-report instrument: A preliminary psychometric analysis. *Behaviour Research and Therapy, 40,* 701–715.

Bakken, K., Landheim, A. S., & Vaglum, P. (2005). Substance-dependent patients with and without social anxiety disorder: Occurrence and clinical differences. A study of a consecutive sample of alcohol-dependent and poly-substance-dependent patients treated in two counties in Norway. *Drug and Alcohol Dependence, 80,* 321–328.

Baldwin, M. W., & Main, K. J. (2001). Social anxiety and the cued activation of relational knowledge. *Personality and Social Psychology Bulletin, 27,* 1637–1647.

Ball, S. G., Otto, M. W., Pollack, M. H., Ucello, R., & Rosenbaum, J. F. (1995). Differentiating social phobia and panic disorder: A test of core beliefs. *Cognitive Therapy and Research, 19,* 473–482.

Bandura, A. (1977). Self-efficacy: Toward a unifying theory of behavioral change. *Psychological Review, 84,* 191–215.

Bandura, A. (1983). Self-efficacy determinants of anticipated fears and calamities. *Journal of Personality and Social Psychology, 45,* 464–469.

Bandura, A. (1984). Recycling misconceptions of perceived self-efficacy. *Cognitive Therapy and Research, 8,* 231–255.

Bandura, A. (1986). *Social foundations of thought and action: A social cognitive theory.* Englewood Cliffs, NJ: Prentice-Hall.

Barber, J. P., & DeRubeis, R. J (1989). On second thought: Where the action is in cognitive therapy for depression. *Cognitive Therapy and Research, 13,* 441–457.

Barkow, J. H. (1989). *Darwin, sex, and status: Biological approaches to mind and culture.* Toronto: University of Toronto Press.

Barlow, D. H. (2002). *Anxiety and its disorders* (2nd ed.). New York: Guilford Press.

Barlow, D. H., Allen L. B., & Choate, M. L. (2004). Toward a unified treatment for emotional disorders. *Behavior Therapy, 35,* 205–230.

Barlow, D. H., & Craske, M. G. (2000). *Mastery of your anxiety and panic (MAP-3): Therapists guide for anxiety, panic, and agoraphobia* (3rd ed.). Oxford: Oxford University Press.

Basoğlu, M., Marks, I. M., Kilic, C., Brewin, C. R., & Swinson, R. P. (1994). Alprazolam and exposure for panic disorder with agoraphobia. Attributions of improvement to medication predicts subsequent relapse. *British Journal of Psychiatry, 164,* 652–659.

Battersby, M. (2000). Response to "Does reducing safety behaviours improve treatment response in patients with social phobia?" *Australian and New Zealand Journal of Psychiatry, 34,* 871–872.

Baumeister, R. F., & Leary, M. R. (1995). The need to belong: Desire for interpersonal attachments as a fundamental human motivation. *Psychological Bulletin, 117,* 497–529.

Baumeister, R. F., & Tice, D. M. (1990). Anxiety and social exclusion. *Journal of Social and Clinical Psychology, 9,* 165–195.

Baumgardner, A. H., & Brownlee, E. A. (1987). Strategic failure in social interaction: Evidence for expectancy disconfirmation processes. *Journal of Personality and Social Psychology, 52,* 525–535.

Beaumont, G. (1977). A large open multicenter trial of clomipramine in the management of phobic disorders. *Journal of International Medical Research, 5,* 116–129.

Beck, A. T. (1979). *Cognitive therapy of emotional disorders.* New York, NY: Meridian.

Beck, A. T. (1985). *Anxiety disorders as phobias: A cognitive perspective.* New York, NY: Basic Books.

Beck, A. T., & Emery, G. (1985). *Anxiety disorders and phobias: A cognitive perspective.* New York: Basic Books.

Beck, A. T., & Steer, G. (1987). *Manual for the revised Beck Depression Inventory.* San Antonio, TX: The Psychological Corporation.

Beidel, D. C., & Turner, S. M. (2007). *Shy children, phobic adults. Nature and treatment of social phobia* (2nd ed.). Washington, DC: American Psychological Association.

Beidel, D. C., Turner, S. M., & Morris, T. L. (1995). A new inventory to assess childhood social anxiety and phobia: The Social Phobia and Anxiety Inventory for Children. *Psychological Assessment, 7,* 73–79.

Benca, R., Matuzas, W., & Al-Sadir, J. (1986). Social phobia, MVP, and response to imipramine. *Journal of Clinical Psychopharmacology, 6,* 50–51.

Black, B., Uhde, T. W., & Tancer, M. E. (1992). Fluoxetine for the treatment of social phobia [Letter to editor]. *Journal of Clinical Psychopharmacology, 12,* 293–295.

Blomhoff, S., Haug, T. T., Hellstrom, K., Hohme, I., Humble, M., Madsbu, H. P., & Wold, J. E. (2001). Randomised controlled general practice trial of sertraline exposure therapy and combined treatment in generalised social phobia. *British Journal of Psychiatry, 179,* 23–30.

Bögels, S. M., Alberts, M., & De Jong, P. J. (1996). Self-consciousness, self-focused attention, blushing propensity, and fear of blushing. *Personality and Individual Differences, 21,* 573–581.

Bögels, S. M., & Mansell, W. (2004). Attention processes in the maintenance and treatment of social phobia: Hypervigilance, avoidance, and self-focused attention. *Clinical Psychology Review, 24,* 827–856.

Bögels, S. M., & Reith, W. (1999). Validity of two questionnaires to assess social fears: The Dutch Social Phobia and Anxiety Inventory and the Blushing, Trembling and Sweating Questionnaire. *Journal of Psychopathology and Behavioral Assessment, 21,* 51–66.

Boone, M. L., McNeil, D. W., Masia, C. L., Turk, C. L., Carter, L. E., Ries, B. J., & Lewin, M. R. (1999). Multimodal comparisons of social phobia subtypes and avoidant personality disorder. *Journal of Anxiety Disorders, 13,* 271–292.

Borkovec, T. D. (1978). Self-efficacy: Cause or reflection of behavioural change? *Advances in Behaviour Research and Therapy, 1,* 177–193.

Bouton, M. E., Mineka, S., & Barlow, D. H. (2000). A modern learning-theory perspective on the etiology of panic disorder. *Psychological Review, 108,* 4–32.

Broken heartthrob. (1999, May 17). *People,* 109–111.

Brown, E. J., Heimberg, R. G., & Juster, H. R. (1995). Social phobia subtype and avoidant personality disorder: Effect on severity of social phobia, impairment, and outcome of cognitive behavioral treatment. *Behavior Therapy, 26,* 467–489.

Brown, T. A., Campbell, L. A., Lehman, C. I., Grisham, J. R., & Mancill, R. B. (2001). Structural relationships among dimensions of the DSM-IV anxiety and mood disorders and dimensions of negative affect, positive affect, and autonomic arousal. *Journal of Abnormal Psychology, 110,* 585–599.

Bruce, S. E., Yonkers, K. A., Otto, M. W., Eisen, J. L., Weisberg, R. B., Pagano, M., Shea, M. T., & Keller, M. B. (2005). A 12-year prospective study of, generalized anxiety disorder, social phobia and panic disorder: Psychiatric comorbidity as predictors of recovery and recurrence. *American Journal of Psychiatry, 162,* 1179–1187.

Bruch, M. A., Mattia, J. I., Heimberg, R. G., & Holt, C. S. (1993). Cognitive specificity in social anxiety and depression: Supporting evidence and qualifications due to affective confounding. *Cognitive Therapy and Research, 17,* 1–21.

Buss, A. H. (1980). *Self-consciousness and social anxiety.* San Francisco: Freeman.

Butler, G. (1985). Exposure and treatment of social phobia: Some instructive difficulties. *Behaviour Research and Therapy, 23,* 651–657.

Butler, G., Cullington, A., Munby, M., Amies, P., & Gelder, M. (1984). Exposure and anxiety management in the treatment of social phobia. *Journal of Consulting and Clinical Psychology, 52,* 642–650.

Cervone, D., Kopp, D. A., Schaumann, L., & Scott, W. D. (1994). Mood, self-efficacy, and performance standards: Lower moods induce higher standards for performance. *Journal of Personality and Social Psychology, 67,* 499–512.

Chambless, D. L., Tran, G. Q., & Glass, C. R. (1997). Predictors of response to cognitive-behavioral group therapy for social phobia. *Journal of Anxiety Disorders, 11,* 221–240.

Clark, D. B., & Agras, W. S. (1991). The assessment and treatment of performance anxiety in musicians. *American Journal of Psychiatry, 148,* 598–605.

Clark, D. M. (2001). *A cognitive perspective on social phobia.* In W. R. Crozier & L. E. Alden (Eds.), *International handbook of social anxiety: Concepts, research and interventions relating to the self and shyness* (pp. 405–430). New York: John Wiley.

Clark, D. M., Ehlers, A., Hackmann, A., McManus, F., Fennell, M., Grey, N., Waddington, L., & Wild, J. (2006). Cognitive therapy versus exposure and applied relaxation in social phobia: A randomized controlled trial. *Journal of Consulting and Clinical Psychology, 74,* 568–578.

Clark, D. M., Ehlers, A., McManus, F., Hackmann, A., Fennell, M., Campbell, H., Flower, T., Davenport, C., & Louis, B. (2003). Cognitive therapy versus fluoxetine in generalized social phobia: A randomized placebo-controlled trial. *Journal of Consulting and Clinical Psychology, 71,* 1058–1067.

Clark, D. M., & McManus, F. (2002). Information processing in social phobia. *Biological Psychology, 51,* 92–100.

Clark, D. M., & Wells, A. (1995). A cognitive model of social phobia. In R. G. Heimberg, M. R. Liebowitz, D. A. Hope, & F. R. Schneier (Eds.), *Social phobia: Diagnosis, assessment, and treatment* (pp. 69–93). New York: Guilford Press.

Clark, J. V., & Arkowitz, H. (1975). Social anxiety and self-evaluation of interpersonal performance. *Psychological Report, 36,* 211–221.

Cloitre, M., Cancienne, J., Heimberg, R. G., Holt, C. S. & Liebowitz, M. R. (1995). Memory bias does not generalize across anxiety disorders. *Behaviour Research and Therapy, 33,* 305–307.

Cloitre, M., Heimberg, R. H., Liebowitz, M. R., & Gitow, A. (1992). Perceptions of control in panic disorder and social phobia. *Cognitive Therapy and Research, 16,* 569–577.

Craske, M. G. (1991). Phobic fear and panic attacks: The same emotional states triggered by different cues? *Clinical Psychology Review, 2,* 599–620.

Davidson, J. R. T., Foa, E. B., Huppert, J. D., Keefe, F., Franklin, M., Compton, J., Zhao, N., Connor, K., Lynch, T. R., & Kishore, G. (2004). Fluoxetine, comprehensive cognitive behavioral therapy, and placebo in generalized social phobia. *Archives of General Psychiatry, 61,* 1005–1013.

Davidson, J. R. T., Hughes, D. L., George, L. K., & Blazer, D. G. (1993). The epidemiology of social phobia: Findings from the Duke Epidemiological Catchment Area Study. *Psychological Medicine, 23,* 709–718.

Davidson, J. R. T., Potts, N. L. S., Richichi, E. A., Ford, S. M., Krishnan, R. R., Smith, R., & Wilson, W. (1991). The Brief Social Phobia Scale. *Journal of Clinical Psychiatry, 52,* 48–51.

Davis, M., Myers, K. M., Ressler, K. J., & Rothbaum, B. O. (2005). Facilitation of extinction of conditioned fear by D-cycloserine: Implications for psychotherapy. *Current Directions in Psychological Science, 14,* 214–219.

Davis, M., Ressler, K., Rothbaum, B.O., & Richardson, R. (2006): Effects of D-cycloserine on extinction: Translation from preclinical to clinical work. *Biological Psychiatry, 60,* 369–375.

Dimberg, U. (1982). Facial reactions to facial expressions. *Psychophysiology, 19,* 643–647.

Dimberg, U., & Öhman, A. (1983). The effects of directional facial cues on electrodermal conditioning to facial stimuli. *Psychophysiology, 20,* 160–167.

Dreessen, L., & Arntz, A. (1998). The impact of personality disorders on treatment outcome of anxiety disorders: Best-evidence synthesis. *Behaviour Research and Therapy, 36,* 483–504.

Edelman, R. E., & Chambless, D. L. (1995). Adherence during sessions and homework in cognitive-behavioral group treatment of social phobia. *Behaviour Research and Therapy, 33,* 573–577.

Ehlers, A., Hofmann, S. G., Herda, C. A., & Roth, W. T. (1994). Clinical characteristics of driving phobia. *Journal of Anxiety Disorders, 8,* 323–339.

Eisenthal, S., Emery, R., Lazare, A., & Udin, H. (1979). "Adherence" and the negotiated approach to patienthood. *Archives of General Psychiatry, 36,* 393–398.

Emmanuel, N. P., Johnson, M., & Villareal, G. (1998). *Imipramine in the treatment of social phobia, a double-blind study.* Poster presented at the 36th Meeting of the American College of Neuropsychopharmacology, Waikoloa, Hawaii.

Emmanuel, N. P., Lydiard, R. B., & Ballenger, J. C. (1991). Treatment of social phobia with bupropion. *Journal of Clinical Psychopharmacology, 11,* 276–277.

Eng, W., Heimberg, R. G., Coles, M. E., Schneier, F. R., & Liebowitz, M. R. (2000). An empirical approach to subtype identification in individuals with social phobia. *Psychological Medicine, 30,* 1345–1357.

Erwin, B. A., Heimberg, R. G., Juster, H. R., & Mindlin, M. (2002). Comorbid anxiety and mood disorders among persons with social anxiety disorder. *Behaviour Research and Therapy, 40,* 19–35.

Evans, M. D., & Hollon, S. D. (1988). Patterns of personal and causal inference: Implications for cognitive therapy of depression. In L. B. Alloy (Ed.), *Cognitive processes in depression* (pp. 344–377). New York: Guilford Press.

Fava, G. A., Rafanelli, C., Cazzaro, M., Conti, S., Grandi, S. (1998). Well-being therapy. A novel psychotherapeutic approach for residual symptoms of affective disorders. *Psychological Medicine, 28,* 475–480.

Fava, G. A., Rafanelli, C., Ottolini, F., Ruini, C., Cazzaro, M., & Grandi, S. (2001). Psychological well-being and residual symptoms in remitted patients with panic disorder and agoraphobia. *Journal of Affective Disorders, 65,*185–190.

Fava, G. A., Ruini, C., Rafanelli, C., Finos, L., Salmaso, L., Mangelli, L., & Sirigatti, S. (2005). Well-being therapy of generalized anxiety disorder. *Psychotherapy and Psychosomatics, 74,* 26–30.

Feske, U., & Chambless, D. L. (1995). Cognitive behavioral versus exposure only treatment for social phobia: A meta-analysis. *Behavior Therapy, 26,* 695–720.

Feske, U., Perry, K. J., Chambless, D. L., Renneberg, B., & Goldstein, A. J. (1996). Avoidant personality disorder as predictor for severity and treatment outcome among generalized social phobics. *Journal of Personality Disorder, 10,* 174–184.

Foa, E. B. (1979). Failure in treating obsessive-compulsives. *Behaviour Research and Therapy, 17,* 169–176.

Foa, E. B., Franklin, M. E., & Moser, J. (2002). Context in the clinic: How well do cognitive-behavioral therapies and medications work in combination? *Biological Psychiatry, 52,* 987–997.

Foa, E. B., Franklin, M. E., Perry, K. J., & Herbert, J. D. (1996). Cognitive biases in generalized social phobia. *Journal of Abnormal Psychology, 105,* 433–439.

Foa, E. B., & Kozak, M. J. (1986). Emotional processing of fear: Exposure to corrective information. *Psychological Bulletin, 99,* 20–35.

Furmark, T. (2002). Social phobia: Overview of community surveys. *Acta Psychiatrica Scandinavica, 105,* 84–93.

Fyer, A. J., Mannuzza, S., Chapman, T. F., Liebowitz, M. R., & Klein, D. F. (1993). A direct interview family study of social phobia. *Archives of General Psychiatry, 50,* 286–293.

Gaynes, B. N., Magruder, K. M., Burns, B. J., Wagner, H. R., Yarnall, K. S., & Broadhead, W. E. (1999). Does a coexisting anxiety disorder predict persistence of depressive illness in primary care patients with major depression? *General Hospital Psychiatry, 21,* 158–167.

Geer, J. H., Davison, G. C., & Gatchel, R. I. (1970). Reduction of stress in humans through nonverdical perceived control of aversive stimulation. *Journal of Personality and Social Psychology, 16,* 731–738.

Gelernter, C. S., Stein, M. B., Tancer, M. E., & Uhde, T. W. (1992). An examination of syndromal validity and diagnostic subtypes in social phobia and panic disorder. *Journal of Clinical Psychiatry, 53,* 23–27.

Gelernter, C. S., Uhde, T. W., Cimbolic, P., Arnkoff, D. B., Vittone, B. J., Tancer, M. E., & Bartko, J. J. (1991). Cognitive-behavioral and pharmacological treatment for social phobia: A controlled study. *Archives of General Psychiatry, 48,* 938–945.

Gilbert, P. (2001). Evolution and social anxiety: The role of attraction, social competition, and social hierarchies. *The Psychiatric Clinics of North America, 24,* 723–751.

Glasgow, R. E., & Arkowitz, H. (1975). The behavioral assessment of male and female social competence in dyadic interactions. *Behavior Therapy, 6,* 488–498.

Glass, C. R., Merluzzi, T. V., Biever, J. L., & Larsen, K. H. (1982). Cognitive assessment of social anxiety: Development and validation of a self-statement questionnaire. *Cognitive Therapy and Research, 6,* 37–55.

Glass, D. C., & Singer, J. E. (1970). *Urban stress.* New York: Academic Press.

Gollwitzer, P. M., & Moskowitz, G. B. (1996). *Goal effects on action and cognition.* In E. T. Higgins & A. W. Kruglanski (Eds.), *Social psychology: Handbook of basic principles* (pp. 361–399). New York: Guilford Press.

Gordon, A. J., & Zrull, M. (1991). Social networks and recovery: One year after inpatient treatment. *Journal of Substance Abuse Treatment, 8,* 143–152.

Gorman, J. M., Liebowitz, M. R., Fyer, A. J., Campeas, R., & Klein, D. F. (1985). Treatment of social phobia with atenolol. *Journal of Clinical Psychopharmacology, 5,* 298–301.

Gottschalk, L. A., Stone, W. N., & Gleser, C. G. (1974). Peripheral versus central mechanisms accounting for antianxiety effects of propranolol. *British Journal of Psychiatry, 36,* 47–51.

Gould, R. A., Buckminster, S., Pollack, M. H., Otto, M. W., & Yap, L. (1997). Cognitive-behavioral and pharmacological treatment for social phobia: A meta-analysis. *Clinical Psychology: Science and Practice, 4,* 291–306.

Guy, W. (1976). *Early Clinical Drug Evaluation Unit (ECDEU) assessment manual for psychopharmacology* (Rev. ed.). Publication no. 76-338. Rockville, MD: National Institute of Mental Health; Department of Health, Education and Welfare.

Hackmann, A., Clark, D. M., & McManus, F. (2000). Recurrent images and early memories in social phobia. *Behaviour Research and Therapy, 38,* 601–610.

Hackmann, A., Surawy, C., & Clark, D. M. (1998). Seeing yourself through others' eyes: A study of spontaneously occurring images in social phobia. *Behavioural and Cognitive Psychotherapy, 26,* 3–12.

Halford, K., & Foddy, M. (1982). Cognitive and social skills correlates of social anxiety. *British Journal of Clinical Psychology, 21,* 17-28.

Harvey, A. G., Clark, D. M., Ehlers, A., & Rapee, R. M. (2000). Social anxiety and self-impression: Cognitive preparation enhances the beneficial effects of video feedback following a stressful social task. *Behaviour Research and Therapy, 38,* 1183–1192.

Haug, T. T., Blomhoff, S., Hellström, K., Holme, I., Humble, M., Madsbu, H. P., & Wold, J. E. (2003). Exposure therapy and sertraline in social phobia: 1-year follow-up of a randomised controlled trial. *British Journal of Psychiatry, 182,* 312–318.

Hayes, S. C., Strosahl, K. D., & Wilson, K. G. (1999). Acceptance and commitment therapy: An experimental approach to behavioral change. New York, NY: Guilford Press.

Heimberg, R. G. (1996). Social phobia, avoidant personality disorder and the multiaxial conceptualization of interpersonal anxiety. In P. M. Salkovskis (Ed.), *Trends in cognitive and behavioural therapies* (pp. 43–61). New York: John Wiley & Sons.

Heimberg, R. G., & Becker, R. E. (1991). *Cognitive behavioral treatment of social phobia in a group setting: A treatment manual.* Unpublished treatment manual, Center for Stress and Anxiety Disorders, State University of New York at Albany.

Heimberg, R. G., & Becker, R. E. (2002). *Cognitive behavioral group therapy for social phobia: Basic mechanisms and clinical strategies.* New York: Guilford Press.

Heimberg, R. G., Becker, R. E., Goldfinger, K., & Vermilyea, J. A. (1985). Treatment of social phobia by exposure, cognitive restructuring, and homework assignments. *Journal of Nervous and Mental Disease, 173,* 236–245.

Heimberg, R. G., Dodge, C. S., Hope, D. A., Kennedy, C. R., Zollo, L. J., & Becker, R. E. (1990). Cognitive behavioral treatment for social phobia: Comparison with a credible placebo control. *Cognitive Therapy and Research, 14,* 1–23.

Heimberg, R. G., Holt, C. S., Schneier, F. R., Spitzer, R. L., & Liebowitz, M. R. (1993). The issue of subtypes in the diagnosis of social phobia. *Journal of Anxiety Disorders, 7,* 249–269.

Heimberg, R. G., Hope, D. A., Dodge, C. S., & Becker, R. E. (1990). DSM-III-R subtypes of social phobia: Comparison of generalized social phobics and public speaking phobics. *The Journal of Nervous and Mental Disease, 176,* 172–179.

Heimberg, R. G., & Juster, H. R. (1995). Cognitive-behavioral treatments: Literature review. In R. G. Heimberg, M. R. Liebowitz, D. A. Hope, & F. R. Schneier (Eds.), *Social phobia: Diagnosis, assessment, and treatment* (pp. 261–309). New York: Guilford Press.

Heimberg, R. G., Liebowitz, M. R., Hope, D. A., Schneier, F. R., Holt, C. S., Welkowitz, L. A., Juster, H. R., Campeas, R., Bruch, M. A., Cloitre, M., Falloon, B., & Klein, D. F. (1998). Cognitive behavioral group therapy vs. phenelzine therapy for social phobia. *Archives of General Psychiatry, 55,* 1133–1141.

Heimberg, R. G., Salzman, D. G., Holt, C. S., & Blendell, K. A. (1993). Cognitive behavioral group treatment for social phobia: Effectiveness at five-year follow-up. *Cognitive Therapy and Research, 17,* 325–339.

Heinrichs, N., & Hofmann, S. G. (2001). Information processing in social phobia: A critical review. *Clinical Psychology Review, 21,* 751–770.

Heinrichs, N., Rapee, R. M., Alden, L. A., Bögels, S., Hofmann, S. G., Oh, K. J., & Sakano, Y. (2006). Cultural differences in perceived social norms and social anxiety. *Behaviour Research and Therapy, 4,* 1187–1197.

Heldt, E., Manfro, G. G., Kipper, L., Blaya, C., Isolan, L., & Otto, M. W. (2006). One-year follow-up of pharmacotherapy-resistant patients with panic disorder treated with cognitive behavioral therapy: Outcome and predictors of remission. *Behaviour Research and Therapy, 44,* 657–665.

Herbert, J. D., Bellack, A. S., Hope, D. A., & Mueser, K. T. (1992). Scoring the Social Phobia and Anxiety Inventory: Reply to Beidel and Turner. *Journal of Psychopathology and Behavioral Assessment, 14,* 381–383.

Herbert, J. D., Hope, D. A., & Bellack, A. S. (1992). Validity of the distinction between generalized social phobia and avoidant personality disorder. *Journal of Abnormal Psychology, 101,* 332–339.

Hiemisch, A., Ehlers, A., & Westermann, R. (2002). Mindsets in social anxiety: A new look at selective information processing. *Journal of Behavior Therapy and Experimental Psychiatry, 33,* 103–114.

Higgins, E. T. (1987). Self-discrepancy: A theory relating self and affect. *Psychological Review, 94,* 319–340.

Himle, J. A., Crystal, D., Curtis, G. C., & Fluent, T. E. (1991). Mode of onset of simple phobia subtypes: Further evidence of heterogeneity. *Psychiatry Research, 36,* 37–43.

Hirsch, C. R., & Clark, D. M. (2004). Information-processing bias in social phobia. *Clinical Psychology Review, 24,* 799–825.

Hirsch, C. R., Clark, D. M., Matthews, A., & Williams, R. (2003). Self-images play a causal role in social phobia. *Behaviour Research and Therapy, 41,* 909–921.

Hirsch, C. R., & Matthews, A. (2000). Impaired positive inferential bias in social phobia. *Journal of Abnormal Psychology, 109,* 705–712.

Hofmann, S. G. (2007). Cognitive factors that maintain social anxiety disorder: A comprehensive model and its treatment implications. *Cognitive Behaviour Therapy, 36,* 195–209.

Hofmann, S. G. (in press-a). Cognitive processes during fear acquisition and extinction in animals and humans: Implications for exposure therapy of anxiety disorders. *Clinical Psychology Review.*

Hofmann, S. G. (in press-b). Treating avoidant personality disorder: The case of Paul. *Journal of Cognitive Psychotherapy.*

Hofmann, S. G. (2000a). Self-focused attention before and after treatment of social phobia. *Behaviour Research and Therapy, 38,* 717–725.

Hofmann, S. G. (2000b). Treatment of social phobia: Potential mediators and moderators. *Clinical Psychology: Science and Practice, 7,* 5–18.

Hofmann, S. G. (2004). Cognitive mediation of treatment change in social phobia. *Journal of Consulting and Clinical Psychology, 72,* 392–399.

Hofmann, S. G. (2005). Perception of control over anxiety mediates the relation between catastrophic thinking and social anxiety in social phobia. *Behaviour Research and Therapy, 43,* 885–895.

Hofmann, S. G. (2006). The emotional consequences of social pragmatism: The psychophysiological consequences of self-monitoring. *Biological Psychology, 73,* 169–173.

Hofmann, S. G. (2007). Enhancing exposure-based therapy from a translational research perspective. *Behaviour Research and Therapy, 45,* 1987–2001.

Hofmann, S. G., & Barlow, D. H. (2002). Social phobia (social anxiety disorder). In D. H. Barlow (Ed.), *Anxiety and its disorders: The nature and treatment of anxiety and panic* (2nd ed., pp. 454–476). New York: Guilford Press.

Hofmann, S. G., & Bitran, S. (2007). Sensory-processing sensitivity in social anxiety disorder: Relationship to harm avoidance and diagnostic subtypes. *Journal of Anxiety Disorders, 21,* 944–954.

Hofmann, S. G., & DiBartolo, P. M. (2000). An instrument to assess self-statements during public speaking: Scale development and preliminary psychometric properties. *Behavior Therapy, 31,* 499–515.

Hofmann, S. G., & DiBartolo, P. M. (Eds.). (2001). *From social anxiety to social phobia: Multiple perspectives.* Needham Heights, MA: Allyn & Bacon.

Hofmann, S. G., DiBartolo, P. M., Holaway, R. M., & Heimberg, R. G. (2004). Scoring error of social avoidance and distress scale and its psychometric implications. *Depression and Anxiety, 19,* 197–198.

Hofmann, S. G., Ehlers, A., & Roth, W. T. (1995). Conditioning theory: A model for the etiology of public speaking anxiety? *Behaviour Research and Therapy, 33,* 567–571.

Hofmann, S. G., Gerlach, A., Wender, A., & Roth, W. T. (1997). Speech disturbances and gaze behavior during public speaking in subtypes of social phobia. *Journal of Anxiety Disorders, 11,* 573–585.

Hofmann, S. G., & Heinrichs, N. (2003). Differential effect of mirror manipulation on self-perception in social phobia subtypes. *Cognitive Therapy and Research, 27,* 131–142.

Hofmann, S. G., Heinrichs, N., & Moscovitch, D. A. (2004). The nature and expression of social phobia: Toward a new classification. *Clinical Psychology Review, 24,* 769–797.

Hofmann, S. G., & Kim, H.-J. (2006). Anxiety goes under the skin: Behavioral inhibition, anxiety, and autonomic arousal in speech anxious males. *Personality and Individual Differences, 40,* 1441–1451.

Hofmann, S. G., & Loh, R. (2006). The Tridimensional Personality Questionnaire: Changes during psychological treatment of social phobia. *Journal of Psychiatric Research, 40,* 214–220.

Hofmann S. G., Meuret, A. E., Smits, J. A. J., Simon, N. M., Pollack, M. H., Eisenmenger, K., Shiekh, M., & Otto, M. W. (2006). Augmentation of exposure therapy for social anxiety disorder with D-cycloserine. *Archives of General Psychiatry, 63,* 298–304.

Hofmann, S. G., Moscovitch, D. A., & Kim, H.-J. (2006). Autonomic correlates of social anxiety and embarrassment in shy and non-shy individuals. *International Journal of Psychophysiology, 61,* 134–142.

Hofmann, S. G., Moscovitch, D. A., Kim, H.-J., & Taylor, A. N. (2004). Changes in self-perception during treatment of social phobia. *Journal of Consulting and Clinical Psychology, 72,* 588–596.

Hofmann, S. G., Newman, M. G. Becker, E., Taylor, C. B., & Roth, W. T. (1995). Social phobia with and without avoidant personality disorder: Preliminary behavior therapy outcome findings. *Journal of Anxiety Disorders, 9,* 427–438.

Hofmann, S. G., Newman, M. G., Ehlers, A., & Roth, W. T. (1995). Psychophysiological differences between subtypes of social phobia. *Journal of Abnormal Psychology, 104,* 224–231.

Hofmann, S. G., & Roth, W. T. (1996). Issues related to social anxiety among controls in social phobia research. *Behavior Therapy, 27,* 79–91.

Hofmann, S. G., & Scepkowski, L. A. (2006). Social self-reappraisal therapy for social phobia: Preliminary findings. *Journal of Cognitive Psychotherapy, 20,* 45–57.

Hofmann, S. G., Schulz, S. M., Meuret, A. M., Moscovitch, D. M., & Suvak, M. (2006). Sudden gains during therapy of social phobia. *Journal of Consulting and Clinical Psychology, 74,* 687–697.

Hofmann, S. G., & Suvak, M. (2006). Treatment attrition during group therapy for social phobia. *Journal of Anxiety Disorders, 20,* 961–972.

Hollon, S. D., Evans, M. D., & DeRubeis, R. J. (1990). Cognitive mediation of relapse prevention following treatment for depression: Implications of differential risk. In R. E. Ingram (Ed.), *Contemporary psychological approaches to depression* (pp. 117–136). New York: Plenum Press.

Holt, C. S., Heimberg, R. G., & Hope, D. A. (1992). Avoidant personality disorder and the generalized subtype of social phobia. *Journal of Abnormal Psychology, 101,* 318–325.

Holt, C. S., Heimberg, R. G., Hope, D. A., & Liebowitz, M. R. (1992). Situational domains of social phobia. *Journal of Anxiety Disorders, 6,* 63–77.

Hook, J. N., & Valentiner, D. P. (2002). Are specific and generalized social phobias qualitatively distinct? *Clinical Psychology: Science and Practice, 9*, 379–395.

Hope, D. A., Heimberg, R. G., & Bruch, M. A. (1995). Dismantling cognitive-behavioral group therapy for social phobia. *Behaviour Research and Therapy, 33*, 637–650.

Hope, D. A., Herbert, J. D., & White, C. (1995). Diagnostic subtype, avoidant personality disorder, and efficacy of cognitive-behavioral group therapy for social phobia. *Cognitive Therapy and Research, 19*, 399–417.

Hopko, D. R., Lejuez, C. W., & Hopko, S. D. (2004). Behavioral activation as an intervention for co-existent depressive and anxiety symptoms. *Clinical Case Studies, 3*, 37–48.

Hopko, D. R., Lejuez, C. W., Ruggiero, K. J., & Eifert G. H. (2003). Contemporary behavioral activation treatments for depression: Procedures, principles, and progress. *Clinical Psychology Review, 23*, 699–717.

Horwarth, E., Wolk, S. I., Goldrein, R. B., Wickramaratne, P., Sobin, C., Adams, P., Lish, J. D., & Weissman, M. M. (1995). Is the comorbidity between social phobia and panic disorder due to familial cotransmission or other factors? *Archives of General Psychiatry, 52*, 574–582.

Juster, H. R., Heimberg, R., & Holt, C. S. (1996). Social phobia: Diagnostic issues and review of cognitive-behavioral treatment strategies. In M. Hersen, R. Eisler, & P. Miller (Eds.), *Progress in behavior modification.* Vol. 30 (pp. 74–98). Pacific Grove, CA: Brooks/Cole.

Kagan, J., Reznick, J. S., & Snidman, N. (1988). Biological bases of childhood shyness. *Science, 240*, 167–171.

Kashdan, T. B., & Hofmann, S. G. (in press). The high novelty seeking subtype of generalized social anxiety disorder. *Depression and Anxiety.*

Katzelnick, D. J., Kobak, K. A., Greist, J. H., Jefferson, J. W., Mantle, J. M., & Serlin, R. C. (1995). Sertraline for social phobia: A double-blind, placebo-controlled crossover study. *American Journal of Psychiatry, 152*, 1368–1371.

Kendler, K. S., Neale, M. C., Kessler, R. C., Heath, A. C., & Eaves, L. J. (1992). The genetic epidemiology of phobias in women: The interrelations of agoraphobia, social phobia, situational phobia, and simple phobia. *Archives of General Psychiatry, 49*, 273–281.

Kessler, R. C., Berglund, P., Demler, O., Jin, R., & Walters, E. (2005). Lifetime prevalence and age-of-onset distributions of DSM-IV disorders in the National Comorbidity Survey—Replication. *Archives of General Psychiatry, 62*, 593–602.

Kessler, R. C., Stein, M. B., & Berglund, P. (1998). Social phobia subtypes in the National Comorbidity Survey. *American Journal of Psychiatry, 155,* 613–619.

Kim, H-Y., Lundh, L.-G., & Harvey, A. G. (2002). The enhancement of video feedback by cognitive preparation in the treatment of social anxiety. *Journal of Behavior Therapy and Experimental Psychiatry, 33,* 19–37.

Kollman, D. M., Brown, T. A., Liverant, G. I., & Hofmann, S. G. (2006). A taxometric investigation of the latent structure of social anxiety disorder in outpatients with anxiety and mood disorders. *Depression and Anxiety, 23,* 190–199.

Kushner, M. G., Kim, S. W., Donahue, C., Thuras, P., Adson, D., Kotlyar, M., McCabe, J., Peterson, J., Foa, E. B. (2007). D-cycloserine augmented exposure therapy for obsessive-compulsive disorder. *Biological Psychiatry, 62,* 835–838.

Kushner, M. G., Sher, K. J., & Beitman, B. D. (1990). The relation between alcohol problems and the anxiety disorders. *American Journal of Psychiatry, 147,* 685–695.

Lam, D. H., Watkins, E. R., Hayward, P., Bright, J., Wright, K., Kerr, N., Parr-Davis, G., & Sham, P. (2003). A randomized controlled study of cognitive therapy of relapse prevention for bipolar affective disorder: Outcome of the first year. *Archives of General Psychiatry, 60,* 145–152.

Lang, P. J. (1985). The cognitive psychophysiology of emotion: Fear and anxiety. In A. H. Tuma & J. D. Maser (Eds.), *Anxiety and the anxiety disorders* (pp. 131–170). Hillsdale, NJ: Erlbaum.

Leary, M. R. (1983). A brief version of the Fear of Negative Evaluation Scale. *Personality and Social Psychology Bulletin, 9,* 371–375.

Leary, M. R. (2001). Social anxiety as an early warning system: A refinement and extension of the self-presentation theory. In S. G. Hofmann & P. M. DiBartolo (Eds.), *From social anxiety to social phobia: Multiple perspectives* (pp. 321–334). Boston: Allyn & Bacon.

Leung, A. W., & Heimberg, R. H. (1996). Homework compliance, perceptions of control, and outcome of cognitive-behavioral treatment of social phobia. *Behaviour Research and Therapy, 34,* 423–432.

Levin, A. P., Saoud, J. B., Strauman, T. J., Gorman, J. M., Fyer, A. J., Crawford, R., & Liebowitz, M. R. (1993). Responses of "generalized" and "discrete" social phobics during public speaking. *Journal of Anxiety Disorders, 7,* 202–221.

Liebowitz, M. R. (1987). Social phobia. *Modern Problems in Pharmacopsychiatry, 22,* 141–173.

Liebowitz, M. R., Gorman, J. M., Fyer, A. J., & Klein, D. F. (1985). Social phobia: Review of a neglected anxiety disorder. *Archives of General Psychiatry, 42,* 729–736.

Liebowitz, M. R., Schneier, F., Campeas, R., Hollander, E., Hatterer, J., Fyer, A., Gorman, J., Papp, L., Davies, S., Gully, R., & Klein, D. F. (1992). Phenelzine vs. atenolol in social phobia: A placebo-controlled comparison. *Archives of General Psychiatry, 49,* 290–300.

Lincoln, T. M., & Rief, W. (2004). How much do sample characteristics affect the effect size? An investigation of studies testing the treatment effects for social phobia. *Journal of Anxiety Disorders, 18,* 515–529.

Lucock, M. P., & Salkovskis, P. M. (1988). Cognitive factors in social anxiety and its treatment. *Behaviour Research and Therapy, 26,* 297–302.

Lundh, L.-G., & Öst, L.-G. (1996). Recognition bias for critical faces in social phobics. *Behaviour Research and Therapy, 34,* 787–794.

Lundh, L.-G., & Sperling, M. (2002). Social anxiety and the post-event processing of socially distressing events. *Cognitive Behaviour Therapy, 31,* 129–134.

Mancini, C., van Ameringen, M., Szatmari, P., Fugere, C., & Boyle, M. (1996). A high-risk pilot study of the children of adults with social phobia. *Journal of the American Academy of Child and Adolescent Psychiatry, 35,* 1511–1517.

Mannuzza, S., Schneier, F. R., Chapman, T. F., Liebowitz, M. R., Klein, D. F., & Fyer, A. J. (1995). Generalized social phobia. Reliability and validity. *Archives of General Psychiatry, 52,* 230–237.

Mansell, W. & Clark, D. M. (1999). How do I appear to others? Social anxiety and processing of the observable self. *Behaviour Research and Therapy, 37,* 419–434.

Marks, I. M. (1987). *Fears, phobias, and rituals: Panic, anxiety, and their disorders.* New York: Oxford University Press.

Marks, I. M., & Gelder, M. G. (1966). Different ages of onset in varieties of phobias. *American Journal of Psychiatry, 123,* 218–221.

Masia, C. L., & Morris, T. L. (1998). Parental factors associated with social anxiety: Methodological limitations and suggestions for integrated behavioral research. *Clinical Psychology: Science and Practice, 5,* 211–228.

Mattick, R. P., & Clarke, J. C. (1998). Development and validation of measures of social phobia scrutiny fear and social interaction anxiety. *Behaviour Research and Therapy, 36,* 455–470.

Mattick, R. P., & Peters, L. (1988). Treatment of severe social phobia: Effects of guided exposure with and without cognitive restructuring. *Journal of Consulting and Clinical Psychology, 56,* 251–260.

McManus, F., Clark, D. M., & Hackmann, A. (2000). Specificity of cognitive biases in social phobia and their role in recovery. *Behavioural and Cognitive Psychotherapy, 28,* 201–209.

McNally, R. J., & Steketee, G. S. (1985). The etiology and maintenance of severe animal phobias. *Behaviour Research and Therapy, 23,* 431–435.

McNeil, D. W. (2001). Terminology and evolution of the constructs. In S. G. Hofmann & P. M. DiBartolo (Eds.), *From social anxiety to social phobia: Multiple perspectives* (pp. 8–19). Needham Heights, MA: Allyn & Bacon.

McNeil, D. W., Ries, B. J., Taylor, L. J., Boone, M. L., Carter, L. E., Turk, C. L., & Lewin, M. R. (1995). Comparison of social phobia subtypes using Stroop tests. *Journal of Anxiety Disorders, 9,* 47–57.

Mellings, M. B., & Alden, L. E. (2000). Cognitive processes in social anxiety: The effects of self-focus, rumination, and anticipatory processing. *Behaviour Research and Therapy, 38,* 243–257.

Merckelbach, H., van Hout, W., van den Hout, M. A., & Mersch, P. P. (1989). Psychophysiological and subjective reactions of social phobics and normals to facial stimuli. *Behaviour Research and Therapy, 27,* 289–294.

Mersch, P. P. A., Emmelkamp, P. M. G., Bögels, S. M., & van der Sleen, J. (1989). Social phobia: Individual response patterns and the effects of behavioral and cognitive interventions. *Behaviour Research and Therapy, 27,* 421–434.

Mersch, P. P. A., Emmelkamp, P. M. G., & Lips, C. (1991). Social phobia: Individual response patterns and the long-term effects of behavioral and cognitive interventions: A follow-up study. *Behaviour Research and Therapy, 29,* 357–362.

Mersch, P. P. A., Jansen, M. A., & Arntz, A. (1995). Social phobia and personality disorder: Severity of complaint and treatment effectiveness. *Journal of Personality Disorders, 9,* 143–159.

Mick, M. A., & Telch, M. J. (1998). Social anxiety and history of behavioral inhibition in young adults. *Journal of Anxiety Disorders, 12,* 1–20.

Miklowitz, D. J., Otto, M. W., Frank, E., Reilly-Harrington, N. A., Wisniewski, S. R., Kogan, J. N., Nierenberg, A. A., Calabrese, J. R., Marangell, L. B., Gyulai, L., Araga, M., Gonzalez, J. M., Shirley, E. R., Thase, M. E., & Sachs, G. S. (2007). Psychosocial treatments for bipolar depression: A 1-year randomized trial from the Systematic Treatment Enhancement Program. *Archives of General Psychiatry, 64,* 419–426.

Mills, I., & Salkovskis, P. (1988). Mood and habituation to phobic stimuli. *Behaviour Research and Therapy, 26,* 435–439.

Mineka, S. (1985). Animal models of anxiety disorders: Their usefulness and limitations. In A. H. Tuma & J. D. Maser (Eds.), *Anxiety and the anxiety disorders* (pp. 199–244). Hillsdale, NJ: Erlbaum.

Morgan, H., & Raffle, C. (1999). Does reducing safety behaviours improve treatment response in patients with social phobia? *Australian and New Zealand Journal of Psychiatry, 33*, 503–510.

Moscovitch, D. A., Hofmann, S. G., Suvak, M., & In-Albon, T. (2005). Mediation of changes in anxiety and depression during treatment for social phobia. *Journal of Consulting and Clinical Psychology, 75*, 945–952.

Moutier, C. Y., & Stein, M. B. (1999). The history, epidemiology, and differential diagnosis of social anxiety disorder. *Journal of Clinical Psychiatry, 60*, 4–8.

Munjack, D. J., Baltazar, P. L., Bohn, P. B., Cabe, D. D., & Appleton, A. A. (1990). Clonazepam in the treatment of social phobia: A pilot study. *Journal of Clinical Psychiatry, 51*, 35–40.

Newman, M. G., Hofmann, S. G., Trabert, W., Roth, W. T., & Taylor, C. B. (1994). Does behavioral treatment of social phobia lead to cognitive changes? *Behavior Therapy, 25*, 503–517.

Norton, P. J., & Hope, D. A. (2001). Kernels of truth or distorted perceptions: Self and observer ratings of social anxiety and performance. *Behavior Therapy, 32*, 765–786.

Öhman, A. (1986). Face the beast and fear the face: Animal and social fears as prototypes for evolutionary analyses of emotion. *Psychophysiology, 23*, 123–145.

Öhman, A., & Dimberg, U. (1978). Facial expressions as conditioned stimuli for electrodermal responses: A case of "preparedness"? *Journal of Personality and Social Psychology, 36*, 1251–1258.

Öhman, A., Dimberg, U., & Öst, L.-G. (1985). Animal and social phobias: Biological constraints on learned fear responses. In S. Reiss & R. R. Bootzin (Eds.), *Theoretical issues in behavior therapy* (pp. 123–178). Orlando, FL: Academic Press.

Ontiveros, A., & Fontaine, R. (1990). Social phobia and clonazepam. *Canadian Journal of Psychiatry, 35*, 439–441.

Öst, L. G. (1989). A maintenance program for behavioral treatment of anxiety disorders. *Behaviour Research and Therapy, 27*, 123–130.

Öst, L. G., & Hugdahl, K. (1981). Acquisition of phobia and anxiety response patterns in clinical patients. *Behaviour Research and Therapy, 19*, 437–471.

Öst, L. G., & Hugdahl, K. (1983). Acquisition of agoraphobia, mode of onset, and anxiety response patterns. *Behaviour Research and Therapy, 21*, 623–631.

Otto, M. W. (2000). Stories and metaphors in cognitive behavioral therapy. *Cognitive and Behavioral Practice, 7,* 166–172.

Otto, M. W., Basden, S., Leyro, T. M., McHugh, R. K., & Hofmann, S. G. (2007). Clinical perspectives on the combination of D-cycloserine and CBT for the treatment of anxiety disorders. *CNS Spectrums, 12,* 51–61.

Otto, M. W., Fava, M., Penava, S. A., Bless, E., Muller, R. T., & Rosenbaum, J. F. (1997). Life event and cognitive predictors of perceived stress before and after treatment for major depression. *Cognitive Therapy and Research, 21,* 409–420.

Otto, M. W., Jones, J. C., Craske, M. G., & Barlow, D. H. (1996) *Stopping anxiety medication: Panic control therapy for benzodiazepine discontinuation (Therapist guide).* Oxford, UK: Oxford University Press.

Otto, M. W., Pollack, M. H., Gould, R. A., Worthington, J. J., Heimberg, R. G., McArdle, E. T., & Rosenbaum, J. F. (2000). A comparison of the efficacy of clonazepam and cognitive-behavioral group therapy for the treatment of social phobia. *Journal of Anxiety Disorders, 14,* 345–358.

Otto, M. W., Pollack, M. H., Penava, S. J., & Zucker, B. G. (1999). Cognitive behavioral therapy for patients failing to respond to pharmacotherapy for panic disorder: A clinical case series. *Behaviour Research and Therapy, 37,* 763–770.

Otto, M. W., Powers, M. B., Stathopoulou, G., & Hofmann, S. G. (in press). In M. A. Whisman (Ed.), *Cognitive therapy for complex and comorbid depression: Conceptualization, assessment, and treatment.* New York: Guilford Press.

Otto, M. W., Simon, N. S., Wisniewski, S. R., Miklowitz, D. J., Kogan, J. N., Reilly-Harrington, N. A., Frank, E., Nierenberg, A. A., Marangell, L. B., Sagduyu, K., Weiss, R. D., Miyahara, S., Thase, M. E., Sachs, G. S., & Pollack, M. H. for STEP-BD Investigators. (2006). Prospective 12-month course of bipolar disorder in outpatients with and without comorbid anxiety disorders. *British Journal of Psychiatry, 189,* 20–25.

Otto, M. W., Smits, J. A. J., & Reese, H. E. (2005). Combined psychotherapy and pharmacotherapy for mood and anxiety disorders in adults: Review and analysis. *Clinical Psychology: Science and Practice, 12,* 72–86.

Paris, J. (2007). Intermittent psychotherapy: An alternative to continuous long-term treatment for patients with personality disorders. *Journal of Psychiatric Practice, 13,* 153–158.

Pecknold, J. C., McClure, D. J., Appeltauer, L., Allan, T., & Wrzesinski, L. (1982). Does tryptophan potentiate clomipramine in the treatment of agoraphobic and social phobic patients? *British Journal of Psychiatry, 140,* 484–490.

Plomin, R., & Daniels, D. (1985). Origins of individual differences in infant shyness. *Developmental Psychology, 21,* 118–121.

Pohl, R. B., Balon, R., Chapman, P., & McBride, J. (1998). *A new patient diary to study performance anxiety.* Poster presented at the 151st Annual Meeting of the American Psychiatric Association, Toronto, ON, Canada.

Pollard, C. A., & Henderson, J. G. (1988). Four types of social phobia in a community sample. *Journal of Nervous and Mental Disorders, 176,* 440–445.

Powers, M. B., Smits, J. A. J., Leyro, T. M., & Otto, M. (2006). Translational research perspectives on maximizing the effectiveness of exposure therapy. In D. C. S. Richard & D. L. Lauterbach (Eds.), *Comprehensive handbook of exposure therapies* (pp. 109–126). Boston: Academic Press.

Powers, M. B., Smits, J. A. J., & Telch, M. J. (2004). Disentangling the effects of safety-behavior utilization and safety-behavior availability during exposure-based treatment: A placebo-controlled trial. *Journal of Consulting and Clinical Psychology, 72,* 448–454.

Rachmann, S., Grüter-Andrew, J., & Shafran, R. (2000). Post-event processing in social anxiety. *Behaviour Research and Therapy, 38,* 611–617.

Rapee, R. M., & Hayman, K. (1996). The effects of video feedback on the self-evaluation of performance in socially anxious subjects. *Behaviour Research and Therapy, 34,* 315–322.

Rapee, R. M., & Heimberg, R. G. (1997). A cognitive-behavioral model of anxiety in social phobia. *Behaviour Research and Therapy, 35,* 741–756.

Rapee, R. M., & Lim, L. (1992). Discrepancy between self- and observer ratings of performance in social phobics. *Journal of Abnormal Psychology, 101,* 728–731.

Rapee, R. M., McCallum, S. L., Melville, L. F., Ravenscroft, H., & Rodney, J. M. (1994). Memory bias in social phobia. *Behaviour Research and Therapy, 32,* 89–99.

Reich, J., & Yates, W. (1988). A pilot study of treatment of social phobia with alprazolam. *American Journal of Psychiatry, 145,* 590–594.

Reiter, S. R., Pollack, M. H., Rosenbaum, J. F., & Cohen, L. S. (1990). Clonazepam for the treatment of social phobia. *Journal of Clinical Psychiatry, 51,* 470–472.

Ressler, K. J., Rothbaum, B. O., Tannenbaum, L., Anderson, P., Graap, K., Zimand, E., Hodges, L., & Davis, M. (2004). Cognitive enhancers as adjuncts to psychotherapy: Use of D-cycloserine in phobics to facilitate extinction of fear. *Archives of General Psychiatry, 61,* 1136–1144.

Ries, B. J., McNeil, D. W., Boone, M. L., Turk, C. L., Carter, L. E., & Heimberg, R. G. (1998). Assessment of contemporary social phobia verbal report instruments. *Behaviour Research and Therapy, 36,* 983–994.

Rosenbaum, J. F., Biederman, J., Hirshfeld, D. R., Bolduc, E. A., & Chaloff, J. (1991). Behavioral inhibition in children: A possible precursor to panic disorder and social phobia. *Journal of Clinical Psychiatry, 52,* 5–9.

Rosenbaum, J. F., Biederman, J., Pollock, R. A., & Hirshfeld, D. R. (1994). The etiology of social phobia. *Journal of Clinical Psychiatry, 55,* 10–16.

Rotter, J. B. (1966). Generalized expectancies for internal versus external control of reinforcement. *Psychological Monographs, 80,* 1–28.

Rotter, J. B. (1975). Some problems and misconceptions related to the construct of internal versus external control of reinforcement. *Journal of Consulting and Clinical Psychology, 43,* 56–67.

Safren, S. A., Heimberg, R. G., Horner, K. J., Juster, H. R., Schneier, F. R., & Liebowitz, M. R. (1999). Factor structure of social fears: The Liebowitz Social Anxiety Scale. *Journal of Anxiety Disorders, 13,* 253–270.

Safren, S. A., Heimberg, R. G., & Juster, H. R. (1997). Client's expectancies and their relationship to pretreatment symptomatology and outcome of cognitive-behavioral group treatment for social phobia. *Journal of Consulting and Clinical Psychology, 65,* 694–698.

Sanderson, W. C., Rapee, R. M., & Barlow, D. H. (1989). The influence of perceived control on panic attacks induced via inhalation of 5.5% $CO_2$-enriched air. *Archives of General Psychiatry, 46,* 157–162.

Schadé, A., Marquenie, L. A., van Balkom, A. J., Koeter, M. W., de Beurs, E., van den Brink, W., & van Dyck, R. (2005). The effectiveness of anxiety treatment on alcohol-dependent patients with a comorbid phobic disorder: A randomized controlled trial. *Alcoholism: Clinical and Experimental Research, 29,* 794–800.

Schadé, A., Marquenie, L. A., van Balkom, A. J., Koeter, M. W., de Beurs, E., van Dyck, R., van den Brink, W. (2007). Anxiety disorders: Treatable regardless of the severity of comorbid alcohol dependence. *European Addiction Research, 13,* 109–115.

Schlenker, B. R., & Leary, M. R. (1982). Social anxiety and self-presentation: A conceptualization and model. *Psychological Bulletin, 92,* 641–669.

Schneier, F. R., Heckelman, L. R., Garfinkel, R., Campeas, R., Fallon, B., Gitow, A., Street, L., DelBene, D., & Liebowitz, M. R. (1994). Functional impairment in social phobia. *Journal of Clinical Psychiatry, 55,* 322–331.

Schneier, F. R., Johnson, J., Hornig, C. D., Liebowitz, M. R., & Weissman, M. M. (1992). Social phobia: Comorbidity and morbidity in an epidemiological sample. *Archives of General Psychiatry, 49,* 282–288.

Schneier, F. R., Saoud, J. B., Campeas, R., Fallon, B. A., Hollander E., Coplan J., & Liebowitz, M. R. (1993). Buspirone in social phobia. *Journal of Clinical Psychopharmacology, 13,* 251–256.

Schneier, F. R., Spitzer, R. L., Gibbon, M., Fyer, A. J., & Liebowitz, M. R. (1991). The relationship of social phobia subtypes and avoidant personality disorder. *Comprehensive Psychiatry, 32,* 496–502.

Scholing, A., & Emmelkamp, P. M. G. (1999). Prediction of treatment outcome in social phobia: A cross-validation. *Behaviour Research and Therapy, 37,* 659–670.

Schulberg, H. C., Block, M. R., Madonia, M. J., Scott, C. P., Rodriguez, E., Imber, S. D., Perel, J., Lave, J., Houck, P. R., & Coulehan, J. L. (1996). Treating major depression in primary care practice. Eight-month clinical outcomes. *Archives of General Psychiatry, 53,* 913–919.

Schwartz, C. E., Snidman, N., & Kagan, J. (1999). Adolescent social anxiety as an outcome of inhibited behavior in childhood. *Journal of the American Academy of Child and Adolescent Psychiatry, 38,* 1008–1015.

Scott, W. D., & Cervone, D. (2002). The impact of negative affect on performance standards: Evidence for an affect-as-information mechanism. *Cognitive Therapy and Research, 26,* 19–37.

Siitonen, L., & Tanne, J. (1976). Effect of beta-blockade during bowling competitions. *Annals of Clinical Research, 8,* 393–398.

Simon, N. M., Otto, M. W., Wisniewski, S. R., Fossey M., Sagduyu, K., Frank, E., Sachs, G. S., Nierenberg, A. A., Thase, M. E., & Pollack, M. H. (2007). Anxiety disorder comorbidity in bipolar disorder: Data from the first 500 STEP-BD participants. *American Journal of Psychiatry, 161,* 2222–2229.

Simpson, H. B., Schneier, F. R., Campeas, R. B., Marshall, R. D., Fallon, B. A., Davies, S., Klein, D. F., Liebowitz, M. R. (1998). Imipramine in the treatment of social phobia. *Journal of Clinical Psychopharmacology, 18,* 132–135.

Skre, I., Onstad, S., Torgersen, S., Lygren, S., & Kringlen, E. (1993). A twin study of DSM-III-R anxiety disorders. *Acta Psychiatrica Scandinavica, 88*, 85–92.

Slavkin, S. L., Holt, C. S., Heimberg, R. G., Jaccard, J. J., & Liebowitz, M. R. (1990, November). *The Liebowitz Social Phobia Scale: An exploratory analysis of construct validity.* Paper presented at the annual meeting of the Association for the Advancement of Behavior Therapy, Washington, DC.

Spurr, J. M., & Stopa, L. (2002). Self-focused attention in social phobia and social anxiety. *Clinical Psychology Review, 22*, 947–975.

Stangier, U., Heidenreich, T., Peitz, M., Lauterbach, W., & Clark, D. M. (2003). Cognitive therapy for social phobia: Individual versus group treatment. *Behaviour Research and Therapy, 41*, 991–1007.

Stein, M. B., & Chavira, D. A. (1998). Subtypes of social phobia and comorbidity with depression and other anxiety disorders. *Journal of Affective Disorders, 50*, 11–16.

Stein, M. B., & Kean, Y. M. (2001). Disability and quality of life in social phobia: Epidemiologic findings. *American Journal of Psychiatry, 157*, 1606–1613.

Stein, M. B., Liebowitz, M. R. Lydiard, R. B., Pitts, C. D., Bushnell, W., & Gergel, I. (1998). Paroxetine treatment of generalized social phobia (social anxiety disorder). A randomized clinical trial. *Journal of the American Medical Association, 280*, 708–713.

Stein, M. B., Torgrud, L. J., & Walker, J. (2000). Social phobia symptoms, subtypes, and severity. *Archives of General Psychiatry, 57*, 1046–1052.

Stein, M. B., Walker, J. R., & Forde, D. R. (1996). Public speaking fears in a community sample. Prevalence, impact on functioning, and diagnostic classification. *Archives of General Psychiatry, 53*, 169–174.

Stemberger, R. T., Turner, S. M., Beidel, D. C., & Calhoun, K. S. (1995). Social phobia: An analysis of possible developmental factors. *Journal of Abnormal Psychology, 104*, 526–531.

Sternbach, H. (1990). Fluoxetine treatment of social phobia. *Journal of Clinical Psychopharmacology, 10*, 230–231.

Stopa, L., & Clark, D. M. (1993). Cognitive processes in social phobia. *Behaviour Research and Therapy, 31*, 255–267.

Stopa, L., & Clark, D. M. (2000). Social phobia and interpretation of social events. *Behaviour Research and Therapy, 38*, 273–283.

Strauman, T. J. (1989). Self-discrepancies in clinical depression and social phobia: Cognitive structures that underlie emotional disorders? *Journal of Abnormal Psychology, 98*, 14–22.

Strauman, T. J., & Higgins, E. T. (1987). Automatic activation of self-discrepancies and emotional syndromes: When cognitive structures influence affect. *Journal of Personality and Social Psychology, 53,* 1004–1014.

Stravynski, A., & Amado, D. (2001). Social phobia as a deficit in social skills. In S. G. Hofmann & P. M. DiBartolo (Eds.), *From social anxiety to social phobia: Multiple perspectives* (pp. 107–129). Boston: Allyn & Bacon.

Stravynski, A., Grey, S., & Elie, R. (1987). Outline of the therapeutic process in social skills training with socially dysfunctional patients. *Journal of Consulting and Clinical Psychology, 55,* 224–228.

Stravynski, A., Marks, I., & Yule, W. (1982). Social skills problems in neurotic outpatients: Social skills training with and without cognitive modification. *Archives of General Psychiatry, 39,* 1378–1385.

Tang, T. Z., & DeRubeis, R. J. (2005). Sudden gains and critical sessions in cognitive behavioral therapy for depression. *Journal of Consulting and Clinical Psychology, 67,* 894–909.

Taylor, S. (1996). Meta-analysis of cognitive-behavioral treatments for social phobia. *Journal of Behaviour Therapy and Experimental Psychiatry, 27,* 1–9.

Teasdale, J. D., Moore, R. G., Hayhurst, H., Pope, M., Williams, S., & Segal, Z. V. (2002). Metacognitive awareness and prevention of relapse in depression: Empirical evidence. *Journal of Consulting and Clinical Psychology, 70,* 275–287.

Telch, M. J. (1988). Combined pharmacological and psychological treatments for panic sufferers. In S. Rachman & J. D. Maser (Eds.), *Panic: Psychological perspectives* (pp. 167–187). Hillsdale, NJ: Erlbaum.

Terra, M. B., Barros, H. M., Stein, A. T., Figueira, I., Athayde, L. D., Spanemberg, L., de Aguiar Possa, M., Filho, L. D., & da Silveira, D. X. (2006). Does co-occurring social phobia interfere with alcoholism treatment adherence and relapse? *Journal of Substance Abuse Treatment, 31,* 403–409.

Thomas, S. E., Thevos, A. K., & Randall, C. L. (1999). Alcoholics with and without social phobia: A comparison of substance use and psychiatric variables. *Journal of Studies on Alcohol, 60,* 472–479.

Tooby, J., & Cosmides, L. (1996). Friendship and the banker's paradox: Other pathways to the evolution of adaptations for altruism. *Proceedings of the British Academy, 88,* 119–143.

Trau, G. O., & Chambless, D. L. (1995). Psychopathology of social phobia: Effects of subtype and of avoidant personality disorder. *Journal of Anxiety Disorder, 9,* 489–501.

Trower, P., & Gilbert, P. (1989). New theoretical conceptions of social anxiety and social phobia. *Clinical Psychology Review, 9,* 19–35.

Turner, S. M., & Beidel, D. C. (1988). Some further comments on the measurement of social phobia. *Behaviour Research and Therapy, 26,* 411–413.

Turner, S. M., Beidel, D. C., Cooley, M. R., Woody, S. R., & Messer, S. C. (1994). A multicomponent behavioral treatment of social phobia: Social effectiveness therapy. *Behaviour Research and Therapy, 32,* 381–390.

Turner, S. M., Beidel, D. C., & Cooley-Quille, M. R. (1995). Two year follow-up of social phobics treated with social effectiveness therapy. *Behaviour Research and Therapy, 33,* 553–556.

Turner, S. M., Beidel, D. C., Dancu, C. V., & Stanley, M. A. (1989). An empirically derived inventory to measure social fears and anxiety: The Social Phobia and Anxiety Inventory. *Psychological Assessment, 1,* 35–40.

Turner, S. M., Beidel, D. C., & Jacob, R. G. (1994). Social phobia: A comparison of behavior therapy and atenolol. *Journal of Consulting and Clinical Psychology, 62,* 350–358.

Turner, S. M., Beidel, D. C., & Townsley, R. M. (1990). Social phobia: Relationship to shyness. *Behaviour Research and Therapy, 28,* 497–505.

Turner, S. M., Beidel, D. C., & Townsley, R. M. (1992). Social phobia: A comparison of specific and generalized subtypes and avoidant personality disorder. *Journal of Abnormal Psychology, 101,* 326–331.

Turner, S. M., McCanna, M., & Beidel, D. C. (1987). Discriminative validity of the Social Avoidance and Distress and Fear of Negative Evaluation Scale. *Behaviour Research and Therapy, 25,* 113–115.

Uhde, T. W., Tancer, M. E., Black, B., & Brown, T. M. (1991). Phenomenology and neurobiology of social phobia: Comparison with panic disorder. *Journal of Clinical Psychiatry, 52,* 31–40.

van Ameringen M., Mancini, C., & Streiner, D. L. (1993). Fluoxetine efficacy in social phobia. *Journal of Clinical Psychiatry, 54,* 27–32.

Van Velzen, C. J. M., Emmelkamp, P. M. G., & Scholing, A. (1997). The impact of personality disorders on behavioural treatment outcome for social phobia. *Behaviour Research and Therapy, 35,* 889–900.

van Vliet, I. M., Den Boer, J. A., & Westenberg, H. G. M. (1994). Psychopharmacological treatment of social phobia: A double-blind, placebo-controlled study with fluvoxamine, *Psychpharmacology, 115,* 128–134.

Versiani, M., Mundim, F. D., Nardi, A. E., & Liebowitz, M. R. (1988). Tranylcypromine in social phobia. *Journal of Clinical Psychopharmacology, 8,* 279–283.

Versiani, M., Nardi, A. E., Mundim, F. D., Alves, A. B., Liebowitz, M. R., & Amrein, R. (1992). Pharmacotherapy of social phobia: A controlled study with moclobemide and phenelzine. *British Journal of Psychiatry, 161,* 353–360.

Wallace, S. T., & Alden, L. E. (1991). A comparison of social standards and perceived ability in anxious and nonanxious men. *Cognitive Therapy and Research, 15,* 237–254.

Wallace, S. T., & Alden, L. E. (1995). Social anxiety and standard setting following social success or failure. *Cognitive Therapy and Research, 19,* 613–631.

Wallace, S. T., & Alden, L.E. (1997). Social phobia and positive social events: The price of success. *Journal of Abnormal Psychology, 106,* 416–424.

Watson, D., & Friend, R. (1969). Measurement of social-evaluative anxiety. *Journal of Consulting and Clinical Psychology, 33,* 448–457.

Weilage, M., & Hope, D. A. (1999). Self-discrepancy in social phobia and dysthymia. *Cognitive Theory and Research, 23,* 637–650.

Wells, A., Clark, D. M., & Ahmad, S. (1998). How do I look with my minds eye: Perspective taking in social phobic imagery. *Behaviour Research and Therapy, 36,* 631–634.

Wells, A., Clark, D. M., Salkovskis, P., Ludgate, J., Hackmann, A., & Gelder, M. (1995). Social phobia: The role of in-situation safety behaviors in maintaining anxiety and negative beliefs. *Behavior Therapy, 26,* 153–161.

Wells, A., & Papageorgiou, C. (1998). Social phobia: Effects of external attention on anxiety, negative beliefs, and perspective taking. *Behavior Therapy, 29,* 357–370.

Wells, A., & Papageorgiou, C. (2001). Brief cognitive therapy for social phobia: A case series. *Behaviour Research and Therapy, 39,* 713–720.

Whisman, M. A. (1993). Mediators and moderators of change on cognitive therapy of depression. *Psychological Bulletin, 114,* 248–265.

Williams, S. L, Dooseman, G., & Kleifield, E. (1984). Comparative effectiveness of guided mastery and exposure treatment for intractable phobias. *Journal of Consulting and Clinical Psychology, 52,* 505–518.

Williams, S. L., Kinney, P. J., & Falbo, J. (1989). Generalization of therapeutic changes in agoraphobia: The role of perceived self-efficacy. *Journal of Consulting and Clinical Psychology, 57,* 436–442.

Williams, S. L., Turner, S. M., & Peer, D. F. (1985). Guided mastery and performance desensitization treatment for severe acrophobia. *Journal of Consulting and Clinical Psychology, 53,* 237–247.

Wilson, J. K., & Rapee R. M. (2005). The interpretation of negative social events in social phobia with versus without comorbid mood disorder. *Journal of Anxiety Disorders, 19,* 245–274.

Wlazlo, Z., Schroeder-Hartwig, K., Hand, I., Kaiser, G., & Münchau, N. (1990). Exposure in vivo vs. social skills training for social phobia: Long-term outcome and differential effects. *Behaviour Research and Therapy, 28,* 181–193.

Woody, S. R. (1996). Effects of focus of attention on anxiety levels and social performance of individuals with social phobia. *Journal of Abnormal Psychology, 105,* 61–69.

Woody, S. R., Chambless, D. L., & Glass, C. R. (1997). Self-focused attention in the treatment of social phobia. *Behaviour Research and Therapy, 35,* 117–129.

Zitrin, C. M., Klein, D. F., Woerner, M. G., & Ross, D. C. (1983). Treatment of phobias I: Comparison of imipramine hydrochloride and placebo. *Archives of General Psychiatry, 40,* 125–138.

# Handout 1
## *A CBT Model of Social Anxiety Disorder*

```
┌─────────────────────────────┐
│ High Perceived Social Standards │
│ and Poorly Defined Social Goals │
└─────────────────────────────┘
              ↕
┌──────────────────┐   ┌────────────────────┐   ┌──────────────────┐
│ Social Apprehension │ ← │ Post-Event Rumination │ ← │ Avoidance and    │
│                  │   │                    │   │ Safety Behaviors │
└──────────────────┘   └────────────────────┘   └──────────────────┘
        ↓
┌──────────────┐
│ Heightened    │
│ Self-focused  │
│ Attention     │
└──────────────┘
```

| | |
|---|---|
| | Negative Self-Perception |
| | High Estimated Probability and Cost |
| | Low Perceived Emotional Control |
| | Perceived Poor Social Skills |

# Handout 2
## *Learning Objectives*

- You will realize that people do not expect as much from you as you think they do. Furthermore, you will learn how to define clear goals for yourself during a social situation and how to use this information to determine whether the situation was successful.
- You will learn strategies to understand, but not engage in, anxious feelings and thoughts. Instead, you will learn how to direct your attention toward the situation in order to successfully complete the social task.
- You are more critical toward yourself than other people are toward you. Therefore, it is important that you become comfortable with the way you are (including your imperfections in social performance situations).
- Major social mishaps with serious consequences are rare. Minor social mishaps are normal and happen all the time. But what makes people different is the degree to which these mishaps affect a person's life. You will realize that even if a social encounter objectively did not go well, it just doesn't matter that much.
- You will realize that you have more control over your anxious feelings than you think. Your feeling of anxiety is a very private experience; other people cannot see your racing heart, your sweaty palms, or your shaky knees. You will realize that you overestimate how much other people can see what's going on in your body.
- You will realize that your actual social performance is not nearly as bad as you think it is.

- You will learn that using avoidance strategies (either active or passive) is part of the reason why social anxiety is so persistent and tends to spread.
- You will realize that ruminating about past situations does no one any good. What happened, happened! Ruminating only makes it worse and makes it harder to feel comfortable in future social situations.

# Handout 3
## *Approach to Social Situations Scale*

Please answer the following questions as honestly as you can. Your honest answers will help us tailor the treatment that you are about to receive to your specific needs. Please rate how much you agree with the following statements on a scale from 0 (I don't agree at all/this is not typical of me) to 10 (I agree very much/this is very typical of me).

1. I believe that the expectations of me in social situations are very high.

    0—1—2—3—4—5—6—7—8—9—10

2. I am often not quite clear about what I personally want to achieve in a social situation.

    0—1—2—3—4—5—6—7—8—9—10

3. I tend to focus my attention toward myself when I am in a social situation.

    0—1—2—3—4—5—6—7—8—9—10

4. I tend to overestimate how bad a social situation can turn out.

    0—1—2—3—4—5—6—7—8—9—10

5. I believe that my social skills to handle social situations are poor.

    0—1—2—3—4—5—6—7—8—9—10

6. I don't like myself very much when it comes to social situations.

0—1—2—3—4—5—6—7—8—9—10

7. I have little control over my anxiety in social situations.

0—1—2—3—4—5—6—7—8—9—10

8. I think that people can tell when I am anxious in social situations.

0—1—2—3—4—5—6—7—8—9—10

9. I usually expect that something bad will happen to me in a social situation.

0—1—2—3—4—5—6—7—8—9—10

10. I tend to dwell about social situations after they have happened.

0—1—2—3—4—5—6—7—8—9—10

11. I often avoid social situations.

0—1—2—3—4—5—6—7—8—9—10

12. I often do things that make me feel less uncomfortable when I am in social situations.

0—1—2—3—4—5—6—7—8—9—10

Reprinted from Hofmann, S.G. (in press-a). Cognitive factors that maintain social anxiety disorder: A comprehensive model and its treatment implications. *Cognitive Behaviour Therapy.* (With permission from Routledge.)

# Handout 4
## *Daily Record of Social Situations (DRSS)*

### INSTRUCTIONS ON HOW TO COMPLETE THE DAILY RECORD OF SOCIAL SITUATIONS (DRSS)

1. Don't avoid situations. Go at least five times per week into a fearful situation that you previously avoided.
2. On the Daily Record of Social Situations, describe the fearful situation (second column) and record the date and time (first column).
3. Rate your anticipatory anxiety and specify what signs of anxiety you expect to experience (third column).
4. How bad do you think it would be if the situation did not go well on a scale from 0 (not bad at all) to 10 (very bad)? Also, please specify what "not going well" exactly means in this context (fourth column).
5. How much could you cope with the bad outcome, and what are the ways you could cope with it (fifth column)?
6. What is the likelihood that this bad outcome will in fact happen on a scale from 0% (not likely at all) to 100% (very likely; sixth column)?

**Remember:** An ideal exposure task is a situation that induces a lot of anxiety for a long period of time. The more often you do it and the longer you stay in it, the better it is.

| Date | Social situation | How anxious do you think you will be (0–10)? Specify signs of anxiety. | How bad would it be if the situation didn't go well (0–10)? What does "not going well" mean? | How much could you cope with a bad outcome (0–10)? Specify ways of coping. | How likely is it a bad outcome will happen (0–100%)? |
|------|------------------|------------------|------------------|------------------|------------------|
|      |                  |                  |                  |                  |                  |

# Handout 5
## *Cognitive Preparation for Video Feedback*

### PREDICTION OF SOCIAL PERFORMANCE

The video feedback provides you with the opportunity to thoroughly evaluate your own performance and to examine whether some of your assumptions are correct. In order to do this, I would like you to predict in detail what you think you will see in the video. Please rate your speech on the following dimensions on a scale from 0 (not at all) to 10 (extremely well):

1. Overall, how well you think you came across?

Not at all                                            Extremely well

     0     1     2     3     4     5     6     7     8     9     10

2. How well do you think you performed during the speech

Not at all                                            Extremely well

     0     1     2     3     4     5     6     7     8     9     10

In addition, I would like you to tell me how you would rate the presence of each of the following performance indicators:

| | Not at all present | | | | | | | | | Extremely apparent |
|---|---|---|---|---|---|---|---|---|---|---|
| eye contact | 0 | 1 | 2 | 3 | 4 | 5 | 6 | 7 | 8 | 9 | 10 |
| stuttering | 0 | 1 | 2 | 3 | 4 | 5 | 6 | 7 | 8 | 9 | 10 |
| long pauses | 0 | 1 | 2 | 3 | 4 | 5 | 6 | 7 | 8 | 9 | 10 |
| fidgeting | 0 | 1 | 2 | 3 | 4 | 5 | 6 | 7 | 8 | 9 | 10 |
| ums and ahs | 0 | 1 | 2 | 3 | 4 | 5 | 6 | 7 | 8 | 9 | 10 |
| trembling/shaking | 0 | 1 | 2 | 3 | 4 | 5 | 6 | 7 | 8 | 9 | 10 |
| sweating | 0 | 1 | 2 | 3 | 4 | 5 | 6 | 7 | 8 | 9 | 10 |
| blushing | 0 | 1 | 2 | 3 | 4 | 5 | 6 | 7 | 8 | 9 | 10 |
| face twitching | 0 | 1 | 2 | 3 | 4 | 5 | 6 | 7 | 8 | 9 | 10 |
| voice quivering | 0 | 1 | 2 | 3 | 4 | 5 | 6 | 7 | 8 | 9 | 10 |
| nervous | 0 | 1 | 2 | 3 | 4 | 5 | 6 | 7 | 8 | 9 | 10 |
| boring | 0 | 1 | 2 | 3 | 4 | 5 | 6 | 7 | 8 | 9 | 10 |
| fluent speech | 0 | 1 | 2 | 3 | 4 | 5 | 6 | 7 | 8 | 9 | 10 |
| looking awkward | 0 | 1 | 2 | 3 | 4 | 5 | 6 | 7 | 8 | 9 | 10 |
| looking embarrassed | 0 | 1 | 2 | 3 | 4 | 5 | 6 | 7 | 8 | 9 | 10 |
| were interesting | 0 | 1 | 2 | 3 | 4 | 5 | 6 | 7 | 8 | 9 | 10 |

## IMAGINATION OF SOCIAL PERFORMANCE

Please close your eyes now and form a clear image of how you think you came across during the speech. Please construct an internal video of how you think you appeared.

How vividly were you able to see yourself giving the speech?

Not at all                                                                    Extremely
                                                                              well
     0     1     2     3     4     5     6     7     8     9     10

How was your performance in the image?

Very poor                                                                   Very good
     0     1     2     3     4     5     6     7     8     9     10

## IDENTIFYING AND CHALLENGING
## INCORRECT PREDICTIONS

In order for you to watch the video objectively, please only pay attention to how you looked, not how you felt. Please watch the video as if you were watching a stranger. How was your performance in the video? (Get responses from patient and group members.)

Not at all                                                          Extremely
                                                                    well

0    1    2    3    4    5    6    7    8    9    10

Based on the procedure described in Harvey, A. G., Clark, D. M., Ehlers, A., & Rapee, R. M. (2000). Social anxiety and self-impression: Cognitive preparation enhances the beneficial effects of video feedback following a stressful social task. *Behaviour Research and Therapy, 38,* 1183–1192.

# Self-Defeating Thoughts

## AMPLIFYING COGNITIONS

*Great ways to transform everyday events into a sense of failure*

*Think:*

If I get anxious—I am a loser

If my face flushes—Then I failed

If I flub a word—I am worthless as a speaker

If I act different from others—I am weird

If I lose my train of thought—I am incompetent

# Worksheet for Challenging Automatic Thoughts

Instructions for completing the worksheet:

1. Don't avoid any social situations. Briefly describe the situation in the first column.
2. Name the most disturbing thought (or image) in the second column.
3. In the third column, state what the most feared consequence might be (whether this is realistic or not).
4. Challenge the likelihood that this feared consequence will happen in the fourth column. What evidence do you have that it is going to happen? How likely do you think it is that the worst outcome is going to happen?
5. In the fifth column, challenge your catastrophic thinking. How bad do you think would it be if the situation did not go well? What is the worst outcome? Could you deal with this situation? Were you able to deal with similar situations in the past?
6. Finally, explore more reasonable interpretations of the same situation.

Remember - An ideal exposure task is a situation that induces a lot of anxiety for a long period of time. The more often you do it and the longer you stay in it, the better it is.

| Situation | Most disturbing thoughts | What is the feared consequence? | Challenge probability overestimation: What is the evidence? How likely is the worst outcome going to happen? | Challenge catastrophic thinking; What is the worst outcome? Could you cope? Is this a real catastrophe? | What is a more reasonable interpretation of the situation? |
|---|---|---|---|---|---|
| | | | | | |
| | | | | | |
| | | | | | |
| | | | | | |

# Fear and Avoidance Hierarchy

| Social Situation | Fear (0–100) | Avoidance (0–100) |
|---|---|---|
| My worst fear: | | |
| My 2nd worst fear: | | |
| My 3rd worst fear: | | |
| My 4th worst fear: | | |
| My 5th worst fear: | | |
| My 6th worst fear: | | |
| My 7th worst fear: | | |
| My 8th worst fear: | | |
| My 9th worst fear: | | |
| My 10th worst fear: | | |

# Social Fear Worksheet for Exposure Planning

What sorts of situations best characterize the patient's fears of humiliation or embarrassment? Are they individual interactions, small groups, or large groups; informal or formal; structured or unstructured; work or socially related; dependent on topic; etc.?

*Ask:* Describe for me some of your most feared social scenarios.

_____

_____

_____

_____

What are the actual fears of humiliation? Do they center on social errors, emergence of symptoms, beliefs of incompetence, etc.?

*Ask:* Many times, individuals with social anxiety fear they will make certain social errors. Can you tell me about some of the things you fear will happen in a social situation?

_____

_____

_____

_____

**Are social fears richly dependent on the emergence of symptoms (heart rate, sweating, flushing, dry throat, etc.)?**

*Ask:* Are there any symptoms that intensify your fears of embarrassment when present (blushing, sweating, dry throat, etc.)? Why are these symptoms bothersome?

_____

_____

_____

_____


**What are common safety cues used by the patient?**

*Ask:* What are those things you do, or keep with you, that help you feel less anxious in social situations?

_____

_____

_____

_____


**What are the usual ways in which the patient nullifies adequate performances or self-criticizes after a social performance?**

*Ask:* What do you typically say to yourself after a social situation?

_____

_____

_____

_____


*Ask:* How would you fill in the following statements?
I can't believe I did that (in a social situation), I always …

_____

_____

_____

_____


I blew it. I am such a …

_____

_____

_____

_____

I should have ...

_____
_____
_____
_____


*Ask:* And when you prepare for your next social situation, what are some of the things you worry about or pay attention to?

_____
_____
_____
_____

# The Maintaining Variables of Social Anxiety

THE VICIOUS CYCLE MODEL OF AVOIDANCE

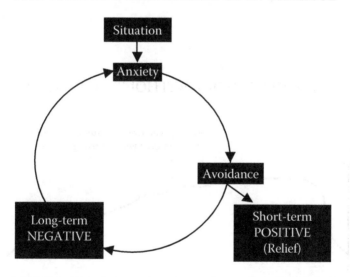

## ANXIETY EPISODE WITH AVOIDANCE

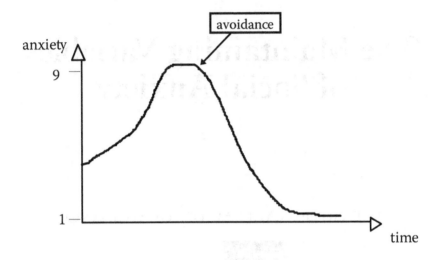

## ANXIETY EPISODE WITHOUT AVOIDANCE

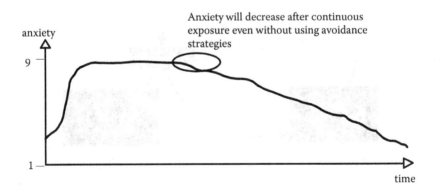

## ANXIETY AFTER REPEATED EXPOSURE
## TO THE SAME SITUATION

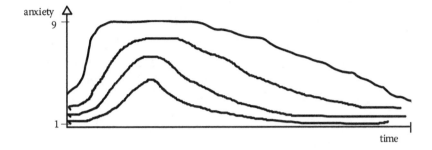

# Examples of In Vivo Exposure Tasks to Challenge Estimated Social Cost

- Ask multiple people (e.g., 10 people over a half hour) in a specific and obvious location (e.g., immediately outside Fenway Park) where to find that location. Say: *Excuse me, I am looking for Fenway Park.*
- Order a sandwich at a takeout restaurant and then tell the cashier you cannot buy it because you do not have enough money. Say without apologizing: *I just realized that I forgot my wallet,* then walk out.
- Order a coffee at a coffee bar and when it is handed to you, say: *Is this decaf?* Add without apologizing: *I would like to have mine decaf.*
- Order a bagel, "accidentally" drop it on the floor and ask for a new one. Say: *I just dropped the bagel on the floor. Could I please have a new one?*
- Go to a restaurant and sit at the bar. When asked if you would like to order something, just ask for tap water. Use the bathroom and then leave without saying anything.
- Go to a restaurant and sit at the bar. Ask a fellow patron whether he has seen the movie *When Harry Met Sally* and who the actors were.
- Go to a hotel and book a room. Walk outside and immediately back in and cancel the room because you *changed your mind.*

- Go to a video rental outlet and rent a DVD. Walk out and immediately back in requesting to return it saying: *I forgot I don't have a DVD player.*
- Stand in a subway station (specify location) and sing "God Bless America" for 30 minutes.
- Ask a female pharmacist for some condoms. When she brings them, ask: *Is this the smallest size you have?*
- Go to every man sitting at a table in a crowded restaurant and ask: *Are you Carl Smith?*
- Go to a bookstore and ask a clerk: *Excuse me, where can I find some books on farting.*
- Ask a bookstore clerk for the following two books: *The Karma Sutra* and *The Joy of Sex*. Ask the clerk which one he would recommend.
- Buy a book and immediately return it because you *changed your mind.*
- Ask the book clerk for his/her opinion about a particular best-seller. Ask: *What did you like about this book, and how many copies have you sold.* Don't buy it. Simply say: *Thank you. I will think about it* and leave.
- Ask a book clerk for a book for a 1-year-old. Find out if and how many children the clerk has, how old they are, what school they attend or attended, and what their favorite color is.
- Go to Store 24, buy a *Playgirl* magazine, and ask the store clerk: *Are there also pictures of naked men in the magazine?* Wait for the answer and put it back on the shelf.
- Wear your shirt backward and inside out and buttoned incorrectly in a crowded store. Goal: Look three people in the eye.
- Walk backward slowly in a crowded street for 3 minutes.

# Booster Worksheet for Exposure Planning

Treatment provided you with strategies for changing some of the core patterns linked to social anxiety disorder (SAD). In reviewing how you are currently doing, please review your need for additional practice with social situations in the following areas:

Currently, what are your most feared social scenarios?

_____

_____

_____

_____

What are the actual fears of humiliation? Do they center on social errors, emergence of symptoms, beliefs of incompetence, etc.?

_____

_____

_____

_____

At present, are there any symptoms that intensify your fears of embarrassment when present (blushing, sweating, dry throat, etc.) such that you would benefit from becoming more comfortable with these symptoms?

_____

_____

_____

_____

Currently, how are you doing in terms of focusing on social goals and noticing whether you meet these goals? In particular, what are some of the ways in which you "coach" (talk to) yourself after social situations?

_____

_____

_____

_____

# Author Index

# Subject Index